Targeted Development

Targeted Development

Industrialized Country Strategy in a Globalizing World

SARAH BLODGETT BERMEO

Oxford University Press is a department of the University of Oxford. It furthers the University's objective of excellence in research, scholarship, and education by publishing worldwide. Oxford is a registered trade mark of Oxford University Press in the UK and in certain other countries.

Published in the United States of America by Oxford University Press
198 Madison Avenue, New York, NY 10016, United States of America.

© Oxford University Press 2018

All rights reserved. No part of this publication may be reproduced, stored in a retrieval system, or transmitted, in any form or by any means, without the prior permission in writing of Oxford University Press, or as expressly permitted by law, by license or under terms agreed with the appropriate reproduction rights organization. Inquiries concerning reproduction outside the scope of the above should be sent to the Rights Department, Oxford University Press, at the address above.

You must not circulate this work in any other form
and you must impose this same condition on any acquirer.

Library of Congress Cataloging-in-Publication Data
Names: Bermeo, Sarah Blodgett, 1975- author.
Title: Targeted development : industrialized country strategy in a
globalizing world / Sarah Blodgett Bermeo.
Description: New York, NY, United States of America : Oxford University
Press, [2018] | Includes bibliographical references.
Identifiers: LCCN 2017022989 | ISBN 9780190851828 (hardcover) |
ISBN 9780190851835 (pbk.) | ISBN 9780190851842 (updf) | ISBN 9780190851859 (epub)
Subjects: LCSH: Developed countries–Foreign economic relations–Developing
countries. | Developing countries–Foreign economic relations–Developed
countries. | Economic development–Developing countries. | Economic
assistance–Developing countries. | International economic relations. |
Globalization–Economic aspects.
Classification: LCC HF1413.B47 2018 | DDC 338.9109172/4–dc23
LC record available at https://lccn.loc.gov/2017022989

For Otto, Katerina, Nathan, and Anika

CONTENTS

List of Figures ix
List of Tables xi
Acknowledgments xiii

1. Development as Self-Interest 1

2. Targeted Development in Perspective 17

3. Maximizing Utility vis-à-vis Developing Countries 35

4. Reorienting Foreign Aid 56

5. Preferential Trade Agreements as Development Policy 89

6. Climate Finance for Developing Countries 126

7. Conclusion: Rethinking Development 144

Notes 155
References 167
Index 175

LIST OF FIGURES

2.1 Bilateral Aid, Europe and Central Asia Breakout   28
2.2 Increasing Connections: Migration and GHG Emissions   30
2.3 Increasing Connections: Foreign Direct Investment and Trade   31
3.1 Utility Maximization and Development   41
4.1 Official Development Assistance Commitments, 1970–2014   60
4.2 Official Development Assistance as a Percent of Gross National Income, 1970–2013   61
4.3 Predicted Aid, Recipient Governance, and Distance   81
5.1 Industrialized–Developing Country Dyads with a Signed Trade Agreement   90
5.2 US Foreign Aid to CAFTA-DR Countries   106
5.3 FDI Stock for Members of CAFTA-DR, 1990–2014   108
5.4 GDP per Capita for Members of CAFTA-DR, 1990–2014   110
5.5 Predicted Probability of Signing a Trade Agreement, by Aid Share   117
5.6 Predicted Probability of Signing a Trade Agreement, by Income per Capita   118

LIST OF TABLES

4.1 Predicted Association Between Explanatory Variables and Aid Allocation   65
4.2 Determinants of Dyadic Aid Allocation   71
4.3 Determinants of Dyadic Aid Allocation, Period Interactions   74
4.4 Determinants of Aid Allocation by Donor   76
4.5 Governance and Aid by Sector   85
A4.1 Official Development Assistance by OECD Donor, 2013   88
5.1 Probability of Signing a Preferential Trade Agreement, 1992–2012   116
A5.1 Industrialized–Developing Dyads Signing Preferential Trade Agreements   121
6.1 Determinants of Aid for Climate Adaptation   136
6.2 Determinants of Aid for Climate Adaptation by Distance   138
6.3 Determinants of Aid for Climate Mitigation   141

ACKNOWLEDGMENTS

The origins of this project can be traced to my time in graduate school. My dissertation focused on foreign aid, arguing that development had become a self-interested concern for donor states, which could be observed in aid allocation patterns. At the time of my final defense, I particularly remember Helen Milner asking me about other applications for this framework. I responded that if development has become an important goal of industrialized states, we should see development concerns informing foreign policy in issue areas beyond aid. In many respects this book is an attempt to answer Helen's question by formalizing the concept I now call "targeted development" and examining its explanatory power in multiple issue areas linking industrialized and developing states.

The early stages of my thinking on this were influenced by my advisors and other faculty at Princeton, most notably Helen Milner, Bob Keohane, and Joanne Gowa, with useful insights also provided by Angus Deaton and John Londregan. I benefitted significantly from working with Christina Davis, who was generous in her comments and advice well beyond our co-authored work. I was fortunate to have excellent graduate student colleagues, and appreciate in particular multiple useful discussions with Jeff Colgan, Jessica Green, and Dustin Tingley.

The majority of this work was written while I was an assistant professor in the Sanford School of Public Policy at Duke University. I have benefitted from research funding and the supportive environment at Sanford and Duke. My colleagues and students have provided intellectual stimulation throughout this process. The chapter on climate funding was influenced by a workshop sponsored by the Niehaus Center for Globalization and Governance at Princeton University, which I co-organized with Helen Milner, Tana Johnson, and Dustin Tingley. I thank the Niehaus Center for funding, my co-organizers and conference participants for valuable insights, and Pat Trinity for logistical support for the conference. Interviews carried out with foreign aid agencies and NGOs in Managua, Nicaragua, and Tegucigalpa, Honduras in 2006 informed my research on foreign aid and CAFTA-DR, and I am grateful to the many individuals who spent time answering my questions on those trips.

Several colleagues, from Duke and beyond, read and commented on an early version of the manuscript at a book conference held in October 2014. I am indebted to the Sanford School for funding this workshop. The input I received at the time led to substantial revisions. For this very valuable feedback as well as many other useful conversations, I am grateful to Judith Kelley, who also organized the workshop, and to all the attendees: Tim Büthe, Jeff Frieden, Bruce Jentleson, Tana Johnson, Miles Kahler, Anirudh Krishna, Eddy Malesky, Fritz Mayer, Layna Mosley, and Ken Scheve. I am also grateful to Randy Stone for extensive and useful comments on the manuscript and to David Leblang for providing guidance and suggestions throughout this project. This work also benefitted significantly from conversations with and feedback from Owen Barder, Charlie Clotfelter, Simone Dietrich, Desha Girod, Christopher Kilby, David Leblang, Kevin Morrison, Daniel Nielson, Maggie Peters, Billy Pizer, Seth Sanders, Alastair Smith, Michael Tierney, Jennifer Tobin, Mike Tomz, Jim Vreeland, Erik Wibbels, Matt Winters, Joe Wright, and anonymous reviewers. Seminar audiences at Columbia, Duke, Georgetown, Princeton, Yale and annual meetings of APSA and IPES provided useful feedback.

I thank the editorial team at Oxford University Press, in particular David McBride, Paul Tompsett, Emily MacKenzie, Claire Sibley, and Wendy Walker, for assistance guiding this book from manuscript through completion.

I thank Cambridge University Press for permission to use material from my article Aid Allocation and Targeted Development in an Increasingly Connected World," published in *International Organization*. Some of the main results from Chapter 4 are reproduced from this article, and part of the theory developed in more detail here is applied there to the case of aid. The overlapping portions are reprinted with permission from Cambridge University Press. All remaining chapters and results are unique to this book.

Finally, and most importantly, I acknowledge with deep gratitude the support of my family, without whom I would never have been able to complete this project. My parents, David and Ruth Blodgett, always encouraged me to tackle difficult projects, work hard, and never give up—lessons I drew on repeatedly while writing this book. My siblings—Matt, Seth, Bethany, Zachary, and Luke—can somehow always remind me not to take myself too seriously, in a supportive and humorous way.

My husband, Otto, has been a source of support and encouragement throughout my career, making it possible to juggle a professional and family life. For this, I am more grateful than I can express. Our children, Katerina, Nathan, and Anika, are a source of joy, and watching them grow and achieve their goals is inspirational. This book is dedicated to my family, whose constant love and support made it possible.

Targeted Development

1

Development as Self-Interest

> More than half the people of the world are living in conditions approaching misery. Their food is inadequate. They are victims of disease. Their economic life is primitive and stagnant. Their poverty is a handicap and a threat both to them and to more prosperous areas.
> —US President Harry Truman, 1949[1]

> It is not only a moral obligation that the better-off countries have to tackle poverty in our world when we still have over a billion people living on less than a dollar a day, but it's also in our interests that we build a more prosperous world. If we don't, the problems of conflict, the problems of mass migration, the problems of uncontrollable climate change are problems that will come and visit us at home.[2]
> —UK Prime Minister David Cameron, 2012

The two quotes opening this study span more than sixty years. One is from 1949 as the world recovered from World War II and the West took up the fight to contain communism, the beginning of what became the Cold War. The other was declared in 2012, well after the Cold War was over, the war on terror under way, and the world recovering from a global recession. Both were spoken by leaders of industrialized states, linking poverty abroad to well-being at home. Both are taken from speeches seeking support for foreign aid programs. Their juxtaposition could easily lead to the conclusion that not much has changed in the philosophy of rich country governments toward the poorer areas of the world.

It is the argument of this book that such a conclusion is incorrect. The changing international landscape has ushered in a new chapter in relations between industrialized and developing states. Foreign policies are no longer defined by the zero–sum nature of a bipolar power structure. Wealthy states are increasingly unable to insulate themselves from the effects of events in developing countries. While rhetoric may not have shifted much, reality is catching up to the rhetoric: the key to prosperity and peace in wealthy states increasingly depends on conditions in poorer areas. Policies in industrialized states are shifting to reflect this reality.

President Truman's speech announced the beginning of the first modern, organized foreign aid program to developing countries, which came to be known as Point Four.[3] While wrapped with the trappings of development promotion, Point Four was unveiled against the backdrop of the start of the Cold War. The United States, often supported by its Western allies, would soon be pursuing a policy designed to contain the spread of Soviet-influenced communism globally, including in developing countries. This would involve covert CIA operations in states such as Iran, Guatemala, and Cuba, support for non-communist "friendly" dictators like Ferdinand Marcos in the Philippines and Mobutu Sese Seko in Zaire (now the Democratic Republic of Congo), large-scale military intervention in Korea and Vietnam, and funding for rebellions against communist governments, including those in Angola and Nicaragua. Even tools ostensibly designed for development, such as foreign aid, would be subordinated to the overriding foreign policy objectives of the time, a point well articulated by Steven Radelet after the end of the Cold War:

> It should hardly be surprising that aid did not always spur development, however, since that was not its principal aim ... Who believed that Zaire's dictator Mobutu Sese Seko would ever use American largesse to vaccinate children or train teachers? Measured against its true objectives, the supposed failure of aid becomes far less apparent. After all, the United States won the Cold War, the threat of communism has essentially disappeared, and Israel and Egypt have remained at peace with one another since Camp David. If some foreign aid meant throwing money down rat holes, Washington at least made sure they weren't communist ones.[4]

During the Cold War, development and development-oriented tools were a means to an end, tactics to be used when they would further broader strategy and set aside when they would not. When policymakers determined that containment was better served through military intervention, covert action, or channeling "development" resources to corrupt dictators, then these tools were employed to achieve the desired goal. As long as development remains relatively unimportant in its own right, simply one possible tactic in an otherwise unrelated overarching strategy, then it will continue to run the risk of being abandoned. When other tactics appear more apropos, development will take a back seat.

With this history, it is easy to dismiss David Cameron's words at the opening of this chapter, and similar sentiments expressed by other world leaders today, as more of the same. As development goals were superseded by the desire to combat and contain Soviet influence during the Cold War, so too may they be superseded by the security concerns of today. Development rhetoric, as in the

Cold War, may be offered to obfuscate less benign-sounding strategic aims of industrialized states in developing countries.

On the other hand, the rhetoric may be part of an actual shift toward pursuing development promotion abroad. The growing connections between industrialized and developing states increase the likelihood of such a change. In the last few decades globalization has made it increasingly difficult for states to insulate themselves from events that occur even in relatively poor, small countries with which they are interconnected. The effects of many problems associated with and enhanced by underdevelopment—illegal migration, political instability, violence, refugee flows, trafficking in persons and illicit substances, spread of disease, lawlessness and its ability to provide havens for terrorists and criminals, pollution, and others—are not confined within national borders. Underdevelopment increasingly creates spillovers that have an impact on wealthier areas.

There was only a tenuous relationship between the strategy of containment and the tactic of development promotion in poor countries during the Cold War. Communism was not caused by underdevelopment. While some underdeveloped countries turned toward Soviet-style communism, others remained in the Western sphere of influence. The non-aligned movement consisted of dozens of developing states with various forms of government, many of which sought to leverage their non-aligned status to gain favors from both the Western-bloc and Eastern-bloc camps. In some countries the United States and its allies were able to stop communist advances using tools other than development. Indeed, it is not difficult to think of examples where support for corrupt dictators likely thwarted development while preventing communist outcomes. While development was embraced—notably by advocates of modernization theory—as a pathway to democracy (and by extension away from communism), in poor countries this process could take decades to bear fruit. To policymakers determined to thwart the spread of communism, the attitude toward development might well be summed up by borrowing a contemporary quote from the memorable Danny Kaye, "But that takes too long. The problem is here, now."[5] In a world of scarce resources and limited time horizons, long-term strategies are likely to be eschewed for those that have a more immediate effect.

In contrast, many of the key policy issues of today are directly related to underdevelopment. Interconnections between countries—both rich and poor—have leapt forward, raising new concerns regarding the impact of underdevelopment abroad on citizens of industrialized states. As Robert Keohane and Joseph Nye observe, "the increasing thickness of globalism—the density of networks of interdependence—is not just a difference in degree . . . different relationships of interdependence intersect more deeply at more points."[6] It is difficult to envision a comprehensive strategy by which industrialized states battle unwanted migration, human trafficking, international gangs, illicit trade, climate change, and other contemporary problems without enhancing and guiding development in poorer areas. Governments in industrialized countries can talk of securing borders, but every day there is evidence of the implausibility of solving these problems through enhanced rules and security alone. Absent genuinely improving economic opportunities within developing countries, negative spillovers will continue to affect industrialized states. While Cold War strategy often eschewed the use of development in favor of more precise tactics, in an increasingly connected world development promotion has emerged as a strategy in its own right.

A Strategy of Targeted Development

The main goal of this book is to develop and test the theory that industrialized states today pursue a strategy of self-interested development promotion abroad. Development promotion is not the only, and likely not even the most important, strategy pursued by industrialized states toward developing countries. However, it is no longer simply a tactic used in pursuit of non-development ends, or a camouflage of words behind which are hidden other agendas. The interests of industrialized countries are not served by setting development goals aside simply because they do not have short-term usefulness for other objectives. Development promotion abroad is an important strategy for fighting problems faced by industrialized states today. Even considering the limitations of scarce resources, development will be pursued alongside of, rather than be subsumed by, other priorities.

As a strategy pursued by industrialized states to further their own interests, development promotion has attributes in common with other foreign policy strategies. Most importantly, development for self-interest is targeted: countries where development will provide the largest benefit to the policymaking state receive the most attention under this strategy. Governments in industrialized states are motivated by a desire to decrease the negative effects on their own countries of spillovers associated with underdevelopment abroad. The source countries from which the impact of spillovers is expected to be highest are the most likely to receive assistance for development promotion.

This strategy of *targeted development* helps define patterns of engagement by industrialized countries in developing areas in the current international environment. In focusing on this broad concept, I do not claim that it explains all actions of industrialized states toward developing countries, nor do I mean to imply that nuances neglected here are unimportant. Yet this broad-based approach is warranted given the task at hand. This book sets forth and tests the theory that there has been a fundamental, high-level shift in the policies pursued by industrialized states toward their developing counterparts such that development considerations are now a key component—although not the only key component—in determining industrialized country foreign policy toward developing states. If so, this should affect policy in multiple issue areas linking these groups of countries, and the impact should be visible at a macro level.

Self-interest pursued through targeted development is fundamentally different from the more simplistic assertion that industrialized countries pursue their own self-interest vis-à-vis developing states. The latter may require no development for success; the former demands development as a prerequisite for claiming success. In the past, if development occurred as a result of industrialized country interactions with developing states, it was an incidental effect—often welcome, but not the main point of the interaction. Now, development is a key goal pursued with foreign policy. Yet despite the claims of policymakers such as former UK Prime Minister Tony Blair, the argument and evidence presented here suggest that rich countries are not pursuing a policy of "enlightened self-interest." Blair and others argue that wealthy states help others because it is good for themselves, that in an era of globalization, "idealism becomes realpolitik."[7] The theory advanced here argues that industrialized states pursue development *when* and *where* it benefits themselves, not simply *because* it benefits themselves.

The self-interested pursuit of development abroad is similar to rationalist scholarly accounts of military intervention for peacekeeping or humanitarian intervention in developing countries. James Fearon and David Laitin attribute the increase in United Nations peacekeeping operations following the end of the Cold War at least in part to the fact that "[i]ncreasingly ... major powers must worry about bad 'externalities' that result from the combination of the scientific revolution and political disorder, economic collapse, and anger in the third world. These externalities include risks of catastrophic terrorism using WMD [weapons of mass destruction], refugee flows, health threats, enhanced drug smuggling networks, and disruption of oil supplies."[8] With regard to international humanitarian interventions, Jack Snyder argues that "states and even multilateral coalitions intervene with military force for humanitarian purposes only when the intervention also serves some perceived self-interest, typically the national interest of the intervening states."[9] These scholars argue that peacekeeping and humanitarian intervention are important tools to serve the evolving self-interest of intervening states. In Snyder's account, self-interest explains not only the growth in humanitarian interventions but also the choice of where to engage; that is, it explains the targeting of interventions across developing states. The theory of targeted development advanced here suggests that the self-interested approach to engagement with poorer countries goes beyond the traditional security realm of military interventions, significantly influencing the use of development tools as well.

The theory advanced in this book claims that the desire of industrialized states to pursue development abroad has increased in a targeted manner. While the remainder of the book is devoted to examining patterns of engagement across issue areas to test this theory, there are implications of the targeted development framework for thinking about relations between industrialized and developing countries more broadly that are worth previewing up front. First, an increase in the desire to promote development, even for self-interested reasons, suggests that past performance may not be a good benchmark for evaluating the effectiveness of development instruments going forward. If the intentions of industrialized states have changed, it is possible this will lead to a shift in outcomes as well. Second, the targeted nature of development promotion suggests that, while some countries will see increased growth, those not targeted will form a smaller periphery where development increasingly lags behind that in other states. Third, the desire to target also has implications for the role of international institutions in development promotion. To the extent that the preferences for targeting vary across industrialized states, they will be reluctant to delegate development promotion to multilateral decision-making bodies. These implications are further developed throughout the book, and I return to them in the conclusion.

Nuanced Approach Spanning Issue Areas

A serious attempt to promote development must simultaneously use various available tools in a nuanced manner that accounts for the specific circumstances of the targeted state. The mantra "trade not aid" rose to prominence with the 1968 United Nations Conference on Trade and Development (UNCTAD) meeting, suggesting that access to trade, rather than development assistance, would be the key to long-term development for poorer countries. Aid fosters dependence; trade is the path to self-sustaining growth. The decade also saw the rise in popularity of the Chinese proverb "Give a man a fish and feed him for a day. Teach a man to fish and feed him for a lifetime." This, like the rationale for trade, is excellent long-run advice for achieving self-sufficiency. Yet unless the desired result is dead, half-trained fishermen with no equipment in the short run, some upfront provision of food and capital, along with training, is necessary.

The point, of course, is that various development tools should be thought of as complements, rather than as substitutes, for pursuing a development strategy. Countries generating spillovers of concern to industrialized states span a wide range of development levels and include governments of various degrees of legitimacy and efficiency. There is no "one-size-fits-all" development strategy that can work across countries. Some have reached a level of development at which foreign aid can have only limited additional impact, while preferential access to industrialized country trade markets could provide a large boost to growth. In these cases, a well-thought-out aid program can build trade capacity to enhance the development impact of a trade agreement. Other states are so underdeveloped that they do not have the infrastructure in place to benefit from preferential trade agreements even when they are offered; foreign aid can be helpful in these instances, increasing development and preparing states for more productive engagement with world markets. Development assistance can even at times serve as a bandage; when violence, corruption, or poor governance prevents advancement of development, outside assistance can work to prevent back sliding until days of better governance arrive. The type of assistance in these cases will differ from that offered in cases where the developing country government is seen as a partner by those wishing to advance development with outside assistance.

In addition to using development tools, if development promotion has become a high priority for industrialized states then they are likely to divert resources ostensibly earmarked for other purposes to meet these goals. For example, funding meant for climate change mitigation may be diverted from its most efficient use for decreasing greenhouse gas (GHG) concentration in order to help meet the development priorities of industrialized states. Mitigating the extent of climate change is as close to a pure public good as one can imagine: the location of GHG emissions is unimportant—reducing GHGs by a given amount anywhere will have the same impact on global warming. Thus one might expect climate mitigation dollars to be allocated with the intent to maximize emission reductions, regardless of where those occur. In this case, delegation to an international body that shares these goals would most likely produce optimal results. However, in many cases these funds, by design, promote "clean development"; while donors of climate finance may have little preference regarding the location of "clean," the theory predicts that they have targeted preferences regarding development. The expected result is that an industrialized state will allocate resources to the developing states that provide it with the highest total increase in utility, after considering the benefits to itself of both development and climate mitigation produced with the resources. This can result in a decrease in efficiency for the stated goal—combatting climate change—to the extent that the optimal spending areas for mitigating climate change do not align with the development preferences of climate finance donors. This is merely an example; similar skewing can be anticipated any time resources allocated ostensibly for other purposes also have development potential.

As was true for the strategy of containment in the Cold War or the fight against terrorism today, the strategy of targeted development will also affect policy in multiple issue areas. In producing the Commitment to Development Index, which evaluates industrialized countries' development performance in the areas of aid, trade, finance, migration, environment, security, and technology, the Center for Global Development argues that "reducing poverty in developing countries is about far more than giving money."[10] While evaluating each of these areas comprehensively in a single study is not feasible, this book devotes a chapter each to foreign aid, trade agreements between industrialized and developing countries, and external financing related to climate change in developing countries.

Foreign aid is examined as the most obvious issue area for testing a theory related to development. Studying the pattern of trade agreements provides an opportunity to determine if the desire to pursue targeted development extends beyond giving money and into an area where domestic political sensitivity in industrialized countries is more pronounced. Looking at climate finance can generate insight as to whether a targeted development strategy redirects resources when the primary stated purpose is something other than development. In each issue area, the desire to pursue targeted development is expected to affect the allocation of industrialized country resources across developing countries.

Development and Terrorism

Following the terrorist attacks of September 11, 2001, World Bank president James Wolfensohn asserted that it was essential to deal with the "breeding grounds of discontent" caused by poverty as a "necessary step two" in the fight against terrorism.[11] World leaders routinely cite links between poverty and terrorism to justify increased spending on development. Yet if development promotion is a serious goal of governments in industrialized states, this is likely in spite of, rather than because of, rhetoric linking underdevelopment to terrorism. For the same reasons that policymakers combatting the Cold War "ism" looked to other tools, the use of development promotion as part of a short-term counterterrorism strategy seems unlikely.

While there has been significant development in the world since the early years of containment, in many countries it is still unfortunately true that development remains a long-term prospect rather than a short-term goal. On the surface, attempts to link underdevelopment with terrorism seem doomed to relegate it to the same fate observed during the Cold War: given scarce resources, development will be set aside in favor of tactics likely to bring about more immediate results. Therefore, development is more likely to be seen as important if it is also used to pursue goals other than counterterrorism. In that case, rather than development rhetoric providing cover for a non-development security concern, the fight against terrorism is providing the necessary—if not completely warranted—justification for a development strategy primarily tackling problems not directly associated with terrorism.

The creation of the Millennium Challenge Account (MCA) by US President George W. Bush provides an interesting example of both a development program not closely linked with the war on terror and the use of counterterrorism rhetoric as a justification. Speaking at the Conference on Financing for Development in Monterrey, Mexico months after the September 11, 2001 terrorist attacks on his country, President Bush announced the creation of the MCA and pledged $5 billion annually in new aid to fund this program. In making this announcement, Bush claimed that new approaches to development "will challenge the poverty and hopelessness and lack of education and failed governments that too often allow conditions that terrorists can seize and try to turn to their advantage." He also called for aid to be more effective, and declared that the new aid he was announcing would be given to countries that "govern justly, invest in their people and encourage economic freedom."[12] These conditions, which were attached to eligibility for the MCA from its inception, effectively excluded the most important states in the war on terror, as they did not meet the criteria for assistance.[13]

Fighting terrorism is probably the most important foreign policy goal today for the majority of governments in industrialized countries. In the long run, promoting development abroad may decrease the support for terrorist activity against wealthy states. However, as in the Cold War, there are short-term tactics likely to bring about more immediate results. Why, then, in competition for scarce resources, should development promotion fare any better during the war on terror than during the Cold War? While many resources are necessarily used to counter terrorist threats, why are other funds specifically allocated for development? A strategy of development promotion is pursued today, much more vigorously than during the Cold War, because today industrialized states face problems—outside of terrorist threats—for which development promotion is the best strategy.

Development and International Institutions

International institutions have struggled to enact development agendas or increase their role in development promotion. From the World Trade Organization (WTO), to the World Bank, to the Green Climate Fund, large-member multilateral institutions are meeting resistance in their attempts to become or remain relevant on development issues. This may be a symptom of the declining relevance placed on development by the principals of these organizations, and evidence against the argument advanced here that concern for underdevelopment has increased significantly and permeates policy on multiple issues in industrialized states. I will argue instead that it is a predictable result of a move toward targeted development. Furthermore, contrary to frequent lamentations in the policy community, it is unclear that a move away from multilateralism will result in worse development outcomes.

Launched to much fanfare, the Doha Round of negotiations at the World Trade Organization (WTO) was dubbed the "Doha Development Agenda" and claimed to place the "needs and interests" of developing countries "at the heart of the Work Programme" adopted in the 2001 Ministerial declaration.[14] In 2005 then Director-General of the WTO, Pascal Lamy, claimed that "Development is the *raison d'être* of the Doha Round."[15] Yet after fourteen years of negotiation, at the Nairobi Ministerial Conference in 2015 the Round was still not concluded and looked increasingly likely to be abandoned altogether. Multilateral action has been difficult on climate finance as well: following the establishment of the Green Climate Fund in 2010, it took five years for project funding to begin, and the target spending for 2016 was $2.5 billion—a modest sum in light of pledges by industrialized states to work toward allocating $100 billion per year for climate finance in developing countries.[16] Donor states have been reluctant to commit a set percentage of promised funds to be channeled multilaterally, but current evidence suggests the multilateral portion will be underwhelming. In the long standing realm of foreign aid, funding has increased markedly since 2000, but the share going to multilateral institutions has not been rising.[17]

While these trends may be troubling for proponents of multilateralism, they are not in themselves evidence against the importance of development as a foreign policy goal of industrialized states. Multilateral institutions are a policy tool, not an end in themselves.[18] As Barbara Koremenos, Charles Lipson, and Duncan Snidal argue, "States favor some institutions because they are better suited to new conditions or new problems and abandon or downplay those that are not."[19] If development has increased in importance to industrialized states, and if they believe their interests are best served through pursuing development bilaterally, a retreat from large-member multilateral institutions is consistent with industrialized states increasing their focus on development. This will be particularly true when states pursue targeted development, rather than universal development, and when their preferences regarding targeting diverge.

Development has clear characteristics of a public good, in that at least some of the positive outcomes from development in a country for the rest of the world are both non-rival and non-excludable. If a country is less likely to be a safe haven for international criminals or send large numbers of refugees over its borders, many other nations may simultaneously benefit from this without detracting from the benefit of others or excluding others from also benefitting. As such, demand for an international regime seems likely, to overcome market failure stemming from free-riding and the resulting underprovision that often occurs in similar circumstances.[20]

A difficulty arises in that the benefit received from improving development in any particular developing state is likely to vary considerably across industrialized states, based on the relative level of connectivity each has with the developing state. This creates a situation in which the preferences of industrialized states regarding the distribution of development resources across developing countries are not aligned. As preferences diverge, bargaining problems increase[21] and the ability to free-ride decreases.[22] Additionally, the larger the differences in preferences, the smaller the potential gains from coordination. Thus there is a movement away from a coordinated multilateral response, with resources provided to the areas targeted to produce private, rather than collective, benefits for each industrialized state. The increased importance of private benefits can potentially lead to increased resources devoted to development as the ability to free-ride declines, but also results in less incentive for coordination. Mancur Olson and Richard Zeckhauser, in a study that addresses both military alliances and foreign aid, note that as the ratio of private to collective benefits increases, "the degree of coordination among the allies will decline, and this will reduce the efficiency of the alliance forces (in a sense leaving them on a poorer production function), but the alliance forces will be larger."[23]

Those who have observed the sharp increases in foreign aid while lamenting inefficiency from lack of donor coordination will recognize the applicability of this assessment to development today. The cost of closer coordination would be fewer resources; whether the gains in efficiency would outweigh the loss of financing and result in more development is unknown.[24] Similar issues plague the areas of trade agreements and international finance for climate change adaptation and mitigation. As will be discussed in Chapter 5, the particular rules of the WTO enhance this problem in the realm of trade. Chapter 6 addresses the preference for bilateral targeting over a coordinated, multilateral response in climate finance, which results in decreased efficiency of resources in achieving mitigation of and adaptation to climate change.

The lack of delegation to international bodies is an expected outcome of industrialized states pursuing targeted, rather than universal, development outcomes, as long as they have different preferences regarding the cross-national allocation of resources. Given that the focus of this book is on targeted development, which is more likely to occur outside of international institutions, the majority of the focus is on bilateral relations between industrialized and developing states. However, in each issue area some attention is paid to the role (or lack thereof) of relevant institutions. Additionally, the conclusion offers some thoughts regarding the continued relevance of using international institutions for development in an era of targeted, self-interested development promotion.

Quo Vadimus?

It is hardly novel to argue that promoting development abroad can further the interests of industrialized states. As the opening quotations for this chapter show, policymakers have been making such statements for decades. Despite this, we lack a framework for determining when, where, and how industrialized states pursue development abroad. When are development statements merely rhetoric, and when are they indicative of important policy priorities? Which developing countries are likely to attract resources for development from industrialized country governments? How should we expect development priorities to guide policy across multiple issue areas? By developing and testing a theory of targeted development to help answer these questions, this book is an important step toward filling the gaps. This section presents a roadmap for the following chapters.

Chapter 2 places the concept of targeted development in historical context, starting with an overview of the time immediately following the end of World War II. Interestingly, this period contains an excellent example of targeted development that was not targeted at developing countries. The logic for targeted development today has much in common with the decision to target development resources to Europe, rather than the developing world, in the second half of the 1940s. Examining how the dynamics of the Cold War evolved, it becomes clear that regardless of early stated intentions by leaders of the largest industrialized states, interactions with developing countries would often have little to do with development promotion in this time period. It then traces the rise of interconnections between industrialized and developing countries since the end of the Cold War.

This overview lays the groundwork for the formal model that is developed in Chapter 3. The model starts from the assumption that governments in industrialized states seek to maximize their own utility in interactions with developing countries. Development concerns compete with other policy goals for scarce government resources. The amount of resources an industrialized state devotes to development will vary over time to reflect changes in the relative importance the state places on development compared to other goals. Resource allocation across developing countries will vary to reflect industrialized country priorities, as well as the efficiency of developing countries at turning resources into development outcomes that the industrialized state values. As industrialized country governments work to maximize the utility gained per dollar (or euro, yen, etc.) spent, development motives will influence policy in issue areas less specifically tied to development, which can range from the location of a military base to the destination of climate finance. Because industrialized countries have divergent preferences regarding the cross-country allocation of resources, they will prefer bilateral to multilateral approaches for addressing problems in developing states.

Chapters 4, 5, and 6 apply the theory to the issue areas of foreign aid, preferential trade agreements, and climate finance. There are multiple benefits to examining these issues in the context of a single study and overarching theoretical framework. A theoretical expectation of the rising importance of development is that it will have an impact on multiple policy fronts. Additionally, given the heterogeneous characteristics of developing countries, industrialized states are likely to pursue a nuanced approach appropriate for individual states; examining a single policy area could lead to erroneous conclusions regarding the broader development landscape. Incorporating analysis of these issues into a single framework of targeted development provides insights into each that would be missed if they were only examined in isolation from each other. Finally, while each of the areas is related to development, they are not identical: the theory generates unique predictions for each, and testing them empirically in the same study provides context for the extent of influence targeted development exhibits across a spectrum of issue areas.

It is important to note that it is not the intent of this book to provide a complete overview of the issue areas used in the empirical analysis; they are each the main focus of multiple existing studies. The approach here is two-fold. First, it is useful to test the relevance of targeted development as an additional explanation for the patterns observed in each issue area. To do this, attention is paid to existing theories and findings in order to situate the concept of targeted development in the broader debates in each field. Analysis is conducted to determine if observed patterns are consistent with the framework of targeted development, after controlling for existing explanations. To the extent that such evidence is found within and across issue areas, it provides support for the main hypotheses of this book. This is, however, a two-way street. While the issue areas are used to test the theory, each chapter also draws out implications from the theory for better understanding current and likely future outcomes in the issue area.

The empirical analysis begins in Chapter 4 with an examination of foreign aid allocation. The stated purpose of foreign aid is development. At a very rudimentary level, failure to find evidence of a pro-development agenda in foreign aid would render suspect the entire premise of the study. Moving beyond this, targeted development generates multiple observable implications that can be tested by examining foreign aid. Foreign aid should be targeted toward those countries where development can most benefit the donor. As negative spillovers must be transmitted to other states to have an effect, greater connectivity between a donor and recipient—through proximity, trade, migration, or historical ties—increases the likelihood of transmission and should therefore be associated with greater foreign aid. In addition to cross-national targeting, donors pursuing development care about the effectiveness of foreign aid at producing development outcomes. To attain these, they will need to craft a basket of aid that matches the needs and capabilities of chosen recipients. Thus, we should expect systematic variation in the composition of aid across developing countries. Finally, the emphasis on development in foreign aid should increase significantly over time as the priorities of industrialized states shifted from a Cold War strategy of containment to one that includes promoting targeted development abroad.

Preferential trade agreements between industrialized and developing countries are the subject of Chapter 5. Trade is widely regarded as one of the most effective vehicles for growth and development. Virtually nonexistent in 1990, there has been a sharp increase in the percentage of industrialized–developing country pairs covered by preferential trade agreements in the last quarter-century. Yet despite this growth, the majority of industrialized–developing country dyads have not signed a preferential trade agreement. The theory suggests that these agreements are more likely to be signed by an industrialized country with a developing state when it places a high value on promoting development in the state and when the state has reached a level of development that will allow it to further benefit from preferential access to the wealthier market.

The analysis in this chapter begins with an overview of the Dominican Republic–Central American preferential trade agreement (CAFTA-DR), signed between the United States, the Dominican Republic, Costa Rica, Honduras, Nicaragua, Guatemala, and El Salvador. The small size of the developing country markets in this agreement relative to the United States suggests that potential gains from trade for special interests and the broader public in the United States are unlikely to justify the amount of political capital used by members of the George W. Bush administration to gain final passage of this agreement in the US Congress. Promoting development through open markets, however, creates a significant opportunity to decrease the effects of underdevelopment in these countries on the United States and a plausible explanation for the importance of this agreement. The remainder of this chapter analyzes the growth of preferential trade agreements between industrialized and developing countries more generally, focusing on the determinants of these agreements and their relationship with foreign aid as tools in a broader development framework.

The final empirical chapter analyzes the relatively new area of climate finance. Funds are offered by industrialized states to developing countries in an effort to both mitigate the causes of climate change and help these countries adapt to the effects of changes that are already under way. Rather than flowing to countries where mitigation efforts will accomplish the greatest GHG reductions and to those states most in need of assistance for adaptation, the theory predicts that funds will be diverted to areas where their use is likely to have the greatest positive impact on the utility of the financing states. When funds can simultaneously address climate change and development, they will be skewed toward the countries where development provides larger benefits for the donor state. This area provides an important test of the extent to which development priorities influence policy in an issue area where the ultimate (stated) goal is not development, but mitigation of and adaptation to climate change.

Examining a new issue area presents challenges: data availability and quality are not as high as in more established areas, and the quantity of scholarly analysis is lower. Yet it also presents the opportunity to test the theory in an area where policy is still evolving. Implications derived from the analysis are more likely to have an impact here than in the more entrenched areas of foreign aid and trade. A key insight that comes from the analysis is that targeting may be as important as free-riding in presenting a challenge to advancing the the stated purposes of climate finance. The ability to target is likely to lessen concerns of free-riding, but also likely to reduce the efficiency of funding for achieving the stated objectives of adaptation and mitigation. It also suggests that distributional concerns are likely to be much more salient in negotiations over mitigation financing than the public good nature of climate change would lead one to expect.

The concluding chapter synthesizes the findings from the empirical analyses. In each issue area, the pursuit of targeted development is found to be an important contributing factor for understanding observed outcomes, although it is not the only motivation behind industrialized country policies. The desire to promote development in a targeted fashion shapes policy across areas in ways not well explained by existing theories. Beyond those examined here, the targeted development framework is likely to have implications for understanding policy in many realms in which industrialized and developing countries interact.

This chapter also highlights some remaining gaps in our understanding of development promotion. Importantly, this study focuses on understanding the motivations behind policies pursued by industrialized states in their interactions with developing countries. It does not analyze outcomes of these policies. It is unclear whether shifting intent in favor of development promotion will be translated into better development results, and there are reasons for both caution and optimism in assessing this likelihood.

Despite intentions, it is possible that industrialized countries are simply not well equipped to spur development in other countries. Books documenting failed development "knowledge" from the past—including the backlash against the once-heralded "Washington Consensus"—could fill a small library. Additionally, many of the institutions tasked with development promotion, both domestic and international, date from an earlier age when development was significantly less important as a motivating factor in shaping the policies of states. It is unclear whether changes in government intentions will be enough to overcome bureaucratic inertia and force either adaptation to the new motivations or the replacement of existing institutions with ones better aligned with current goals.

On the other hand, a stronger development mandate coupled with increased resources may unleash a new wave of effective ingenuity in development. This book focuses on changes in the motivations guiding industrialized country policies toward developing states. The evolving nature of these motivations has important implications for studying the effectiveness of development policies. If development policies have been ineffective in the past because of the motivations of industrialized countries, changes in motivations should have an impact on outcomes. If policies are still ineffective, we will need to look beyond motivations, including to institutions and abilities, to determine the causes of ineffectiveness.

This final chapter also addresses additional implications from the targeted development strategy. If it is successful, development will increase and negative spillovers from the targeted countries will decrease. Yet some countries—those not targeted—will be left behind. While these states are on the periphery of foreign policy agendas today, growing discontent likely associated with rising disparity may render these states some of the more important security concerns of the future. Related to this, the chapter discusses ways in which international institutions can be used to decrease inefficiencies and fill gaps left when industrialized countries follow a targeted, bilateral development strategy. Rethinking the role of international institutions as complements to bilateral strategies, rather than as substitutes for these strategies, can harness the benefits of both bilateral and multilateral approaches.

Targeted development is a self-interested strategy meant to increase the well-being of the policymaking state. As long as underdevelopment continues to inflict costs on industrialized states, these states will respond by attempting to mitigate these effects. The success or failure of targeted development will be judged, by the state, on the extent to which it furthers this goal.

2

Targeted Development in Perspective

> In concentrating upon the problem of aid to Europe I do not ignore the fact that there are other areas of the world beset by economic problems of tremendous gravity. But the very magnitude of the world problem as a whole requires a careful direction of our assistance to the critical areas where it can be most immediately effective.
> —George Marshall, 1947[1]

In the aftermath of World War II, the administration of US President Harry Truman determined that the security and prosperity of the United States required a rapid return to prosperity in Europe. Members of the administration undertook to develop and gain support for an unprecedented level of peacetime foreign assistance that culminated in the passage of the Economic Cooperation Act of 1948, more commonly referred to as the Marshall Plan. It was the first instance of targeted development used as a foreign policy tool, and provides a useful starting point for placing changes in attitudes toward development in historical context. This book is primarily about relations between industrialized and developing countries today—in the post–Cold War, even post-2001 period. Yet history is important for understanding how the pattern of development targeting currently observed marks a break from the past: why was development promotion—after a stunning reception in the Marshall Plan—sidetracked for decades, and why has it assumed greater importance today?

In reviewing the actions of industrialized countries during the Cold War, this chapter is not meant to be—and is not—a comprehensive history of the time. Instead, this account seeks to highlight international circumstances that explain why pro-development rhetoric in the early Cold War period did not translate into a large-scale pursuit of development in poorer countries, despite the overwhelmingly positive reception to pursuing development in Europe under the Marshall Plan. This discussion is important given the limited ability to interpret foreign policy intentions from statements of government officials. During the Cold War the rhetoric of development was often used to justify non-development interventions, with even the tools of development (such as foreign aid) employed to advance these alternate objectives. Much of today's pro-development statements are reminiscent of those uttered by world leaders operating under a different international landscape. Highlighting changes in this broader landscape facilitates understanding why similar pro-development statements today are significantly more likely to be associated with concrete steps to promote development abroad.

The chapter begins with a discussion of post–World War II Europe, highlighting the nuanced and multipronged approach used to contain the spread of communism in that region including, but not limited to, financial assistance. It then provides a brief overview of main themes guiding relations between industrialized and developing states during the Cold War. As the context is broad, the focus is on the strategies of the most powerful industrialized state, the United States, as the undisputed leader of the "Western" camp during this period; brief mentions are also made of the role of secondary powers such as France, Japan, and the United Kingdom. An overview of foreign policy toward developing countries in the 1990s follows, and attention is drawn to a number of ways in which connections between industrialized and developing states have increased. The chapter concludes by discussing the role of the September 11, 2001, terrorist attacks in focusing the attention of policymakers on the importance of underdevelopment as a foreign policy priority.

Marshall Plan

Within a few years of the ending of World War II, US policymakers became concerned with the economic situation in Europe. Secretary of State George Marshall declared in 1947 that "the recovery of Europe has been far slower than expected."[2] Industrial production was taking too long to rebound to its prewar levels. High rates of unemployment and food shortages were creating discontent. Notably, and worrisome from the US point of view at the time, communist parties were gaining strength in many Western European countries; in France and Italy they were garnering more than one-third of the votes in democratic elections.[3] US President Truman and his advisors believed economic recovery was essential to prevent the spread of Soviet-influenced communism to Western Europe and reintegrate (West) Germany into Europe, and they believed US assistance was necessary to achieve this goal. In 1948 Congress approved the Economic Cooperation Act, giving life to the European Recovery Program, the official name for the Marshall Plan.

US aid to Western Europe under the Marshall Plan amounted to approximately $13 billion between 1948 and 1951. The Plan is widely credited with helping European recovery, although more recent interpretations suggest it did not "jump start" recovery, which had already begun.[4] Rather, the aid provided a cushion, allowing governments some freedom to invest by ameliorating the shortfall of cash necessary to pay for imports and overcoming short-term food shortages. It kept recovery moving and provided a psychological boost to the European public, both of which decreased the appeal of communism—especially as the communist parties, acting on orders from the Soviet Union, opposed the very aid that people saw as essential help in a difficult time.[5] It also created good will toward the United States, and a sense of shared commitment on both sides of the Atlantic.

What made the Marshall Plan successful was not simply the aid attached to it, although that is the most commonly cited element. The overall design and implementation of the program, as well as the simultaneous introduction of complementary initiatives also aimed at promoting recovery, European integration, and containment of Soviet influence, were essential components of success. At the insistence of the United States, the initial draft of the plan was drawn up by European governments working together: they were required to submit a single European plan rather than submitting individual country plans.[6] This fostered a sense of collaboration and common purpose among Western European countries, as well as ownership of the program. The United States required a regional authority to work with its own newly created Economic Cooperation Administration (ECA) to oversee implementation; this led to the creation of the Organization for European Economic Cooperation (OEEC), with representatives from each participating country.[7]

The emphasis on working together to draft and administer the program did not result in a one-size-fits-all aid plan; both the amounts and the purposes of Marshall Plan aid varied by recipient.[8] In France much aid was used to further industrial investment already ongoing under the Monnet Plan. In Britain, where food was in short supply, approximately 30% of aid was spent on food, a much higher fraction than in France. In Germany, Marshall Plan aid was coupled with necessary currency reform; the aid was used to finance imports and assist with industrial recovery. Recognizing that achieving a common goal required a different approach in each country, the Marshall Plan incorporated nuances to reflect differing economic and political situations across recipients.

A broad foreign policy strategy will utilize tools across issue areas; this was particularly evident in Europe in the late 1940s. Responding to pressure from the British and French, and spurred to action by the communist coup in Czechoslovakia in 1948 and the Soviet blockade of Berlin, the United States agreed to move forward with a defensive alliance, resulting in the signing of the North Atlantic Treaty in 1949.[9] This committed the United States to defending Europe, which allowed those countries to focus more on their economic recovery than would have been possible if they had been left alone to deal with the rising threat of the Soviet Union.[10] The common alliance also allayed fears associated with German recovery, particularly for France.[11] The wording of the Marshall Plan itself called for specific actions, placing particular emphasis on "a strong production effort, expansion of foreign trade, the creation and maintenance of internal financial stability, and the development of economic cooperation, including all possible steps to establish and maintain equitable rates of exchange and to bring about the progressive elimination of trade barriers."[12] In keeping with this, the United States embraced France's plan to form the European Coal and Steel Community, linking the productive capacities of France and Germany and laying the groundwork for a more integrated Europe.[13]

This multipronged approach of financial assistance, security, cooperation, and economic integration facilitated economic recovery and political stability in Western Europe, effectively containing the spread of Soviet influence on the continent. The Marshall Plan is often heralded today as an example of cooperation between donor and recipient countries and tailored response to country-specific conditions,[14] as well as for its significant contribution of donor resources. It is also, however, an example of targeting: resources were devoted to Europe not because, of all regions, it had the most need of outside assistance. Rather, it was the region where development would best serve the goals of the donor state, and where resources could reasonably be expected to deliver results for the overarching policy goals within a short timeframe.

Developing Countries and Containment

With the backdrop of the ongoing Marshall Plan, Truman's "Point Four" announcement of assistance for developing countries in January 1949 may have been seen as a logical extension of a successful program. Cold War strategy was still evolving. A plan to prevent communism in the developing world by investing in economic development may have seemed sensible. But events moved quickly over the next few years. By the end of 1949 communists, led by Mao Zedong, had declared victory in China. Less than a year later, North Korea—backed by the Soviet Union and China—invaded South Korea, drawing the United States into war. At the same time the Viet Minh, also with support from Stalin and Mao, were making headway against French colonial forces in Indochina.

Given the success of US strategy in Europe, why did Truman's speech not usher in an era of increased development and integration that embraced the developing areas of the world? The answer almost certainly has to do with the difference in time horizons. Paul Hoffman, who was to become Administrator for the European Recovery Program (Marshall Plan), argued with regard to Europe that "We ought to keep our eyes on just one thing and that is: Will the program build up production and produce a reasonable degree of prosperity in 4 or 5 years?"[15] In Europe, this was an achievable goal and was, in fact, achieved. However, as Hoffman also noted, Marshall Plan aid provided the "critical margin" for participating countries.[16] In the developing world, much more than a "margin" would be needed to raise citizens to a "reasonable degree of prosperity," and it would certainly take more than four or five years. It was also unclear that even with development newly independent states would side with their former colonizers in the West rather than the rapidly industrializing Soviet Union. Given US fears that it was losing ground in the Cold War to the Soviet Union and China—reinforced by both international events and the Soviet development of an atomic bomb in 1949, years sooner than the United States had anticipated—it is perhaps not surprising that short-run, often military solutions would be chosen over a long-run development strategy with uncertain results for Cold War balance.

George Kennan's famous "long telegram" and "X Article" of 1947 brought into common use the idea that the United States should focus on "containment" of Soviet expansion. This, coupled with the need to, as Kennan put it in 1949, "economize with our limited resources and … apply them where we feel that they will do the most good," where "most good" can be thought of in terms of achieving the overarching goal of Soviet containment,[17] led the United States to focus its energy and resources in the developing world primarily in those countries where the possibility of successful Soviet influence was feared. Although containment would take various forms under different US administrations, the basic principle of stopping Soviet advances remained intact for the duration of the Cold War.

That containment included the developing world became clear early on. As Kenneth Waltz famously noted, "[i]n a bipolar world there are no peripheries. With only two powers capable of acting on a world scale, anything that happens anywhere is potentially of concern to both of them."[18] Following Truman's concerns regarding Indochina, US President Dwight Eisenhower invoked the "falling domino" principle: "You have a row of dominoes set up, you knock over the first one, and what will happen to the last one is the certainty that it will go over very quickly." The "loss" of Indochina to the communist Viet Minh would endanger, the president argued, Japan, Australia, New Zealand, and others, making the possible consequences to "the free world" "incalculable."[19] The concerns of the US government at this time were not confined to Indochina. In 1953 the CIA backed a coup against Iranian Prime Minister Muhammad Mossadeq, placing power in the hands of the Shah.[20] Just two months after the "domino" analogy, the CIA backed a coup against the democratically elected, but left-leaning, President Jacobo Arbenz in Guatemala, where the US government also supported the subsequent repression of those not loyal to the new leadership.[21]

What happened to the lofty goals of fighting poverty in the self-interest of the United States and its allies that had been hailed as Truman announced the Point Four program? Scholars were quick to dismiss any notion that Point Four assistance was truly motivated by development concerns. Carl McGuire, writing in 1952, noted that "conceivably Point Four might also be considered successful if it did not stimulate the growth of the retarded economies appreciably, provided that the *attempt* to give economic impetus to the backward areas created a more favorable attitude on the part of their governments and their peoples toward the United States than otherwise would have prevailed."[22] Toward the end of the decade, Milton Friedman argued that "foreign economic aid is widely recognized as a weapon in the ideological war in which the United States is now engaged. Its assigned role is to help win over to our side those uncommitted nations that are also underdeveloped and poor."[23]

At the same time a group of scholars, including Daniel Lerner, Max Millikan, and Walt Rostow, among others, was giving rise to the concept of modernization theory, and advocating its relevance for US foreign policy in the developing world. Proponents of modernization theory argued that the United States could accelerate growth in developing countries, helping them reach a "modern" point of development more quickly, which would lead away from communism and toward liberal democracy.[24] In the mid-1950s Millikan argued to a State Department audience that "A much extended program of American participation in the economic development of the so-called underdeveloped states can and should be one of the most important elements in a program of expanding the dynamism and stability of the Free World and increasing its resistance to the appeals of Communism."[25] Modernization theory held considerable appeal, first for Eisenhower and even more so for the administration of President John F. Kennedy when it took office in 1961; Rostow, a noted scholar in modernization theory, served as Director of Policy Planning in the US Department of State from 1961 to 1966.

After assuming office, Kennedy was quick to announce the Alliance for Progress. Utilizing the theories of the modernization school, the United States wanted to promote development in Latin America and thereby prevent future communist victories in the Western Hemisphere along the lines of Fidel Castro's 1959 revolution in Cuba.[26] However, just as the lofty ambitions of Point Four had given way to the need for containment and stopping dominoes, the turn toward the liberalizing goals of modernization theory was short-lived. Michael Latham summarizes the situation in the 1960s well:

By strongly supporting a string of dictators in Saigon, backing the Shah of Iran's political repression, supporting an anti-Communist, military-driven bloodbath in Indonesia, and embracing right-wing coups across Latin America, the United States steadily turned toward "bureaucratic authoritarian" solutions. Modernization promised stability through long-term progress, but by the mid-1960s US policymakers concluded that the immediate preservation of anti-Communist order required a more direct approach.[27]

This force-based "direct" approach was used in post-colonial situations in which the colonial power and/or the United States feared an unfriendly regime could emerge. The United States and Belgium backed opposition to leader Patrice Lumumba in the newly independent Congo in 1960, and provided military support to help Mobutu Sese Seko defeat rebel strongholds in eastern Congo in 1964.[28] The CIA, with the help of the British colonial power, actively opposed the rule of communist-leaning Cheddi Jagan as Guyana gained independence in the mid-1960s.[29] The United States and other Western-bloc states supported the authoritarian regime of Suharto in Indonesia, which spearheaded a campaign of mass killing against Indonesian communists that left more than half a million people dead in the mid-1960s;[30] major aid donors to the Suharto regime included Australia, Germany, Japan, the Netherlands (the former colonial power), the United States, and in some years Canada, France, Italy, and the United Kingdom.[31] In more established countries there was also intervention to promote governments more friendly to the West. The United States encouraged the organizers of the 1964 military coup in Brazil with promises of recognition and aid, and invaded the Dominican Republic in 1965 to avoid the possibility of a left-leaning government.[32] Of course, while the focus here is on the policies of the Western-bloc industrialized states, both the Soviet Union and China were actively backing governments friendly to themselves as well. Mark Bradley notes that as the Cold War evolved "Soviet, American, and Chinese intervention in postcolonial state-making took an increasingly intrusive and militarized turn, first in Vietnam and later in Angola, Mozambique, Ethiopia, Central America, and Afghanistan."[33]

The most notable engagement of the United States in the developing world in 1960s and early 1970s was, of course, the escalation of hostilities in Vietnam. After winning re-election in 1964, US President Lyndon Johnson was determined to avoid a loss to the communists in Vietnam. Melvyn Leffler notes the influence of the domino theory on Johnson's thinking in the mid-1960: "If they take South Vietnam, they take Thailand, they take Indonesia, they take Burma, they come right back to the Philippines."[34] Leffler also shows that some in the administration feared a global contagion, with implications as far afield as South

America.[35] In 1964 and 1965 Johnson decided to commence bombing against North Vietnam and commited large numbers of US ground forces to the war. By the time the communist North claimed victory in 1975, more than 58,000 US military personnel had lost their lives[36] and in excess of 1.5 million Vietnamese civilian and military deaths had occurred as a result of the war.[37]

Following this experience, the US Congress and the American public had little desire for direct military intervention in developing countries. Throughout the remainder of the 1970s and 1980s different tactics were used to support "friendly" regimes in the West's fight to contain communism. When the end of authoritarian rule in Portugal in 1974 led to rapid independence for its former colonies in southern Africa, the United States relied primarily on covert CIA activity and African allies—such as Zaire and South Africa—to fight (unsuccessfully) against Soviet- and Cuban-backed communist groups in Mozambique and Angola.[38] The authoritarian regime of Ferdinand Marcos in the Philippines received hundreds of millions of dollars in foreign aid annually in the 1970s and 1980s, with large donors including the United States (under presidents Ford, Carter, and Reagan), Japan, Germany, and Australia.[39] The country was seen as a vital location for a US military base in pursuing the containment of Soviet influence in Asia, and the Marcos regime had also taken a tough stand against a communist insurgency in the Philippines.[40]

When the Western-backed government of Mobutu Sese Seko in Zaire was threatened by an invasion of fighters from Angola in 1977, France, Morocco and Saudi Arabia—coordinating their actions through the recently formed "Safari Club"—took the lead in carrying out an operation that led to the retreat of the rebels, with additional aid supplied to Mobutu from the United States. The Safari Club also took the lead in supporting Somalia's invasion of Ethiopia in 1977, with the United States again playing a more permissive and supportive, rather than direct, role.[41] When a second invasion into Zaire from Angola occurred the following year, French and Belgium forces intervened with help from the United States.[42] Support for Mobutu's brutal and corrupt regime in Zaire was widespread in the West, both because of its support for anti-communist groups in the region and the abundance of natural resources in the country; significant aid was provided to Mobutu from Belgium, France, Germany, Italy, the United States, and the European Community.[43]

As these examples demonstrate, while the United States was at the helm in opposing the spread of communism in the developing world, it by no means acted alone. European colonial powers often took the lead or acted as key partners to the United States in supporting the installation and maintenance of pro-Western regimes in their former colonies. Japan and West Germany, with post–World War II limitations on their military capabilities and actions, contributed significant financial resources through foreign aid to pro-Western governments in developing countries. By the end of the 1980s Japan was the largest provider of foreign economic aid, surpassing even the United States in this capacity. Scholars have pointed to the importance of US influence over Japan's policies during the period (*gaiatsu*),[44] as well as Japan's desire to enhance its own economic interests,[45] for understanding Japanese foreign aid policy during the Cold War. West Germany also became a major player in the foreign aid realm, giving substantial aid to strategically placed and/or Western-backed governments in countries such as Brazil, Colombia, Cameroon, Egypt, Ghana, Indonesia, Israel, Jordan, Kenya, Morocco, Mali, Malawi, Sudan, Tunisia, Turkey, Tanzania, Zaire, Zambia, and Zimbabwe during the 1970s and 1980s.[46] As will be seen in Chapter 4, the connection between foreign aid and military importance to the West had an impact on the allocation decisions of multiple OECD aid donors: US military assistance was positively associated with aid from Austria, Denmark, Finland, Germany, Italy, Japan, the Netherlands, New Zealand, Norway, Switzerland, the United Kingdom, and the United States during the Cold War. This suggests that a wide range of industrialized countries were using their "development" assistance to enhance the well-being of militarily important regimes.

What was to become the final decade of the Cold War dawned with several "hot" confrontations continuing in developing countries. In Angola, the United States (with help from Mobutu in Zaire and the apartheid regime in South Africa) continued to back the rebel UNITA forces led by Jonas Savimbi against the Soviet- and Cuban-backed Angolan government of Jose Eduardo dos Santos. In one of the defining confrontations of the late Cold War period, the Soviet Union sent significant forces into Afghanistan in 1979. In response, the United States moved to improve relations with Pakistan, sending large amounts of economic and military aid to the country and training mujahideen forces to fight against the Soviets in Afghanistan. Also in 1979, the leftist Sandinista government came to power in Nicaragua. Within a short time they were receiving foreign support from Cuba, the Soviet Union, and other communist states and supporting leftist guerrillas in neighboring El Salvador.[47] The administrations of Jimmy Carter and Ronald Reagan in the United States, determined to fight further communist advances in the region, aided brutally repressive regimes in El Salvador and (to a lesser extent) Guatemala; the United States even invaded Grenada in 1983 to prevent a leftist government.[48] In what was to become another focal point of the Cold War in developing countries during the 1980s, the Reagan administration secretly (and illegally) sold arms to Iran and used the proceeds to finance the "Contra" rebels fighting the Sandinista regime in Nicaragua.

As the decade drew to a close, the Soviet Union was under increasing domestic pressure to draw back from foreign engagements and focus on domestic economic struggles.[49] With the collapse of the Eastern bloc starting in 1989 and the Soviet Union itself in 1991, the Cold War rationale for intervening in developing states disappeared. Western interest in supporting corrupt regimes in Africa and Central America, or the Islamic-based government in Pakistan, quickly evaporated in the early 1990s.

While far from an exhaustive or detailed account of relations between industrialized and developing countries during the Cold War, in the brief history above a clear picture emerges in which the promotion of development barely even registers as a color on the canvas. Successive governments in the United States, led by both Democrat and Republican presidents and supported by allies as far afield as France, Australia, West Germany, Japan, Belgium, the United Kingdom, and others, devoted significant resources—including "development" resources—to containing the spread of Soviet influence in the developing world. Proxy wars were fought or funded in Vietnam, Angola, the Horn of Africa, Afghanistan, Central America, and elsewhere; the most notable results were significant loss of life and demolished infrastructure, not economic development. The overthrow of governments was encouraged, financed, or assisted covertly by the CIA or overtly by the US military in countries such as Iran, Guatemala, Zaire (Democratic Republic of Congo), the Dominican Republic, Brazil, and Grenada. Corrupt and often brutally repressive regimes received substantial economic and/or military support if they supported the United States and its allies during the Cold War; notable instances include the regimes of Suharto in Indonesia, Mobutu in Zaire, Marcos in the Philippines, Pinochet in Chile, Barre in Somalia, and right-wing military regimes in Central America. Indeed, what is striking is the incredible amount of bloodshed, human rights abuses, and economic devastation that was funded by outside powers during the Cold War. To say that development was not actively promoted is in many cases an understatement of mammoth proportions; reflecting on Cold War interactions with the developing world presents many cases in which development was likely set back significantly as a result of great-power meddling within a country.

The End of the Cold War

Following the collapse of Soviet Union and corresponding end to the Cold War, it was not clear what policies industrialized states would pursue vis-à-vis developing countries. Cold War interactions had been dominated by the desire for containment. Prior to the Cold War, interactions between industrialized and developing areas had often operated through colonial structures. There was no well-articulated roadmap for an alternative, broad-based policy toward developing states. In many instances in the 1990s, industrialized states showed a desire to pull back from engagement with developing countries. Some of this was directly tied to the shift in global priorities that followed from the end of the Cold War. There was little benefit to funneling millions of dollars to brutal, corrupt dictators in developing countries once the threat of the Soviet Union collapsed. However, there was also a sense of policy incoherence toward the developing world. Containment was over, but it was unclear what overarching policy, if any, was rising to take its place.

Complicating the early adoption of a post–Cold War strategy toward developing countries was a renewed emphasis on domestic concerns in the United States and some of its allies. George H.W. Bush lost his 1992 re-election bid to Bill Clinton in a race dominated by discussions of the economy and health care.[50] After decades of Cold War foreign policy concerns, the Clinton administration faced pressure to focus on domestic issues and cut spending, including on overseas development. This pattern was not confined to the United States, as many governments in Europe also increased their focus on domestic concerns and decreased their emphasis on development. Tom Porteous notes the United Kingdom's turn away from developing countries in Africa both under the Conservative government of John Major in the early 1990s and the early years of the Labour Government of Tony Blair that was elected in 1997, preferring to focus on domestic issues.[51]

For many industrialized countries, foreign policy in the early post–Cold War period was dominated by concerns for the future of Europe and relations with Russia following the dissolution of the Soviet Union, rather than with broader concerns for the impact of underdevelopment. Large sums of foreign aid were allocated to former communist states in Eastern Europe and Central Asia while aid to other regions dropped sharply, as shown in Figure 2.1. Discussions began regarding enlargement of both the North Atlantic Treaty Organization (NATO) and the European Union (EU) to bring into their folds countries formerly under the Soviet sphere of influence (or part of the Soviet Union itself). In 1995 NATO published a study on enlargement, which led to membership for the Czech Republic, Hungary, and Poland in 1999, followed by Bulgaria, Estonia, Latvia, Lithuania, Romania, Slovakia, and Slovenia in 2004 and Albania and Croatia in 2009. In 1991 the EU signed the first of the "Europe Agreements," meant to start the process of EU expansion to former communist states in Europe. The European Council, at its Copenhagen meeting in 1993, reaffirmed its intent that "the associated countries in Central and Eastern Europe that so desire shall become members of the European Union" and called for increased access to markets and financial assistance—particularly under the Phare program—to help prepare the countries for accession.[52] Cyprus, the Czech Republic, Estonia, Hungary, Latvia, Lithuania, Malta, Poland, Slovakia, and Slovenia joined the EU in 2004, followed by Bulgaria and Romania in 2007 and Croatia in 2013.

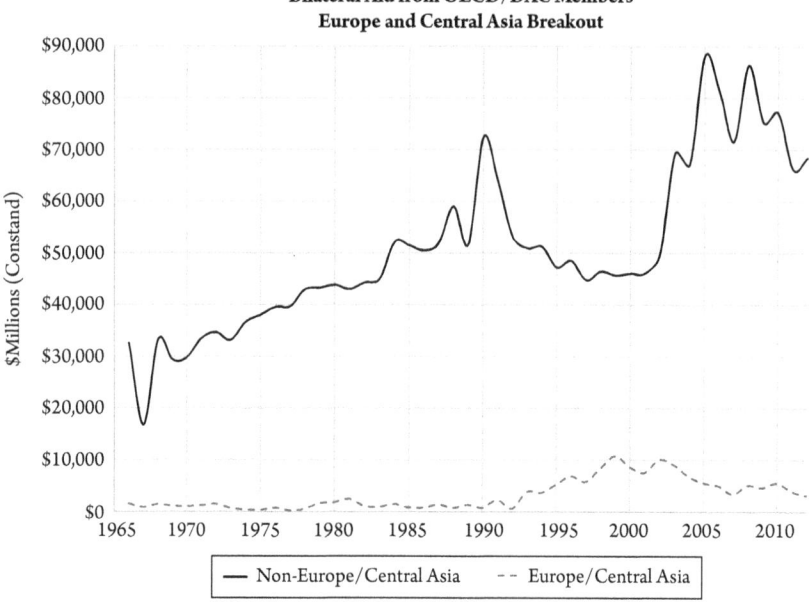

Figure 2.1 Bilateral Aid, Europe and Central Asia Breakout. Data from OECD database DAC3a, for "Total DAC" commitments, breaking out those with the classification of "Europe/Central Asia." Available online at stats.oecd.org; accessed July 15, 2014.

Outside of the plans for NATO and EU enlargement to the east, policies toward developing countries lacked an overarching theme in many industrialized country governments. In the United States, the Clinton administration urged a strategy of "democratic enlargement," arguing that the "overriding purpose must be to expand and strengthen the world's community of market based democracies," which required revitalizing the US economy and opening up world trade.[53] Aside from pursuing trade agreements and promoting democracy, the overall agenda of the Clinton strategy toward developing states lacked focus. The United States, under a mandate from the UN Security Council, in 1992 led a military operation initially aimed at assisting humanitarian goals in Somalia. During the same year, the United States, European countries, and other actors chose not to intervene in Bosnia despite mounting evidence of concentration camps and ethnic cleansing in the heart of Europe.[54] On October 3–4, 1993, the United States fought the Battle of Mogadishu in Somalia, in which eighteen US soldiers were killed, with their bodies paraded through the streets of Mogadishu; on October 7 Clinton announced the withdrawal of all US troops from Somalia by March 1994. Within a week, the US plan to restore democracy in Haiti, again under a mandate from the UN, hit a serious setback as the US warship sent to commence the operation, the USS Harlan County, left Port-au-Prince harbor having never been allowed to dock.[55] The following year the Clinton administration reversed course again, authorizing the use of force in Haiti. The administration's credibility with the regime of Raoul Cédras was low following the US withdrawal the previous year; a force of 20,000 US troops was deployed and the invasion was just hours away before the military government agreed—to a diplomatic team led by former US President Jimmy Carter—to leave the country peacefully.[56] Earlier that year the world had stood by as approximately 800,000 people, most of them ethnic Tutsis, were killed in the Rwandan genocide.[57] NATO would eventually intervene in Bosnia and later in Kosovo, although in neither case would the interventions come in time to prevent large-scale ethnic cleansing.

Regarding development programs like foreign aid, Carol Lancaster notes that the end of the Cold War decreased the rationale for aid at the same time recessions in donor countries and a turn toward fiscal balance in the United States and in Europe, under the terms of the Maastricht Treaty, led to significant cuts in aid budgets.[58] In the United States, Steven Radelet observes that "[w]ith the end of the Cold War, foreign aid lost much of its *raison d'être* and much of its remaining support."[59] The marginalization of development concerns was not confined to the arena of foreign aid: in one of the most important multilateral negotiations of the decade, the interests of developing countries were largely sidelined in the Uruguay Round of trade talks that concluded in 1994, establishing the World Trade Organization.[60]

In a juxtaposition that captures the incoherence of policy toward development in the 1990s, the decrease in resources was often coupled with an increase in concern for the effectiveness of those remaining at promoting development. Studies of aid during the 1990s suggest that it was more effective at promoting growth than in previous periods.[61] The decade ended with the creation of the Millennium Development Goals, setting ambitious targets for development outcomes over the next fifteen years. By the end of the 1990s, industrialized country governments embraced debt relief efforts for heavily indebted poor countries.

The renewed emphasis on development outcomes (if not funding) coincided with a growing realization that globalization was rapidly changing the nature of relations between states in the post–Cold War world. President Bill Clinton remarked in 1999 that "we must embrace the inexorable logic of globalization—that everything, from the strength of our economy to the safety of our cities, to the health of our people, depends on events not only within our borders, but half a world away."[62] Mounting evidence was linking underdevelopment abroad to well-being at home for industrialized states. Tom Porteous writes of the 1990s that "[i]ncreasing numbers of African refugees and

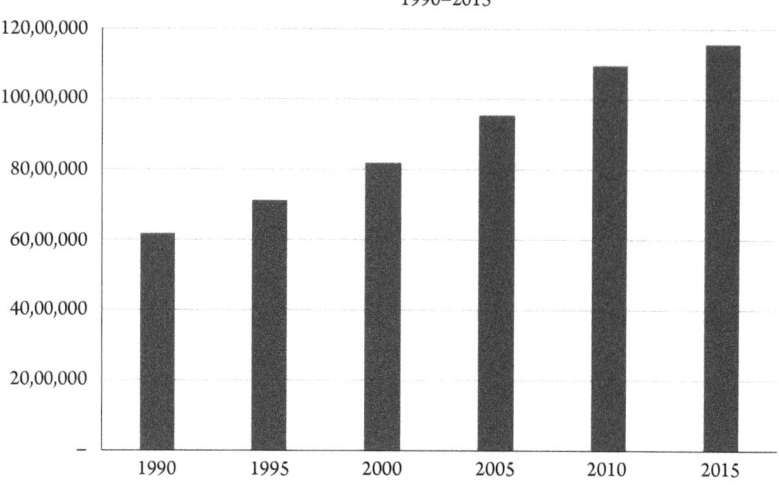

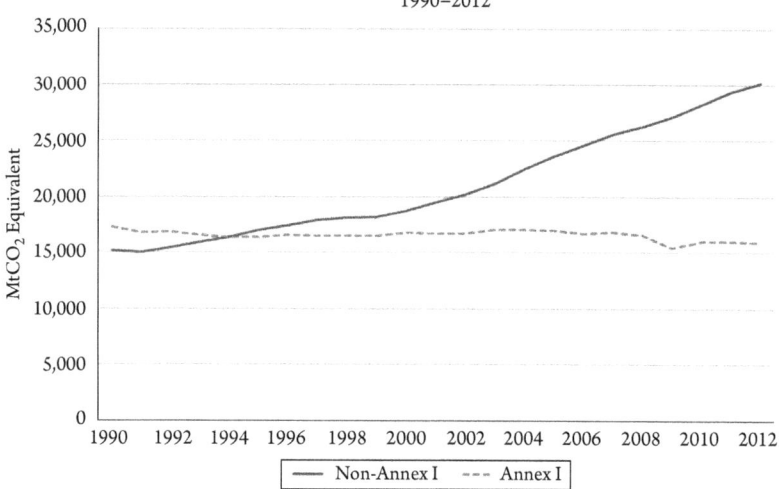

Figure 2.2 Increasing Connections: Migration and GHG Emissions. Data for migration are from the United Nations, Department of Economic and Social Affairs (2015), "Trends in International Migrant Stock: Migrants by Destination and Origin," (United Nations database, POP/DB/MIG/Stock/Rev.2015). Data for GHG emissions are from the CAIT Climate Data Explorer, 2015, Washington, DC: World Resources Institute; available online at: http://cait.wri.org.

economic migrants, many of them escaping very real dangers and hardship in their home countries, were washing up, dead or alive, on the north coasts of the Mediterranean" and that "USA and the Europeans both had good reason to be concerned also about the way in which international criminal cartels

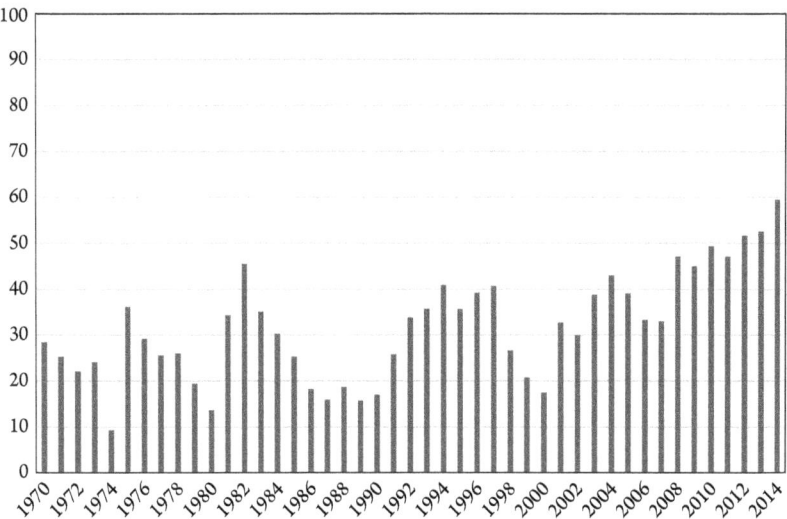

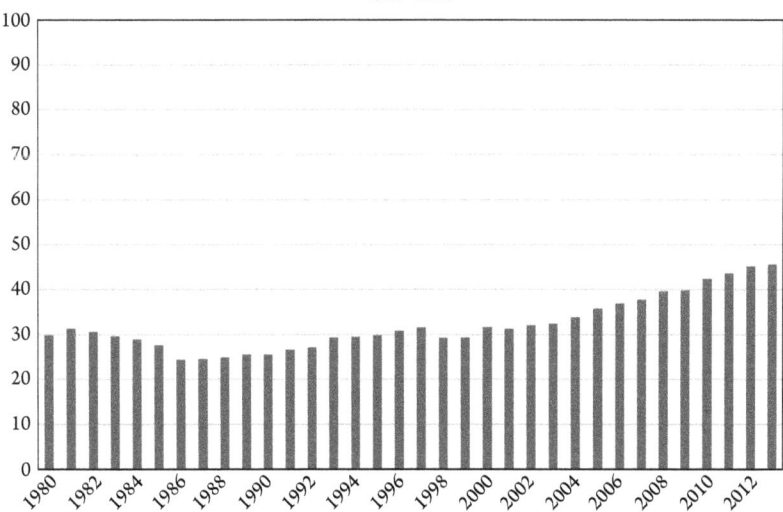

Figure 2.3 Increasing Connections: Foreign Direct Investment and Trade. Data are from The United Nations Conference on Trade and Development (UNCTAD); available online at http://unctadstat.unctad.org.

involved in drugs smuggling, people trafficking, arms dealing and other criminal activities were becoming well established in the conflict zones of Africa"; he also points to the growing foothold of terrorist and extremist organizations in the underdeveloped regions of Africa.[63]

Figures 2.2 and 2.3 show the increased relevance of developing states in the areas of migration, GHG emissions, trade, and foreign direct investment. The stock of migrants from non-OECD countries residing in high-income OECD countries grew throughout the 1990s and continued to grow thereafter.[64] By the mid-1990s developing countries, led by China, were contributing more per year to GHG emissions, including those from land use change, than industrialized states, meaning that their cooperation would be increasingly necessary to thwart the growing menace of climate change. The importance of developing countries as hosts for foreign direct investment was evident by the 1990s, although with a temporary decline following the Asian financial crisis in 1997. Developing countries accounted for about 30% of global trade in the mid-1990s; this percentage would not really begin to take off until after 2000.

While the general sense of an increased connection between underdevelopment abroad and well-being at home led to a shift toward development promotion and debt relief, the response was often ad hoc rather than the result of a coherent foreign policy toward developing countries. It would take a shock to focus the attention of industrialized country governments on the magnitude of the stakes and the need for a new, comprehensive development strategy.

A Renewed Focus on Developing Countries

On September 11, 2001, the United States and the rest of the world awoke to the fact that a relatively small group of individuals, operating out of a poor country thousands of miles away, could within a few hours cause more fatalities within the territory of the United States than had any other single attack by a foreign power in its history. This opened the eyes of the government and the public in the United States, as well as of governments in industrialized states around the world, to the magnitude of the importance of links between poverty and state failure abroad and security at home. The seeds of this understanding were already there, but no coherent policy agenda had been articulated to deal with them. Following the attacks, historian John Lewis Gaddis argued that "10 years into the post-Cold War era, there was very little sign of a comprehensive grand strategy. There were strategies toward particular countries and with regard to particular issues, but very little effort to pull it altogether. 9/11 forced us basically to get our grand strategic act together."[65]

The terrorist attacks of September 11th acted as a trigger, forcing governments in industrialized states to rethink their strategy toward developing countries. The impact on the US strategy toward development became clear early on. As Desha Girod, Stephen Krasner, and Kathryn Stoner-Weiss argue, "[w]hat had been a peripheral concern for the [George W. Bush] Administration when it first came to office, governance and development in poorer countries, assumed much greater prominence after the attacks on the World Trade Center and the Pentagon."[66] As it would turn out, the result would be broader than a strategy focused on terrorism and would seek to deal more comprehensively with the effects of underdevelopment on industrialized states.

That a new strategy was to entail a rethinking of development policy on a global scale, not only in the frontline states of the war on terror, was soon evident. Six months after the September 11th attacks, George W. Bush became the first sitting US president to address the Inter-American Development Bank (IDB) since its establishment in 1959. While not an important region for addressing global terrorism, Latin America is a key source of underdevelopment-related spillovers for the United States. To highlight the importance of his visit, President Bush had with him an entourage including his Secretary of the Treasury, the head of US AID, the US ambassador to the UN, several members of Congress—and U2 singer and development activist Bono.[67] In the two years following the attacks, Bush would announce the largest increases in foreign aid in decades, including the creation of the Millennium Challenge Corporation (MCC) and the President's Emergency Plan for Aids Relief (PEPFAR), neither of which focused on important states in the new war on terror.[68] Carol Lancaster, a deputy administrator for USAID during the Clinton administration, notes that President Bush elevated development to the "first tier of U.S. foreign policy priorities, along with defense and diplomacy," arguing that it was "the first time for many decades that a U.S. president has declared that promoting development abroad is a key priority in U.S. foreign policy."[69]

This rethinking of strategy toward developing countries is not confined to the United States. In the years following the attacks, industrialized states have increasingly responded to the impact of globalization on their national security. While prevention of terrorism plays a key role, it is by no means the only concern raised by industrialized countries with regard to globalization. The Swiss Foreign Policy Strategy notes that "In this age of globalisation, countries have become so interdependent that a conflict or crisis even in a faraway land often has direct consequences for Switzerland: threatening our foreign investments or exports, endangering our nationals living abroad, or destroying natural resources."[70] Japan's National Security Strategy claims that the "cross-border flow of people, goods, capital, information and other items have been facilitated more easily by the advancement of globalization,"[71] while in the United Kingdom policymakers state that "a range of economic, technological and social trends, often grouped under the heading 'globalisation', are increasing the interconnectedness and interdependence between economies, societies, businesses, and individuals."[72] Across industrialized states it has become common for concerns regarding the link between underdevelopment and issues such as the potential for global pandemics and climate change to be mentioned in the official security strategies adopted by governments; these are no longer relegated to foreign aid charters but part of central discussions of national security.

The attacks of September 11, 2001 did not unleash the forces of globalization, but they were instrumental in highlighting their importance for leaders in industrialized states. Ad hoc responses were no longer tenable. A new, comprehensive strategy for dealing with underdevelopment abroad was overdue and has been evolving in the years since the attacks. The remainder of this book will argue that this has taken the form of targeted development, an approach to pursuing development abroad in a manner that advances the self-interest of the policymaking states.

3

Maximizing Utility vis-à-vis Developing Countries

"The faculty of re-solution is possibly much invigorated by mathematical study, and especially by that highest branch of it which, unjustly, and merely on account of its retrograde operations, has been called, as if *par excellence*, analysis. Yet to calculate is not in itself to analyze.[1]
—Edgar Allan Poe, 1841.

Since the beginning of 2015 a migration crisis has affected Europe, with more than 1 million migrants/asylum-seekers fleeing violence in Syria, Afghanistan, Iraq, and other countries.[2] The already tense migration situation in the United States continues to face the prospect of new arrivals from the "Northern Triangle" in Central America; increasing numbers of women with children and unaccompanied minors fleeing violence in El Salvador, Guatemala, and Honduras tax the asylum system on the southern border of the United States.[3] The backlash against migration, including the rise of nationalist sentiment in many industrialized states, suggests the possibility of difficult times ahead as climate-induced migration is likely to add to the already large numbers of people leaving their homelands. The United States and its allies are coping with significant increases in tensions with Russia over its role in Eastern Europe and Syria, and its military buildup, including Russian submarines and warships off the coasts of NATO countries. In the last decade, West Africa has become a major transit route for trafficking illegal drugs into Europe, which has also increased corruption and drug use in the already fragile region.[4] Policymakers across industrialized states struggle to respond to the menace of international terrorism and violence tied to the Islamic State in Iraq and Syria. Concerns of a possible pandemic associated with the worst outbreak of Ebola ever recorded eased just as mounting evidence showed that new complications from the Zika virus pose a wide-ranging threat to global health.[5] Tensions between Saudi Arabia and Iran continue to threaten stability in the Middle East. The future of European integration has been challenged by the financial crisis in Greece, the struggle to find a common solution to the migration crisis, and the uncertain future of EU–UK relations following Brexit. North Korea continues to escalate tensions in Asia with missile tests, leading to the deployment of a US missile defense system in South Korea that China warns could bring an arms race to the region,[6] while states must also decide how to react to China's increasingly assertive stance toward islands in the South China Sea. Commitment of the United States to the 2015 Paris Agreement on climate change, to trade organizations, and to international institutions in general faces an uncertain future following the election of Donald Trump. And these are only a few of the foreign policy issues on the agenda for governments in industrialized states.

At any point in time a government faces a multitude of foreign policy concerns requiring political capital and financial resources. Given a finite ability to respond, strategic choices must be made, prioritizing the most pressing issues. Even when the composition of problems confronting a country remains largely stable, the relative importance can change significantly. This is observed in military strategy as spending fluctuates over time to reflect the magnitude of perceived threats, with the relative emphasis on offensive and defensive capabilities changing. The rise and decline of parties espousing xenophobic platforms in many countries reflects the inconstancy of views toward "foreigners" and on immigration in many states. Moves toward protectionism or free trade also vary over time and across countries. The same is true for concerns with underdevelopment.

Policies designed to promote development abroad must compete with multiple government priorities for attention and funding. If self-interest is motivating state behavior, then development promotion will increase in salience when its importance for addressing key policy concerns increases and/or the opportunity costs of taking resources from other purposes decrease. The highest salience for development promotion should occur when these two conditions coincide. When this occurs, governments in industrialized states will use multiple foreign policy tools to advance development in their own interest. This contrasts with periods when development is a relatively low priority and even tools ostensibly used for development, such as foreign aid, are diverted for other purposes.

This chapter develops a formal model of the theory advanced in the book. As highlighted by the opening quote from Edgar Allan Poe—who has been likened to a Bayesian game theorist by modern statisticians[7]—it is important to lay a sound analytical foundation before launching into the empirics ("calculations") that unfold in the coming chapters. However, those who believe formal models more closely resemble a different allegation from the same source, that "what is only complex is mistaken (a not unusual error) for what is profound,"[8] may wish to skip ahead to the last section of this chapter, which summarizes the main insights from the model and draws implications from it for the empirical chapters to follow. The purpose of the model here is three-fold. First, setting it up requires specifying assumptions, which provides clarity for the reader and precision for the analysis. Second, working through the model provides insights that are not readily apparent *ex ante*. Finally, having laid down the assumptions that go into the model and developed insights that follow from these assumptions, testable implications consistent with the assumptions and insights are derived. The concluding section of this chapter posits several patterns that should appear in the issue areas covered in the empirical chapters—foreign aid, trade agreements, and financing for climate change mitigation and adaptation—if, in fact, industrialized states are pursuing a strategy of targeted development in their interactions with developing countries.

Model Overview

The model allows an industrialized state to interact with developing countries on both development and non-development issues. Expending resources in a developing state (for development or otherwise) takes away from resources available for other purposes. The industrialized state is assumed to maximize its own utility when interacting with developing countries, including when promoting development. In the simplest version, as the value the industrialized state places on development increases, so to do resources used for development promotion. This is true over time and across states: more resources are devoted to development when and where it is most in the interest of the industrialized state.

When the goal of the industrialized state is development it can be mutually beneficial: the governments of both the industrialized and developing state may pursue the same goal of development, with the industrialized country contributing to finance what the developing country cannot afford, or offering concessions in areas that promote development, such as trade. In other situations, the industrialized state may seek to extract a favor or concession from a developing country that is costly for that government to grant. In these cases, the industrialized country can offer compensation in the form of increased development resources, non-development resources, or both.

Perhaps the most surprising insight from the model is that the value states place on development can alter interaction on non-development issues. When an industrialized country considers pursuing a non-development concession from a particular developing state, it must compensate the government of that state, which is costly. If the industrialized state values development promotion in the developing state, and if the developing state government is willing to accept resources geared for development as part of its compensation and able to turn these resources into development outcomes, then the cost of the compensation to the industrialized state is reduced by the value it places on the development outcomes. Thus a non-development transaction will be less costly to the industrialized state—and therefore more likely to be incentive compatible and actually occur—when the industrialized state places a higher value on development in the country, when the developing state also values development and is willing to be compensated through development resources, and when the developing state is capable of turning resources into development outcomes. These same factors will influence the choice of the industrialized state if there are multiple developing countries that could provide a particular non-development concession: the industrialized state will choose as the provider the developing state with the lowest net cost (i.e., where the cost to the industrialized state less the benefit it receives from any resulting development outcomes in the developing state is lowest).

Industrialized states will focus on development when and where it is in their interests to do so, given scarce resources and accounting for opportunity costs. When the costs of underdevelopment increase, more resources will be devoted to development promotion. Development policies, such as large sums of foreign aid or the offer of preferential trade agreements, will be targeted toward those countries where development most benefits the industrialized state. Chapters 4 and 5 test the model's implications in these issue areas, looking at changes over time and differences across countries. There are also implications for issue areas where the stated purpose is not development per se, such as global attempts to limit the atmospheric accumulation of greenhouse gases (GHG). The climatic benefit of limiting GHG emissions does not depend on the location of the emissions. Scholars widely accept that efficient means of limiting GHG emissions include reductions in developing countries, which can be financed by industrialized country programs. From the standpoint of climate change, the most efficient programs are those that achieve the greatest emission reductions for a given cost. However, programs to reduce GHG emissions often involve development projects in poorer countries financed by industrialized states. The model suggests that in these cases development concerns will divert resources from the climate-efficient allocation to one that accounts for the benefits the industrialized state receives *both* from reducing emissions and from promoting development with these programs. While the theoretical finding extends to any area in which development overlaps with other goals, Chapter 6 tests the model in the realm of climate finance.

The Model

The model assumes industrialized states maximize their utility when devoting resources to developing countries. This section develops the model under different possible scenarios, drawing from each the implications for understanding more generally industrialized country interactions with developing states.

Case 1: Development Interactions

To begin simply, I start with a scenario in which an industrialized country interacts with two developing countries only in order to promote development (no non–development based interactions), an assumption that will be relaxed shortly. In this scenario the subscript 1 will be used to differentiate it from others examined below; it is not a time index. The utility of the industrialized country i is given by:

$$U_{i1} = \beta_x k_x [r_{ix1}]^\alpha + \beta_y k_y [r_{iy1}]^\alpha + v_i(R_i - g_{i1}) \qquad (3.1)$$

In this equation r_{ix1} and r_{iy1} are the amounts of resources, both monetary (e.g., foreign aid) and political (e.g., political capital used to negotiate a trade deal), expended on developing countries x and y, respectively, for development purposes by the industrialized country i. It is assumed that the resources can be committed for development, including by bypassing the government in the developing country if necessary. This could be done, for example, by giving foreign aid through nongovernmental organizations. Again, this assumption will be relaxed below. The total amount of resources available to the government of i is given by R_i and the term g_i is the sum of all resources spent by country i in developing countries; in this case $g_{i1} = r_{ix1} + r_{iy1}$. The function $v_i(R_i - g_{i1})$ represents the utility that i receives from spending on purposes other than the interactions with developing countries and is assumed to have the usual property of diminishing returns.

The expressions $k_x[r_{ix1}]^\alpha$ and $k_y[r_{iy1}]^\alpha$ can be thought of as production functions that turn resources into development outcomes; they allow for diminishing returns to resources with $0 \leq \alpha \leq 1$. The effectiveness of the developing country at promoting development (k) is allowed to vary across countries (k_x, k_y). The variable k can be thought of as capturing aspects of the country that make it more efficient at turning resources into development; these may include attributes such as good governance that enhances the effectiveness of foreign aid or strong infrastructure that allows a country to capitalize on trade agreements. Weights are attached to each production function (β_x, β_y), which allow the industrialized country's utility from development to vary across developing countries. These weights capture the idea that development in some countries is more valuable to the industrialized state than development in others.[9] The weights β_x and β_y lie on the interval $[0,1]$ to allow the industrialized country to value \$1 in development less than \$1 in cash.

It is useful to use an example to demonstrate how the utility function works. If the industrialized country expends \$1 in effort in country x ($r_{ix1} = 1$) the production function may turn that into \$3 worth of development ($k_x[r_{ix1}]^\alpha = \$3$), which the industrialized state may value at \$2.50 ($\beta_x k_x[r_{ix1}]^\alpha = \$2.50$). In this example the industrialized state expends \$1 to receive an increase in utility that it values at \$2.50.

In equilibrium, the industrialized state maximizes utility when it divides the total amount of resources, R, between x, y, and other expenditures such that the marginal utility of a dollar spent in x is equal to the marginal utility of a dollar spent in y and to the marginal utility of a dollar spent on other purposes. If this is not the case then the industrialized state can increase its utility by reallocating resources to the purposes yielding a higher marginal utility. Using the above equation, the first-order conditions that satisfy this are given as:

$$\alpha\beta_x k_x[r_{ix1}]^{\alpha-1} = \alpha\beta_y k_y[r_{iy1}]^{\alpha-1} = \frac{\delta v_i}{\delta g_{i1}} \qquad (3.2)$$

The manner in which the industrialized country allocates its resources between promoting development in x, promoting development in y, and other purposes depends on the values of β_x, k_x, β_y, k_y, and diminishing returns to r_{ix1}, r_{iy1}, and $R - g_{i1}$. Figure 3.1 depicts the tradeoffs for a given level of $g_{i1} = r_{ix1} + r_{iy1}$. The curved line represents all possible combinations of development that can be "purchased" with g_{i1}, with the intercepts depicting the points where the entire amount is spent in one country; it can be thought of as the budget constraint, with slope $-\frac{k_y[r_{iy1}]^{\alpha-1}}{k_x[r_{ix1}]^{\alpha-1}}$. The indifference curves in this scenario are straight lines with the slope $-\frac{\beta_x}{\beta_y}$. Point A represents the optimal point in a situation where industrialized country i favors development in country y relatively highly compared to development in country x, while Point B represents the optimum from a different set of indifference curves that show country i placing a higher value on development in country x. As these two points show, changes in the relative value of the βs cause the industrialized state to shift development resources across countries. However, the optimal blend of r_{ix1} and r_{iy1} also rewards countries that use resources more efficiently for development (higher k). An increase in either k_x or k_y would shift the relevant intercept on the budget constraint and result in a reallocation of aid toward the more efficient country for a given set of indifference curves. An overall increase in the utility of development would result in more resources being allocated for development purposes (higher g_{i1}), which would shift the entire budget constraint outward.

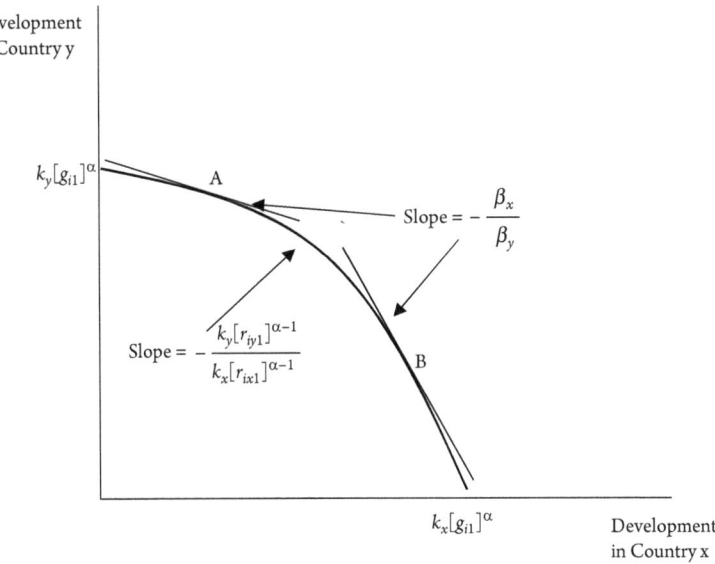

Figure 3.1 Utility Maximization and Development.

In this world the developing country governments always accept resources, since there is no quid pro quo and each developing country government's utility is assumed to be (weakly) increasing in development. The developing country government's utility can be given as:

$$U_{x1} = \gamma_x k_x [r_{ix1}]^\alpha + v_x(R_x) \tag{3.3}$$

and

$$U_{y1} = \gamma_y k_y [r_{iy1}]^\alpha + v_y(R_y) \tag{3.4}$$

where the γs represent the weight the developing country government places on development and $0 \leq \gamma \leq 1$ allows the government to value a \$1 improvement in development outcomes less than it would \$1 in cash. R_x and R_y represent resources available to the governments of x and y from sources other than the industrialized state. It is assumed here (which will be relaxed below) that outside resources are not fungible. Thus r_{ix1} and r_{iy1} fund new development in the countries. The contribution to the developing country government's utility will depend on both its efficiency at translating these resources into development outcomes (k) and the value it places on development (γ); these funds cannot contribute to utility through the $v(\cdot)$ function in developing states.

Key Insights from Case 1

- An industrialized country will target development resources where it gains the most utility from doing so: this will depend on both the relative values the industrialized state attaches to development across developing countries (β_x, β_y) and the relative efficiency of the developing countries at turning resources into development (k_x, k_y).
- The amount of resources devoted to development will vary over time to reflect changes in the relative importance the industrialized state places on development compared to other goals pursued with scarce resources.

Case 2: Non-Development Interactions

This section relaxes both the assumption that the industrialized state pursues only development goals within the developing country and the assumption that all resources granted to the developing state are used for development. Industrialized states pursue a number of non-development goals in developing countries; this was true during the Cold War and remains true today. For example, David Carter and Randall Stone have shown that the United States rewards countries that support it in the UN General Assembly on votes deemed "important" by the State Department.[10] Studies by Ilyana Kuziemko and Eric Werker[11] and by James Vreeland and Axel Dreher[12] show that aid may be used to buy influence with countries occupying one of the rotating seats on the UN Security Council. Vreeland has also shown that Switzerland increases aid to countries that vote in favor of its election to the Board at the World Bank or IMF,[13] while Vreeland and Daniel Lim show that Japan uses its power in the Asian Development Bank in an attempt to influence Asian countries that hold rotating Security Council seats.[14] The United States has used preferential trade agreements with countries such as Israel and Jordan to advance broader foreign policy goals.[15] Several developing countries play an important strategic role in the fight against terrorism, for which they may receive support from industrialized states. For instance, France maintains military bases in African former colonies, which have been helpful in repelling al Qaeda-linked advances in countries such as Mali;[16] the United Kingdom and, most notably, the United States also maintain strategic overseas military bases in developing states. Going forward, industrialized states will need the active participation of developing countries in lowering GHG emissions and limiting climate change, which will benefit industrialized and developing countries alike.

For the purpose of the model, it is useful to separate two categories of non-development interactions between an industrialized state and developing countries. The first includes interactions in which an industrialized state seeks concessions or favors from a developing country that the country is in a unique position to provide. Current interactions of European countries with Turkey over the migrant crisis fit in this category, as did US negotiations with Egypt and Israel at Camp David to bring about peace between those countries—other developing states are not in the position to grant the particular policy concessions desired by the industrialized countries. A second set of interactions concerns issues where there are multiple developing countries that could provide the benefit to the industrialized state: "buying" votes in the UN General Assembly could fit this category, as could climate change mitigation; in both cases the location of the "favor" is not as important as the fact that it is granted.[17] A limited ability to substitute across countries can even influence the location of overseas military bases if, for instance, a base is needed in a region in which any one of several developing countries could serve as a host. It is useful to separately model the role that the desire for development promotion can play in situations in which a developing country is the only potential provider of a non-development favor and in situations in which multiple potential substitute providers are available.

Case 2 models a situation in which industrialized country i desires a concession from developing country x that only country x can provide; this scenario is denoted with the subscript 2. If country i receives the concession, then its utility increases by M_x. There is a cost, C_x, to the leadership of country x if it grants the concession, which can be monetary or political (or both). Because the industrialized state is pursuing a non-development agenda, country x is in a position to demand compensation, either in terms of increased development resources ($r_{ix2} > r_{ix1}$), non-development resources (denoted as f_{ix2}), or both. The term f_{ix2} can be thought of as a no-strings-attached benefit. In reality it could take many forms, including financing something the government of x was planning to finance itself, thus freeing up resources for other purposes. While r_{ix2} is constrained for use in development, f_{ix2} increases the resources available to the government of country x for use on any purpose; the combined resources that country i spends in country x are written as $s_{ix2} = r_{ix2} + f_{ix2}$. The industrialized state continues to place value on development promotion, as in Case 1, in addition to valuing the non-development concession.

A game ensues in which the industrialized state i can choose to make an offer of some combination of f_{ix2} and r_{ix2} to country x in exchange for receiving M_x. Country x decides whether to accept or reject the offer. If no offer is made or if country x rejects the offer, the game defaults to the situation from Case 1 above. Since the game involves only country i and country x in this scenario, the use of development resources in y can best be modeled as one potential use of the remaining $R_i - s_{ix2}$ if an offer is made and accepted. This will only occur if an offer can be crafted that is incentive compatible for both country i and country x. Incentive compatibility for country i includes consideration of the opportunity cost of using some portion of R_i in country x in order to obtain M_x; this extra expenditure in country x will come at the expense of some expenditure in country y and some expenditure on other outcomes of value to country i.[18] The utility functions for countries i and x can be written as:

$$U_{i2} = \beta_x k_x [r_{ix2}]^\alpha + M_x + v_i (R_i - s_{ix2}) \tag{3.5}$$

$$U_{x2} = \gamma_x k_x [r_{ix2}]^\alpha + v_x (R_x + f_{ix2}) - C_x \tag{3.6}$$

In order to observe this outcome, both country i and country x must be at least as well off in Case 2 as in Case 1; in other words, it must be the case that $U_{i2} \geq U_{i1}$ and $U_{x2} \geq U_{x1}$. With respect to country x, incentive compatibility is satisfied for industrialized country i if:

$$M_x \geq \overbrace{v_i(R_i - r_{ix1}) - v_i(R_i - r_{ix2} - f_{ix2})} - \overbrace{\beta_x k_x ([r_{ix2}]^\alpha - [r_{ix1}]^\alpha)} \tag{3.7}$$

This shows that the benefit from M_x must be large enough to overcome the loss in utility from $v(\cdot)$ when additional resources are diverted to country x (the first bracketed expression on the right-hand side in inequality 3.7), less the amount this is offset by any gain in utility that country i receives from enhanced development outcomes (if any) in country x under scenario 2 as compared to scenario 1 (the second bracketed expression on the right-hand side of inequality 3.7). It is possible that $r_{ix2} < r_{ix1}$ if part of the compensation to the government of country x involves moving some resources from development to provide a no-strings-attached transfer; in this case the second expression is negative, adding to the lost utility rather than subtracting from it.

The right-hand side of inequality 3.7 represents the opportunity cost to country i of obtaining M_x. The industrialized country will seek to minimize this cost while making a deal that is incentive compatible for developing country x, which occurs when:

$$\overbrace{\gamma_x k_x ([r_{ix2}]^\alpha - [r_{ix1}]^\alpha)} + \overbrace{v_x(R_x + f_{ix2}) - v_x(R_x)} \geq C_x \tag{3.8}$$

That is, to be incentive compatible the change in utility associated with moving from r_{ix1} to r_{ix2} (the first bracketed expression on the left-hand side of inequality 3.8) plus the increased utility associated with receiving f_{ix2} (the second bracketed expression on the left-hand side of inequality 3.8) must be at least as great as the cost, C_x. Again, it is possible that $r_{ix2} < r_{ix1}$ if part of the compensation to the government of country x involves moving some resources from development to provide a no-strings-attached transfer; in this case the first term in inequality 3.8 is negative.

In a world of complete information, industrialized country i can offer x exactly C_x additional utility in exchange for M_x, leaving x indifferent between Case 1 and Case 2. The industrialized state will make this offer if inequality 3.7 holds after considering the minimum cost of compensation necessary to make Case 2 incentive compatible for x. The government of country i determines the cost-minimizing combination of r_{ix2} and f_{ix2} for which inequality 3.8 holds; that is, it minimizes the right-hand side of inequality 3.7 subject to satisfying inequality 3.8. If inequality 3.7 holds given the cost-minimizing values of r_{ix2} and f_{ix2} determined by this constrained optimization, country i will make the offer and country x will accept, moving from Case 1 to Case 2. Otherwise, the states remain under the scenario in Case 1.

The cost to industrialized country i of a unit of r_{ix2} is less than the cost of a unit of f_{ix2}, as it is offset by some positive benefit that country i receives from development outcomes in x. However, a unit of r_{ix2} may provide less compensation to country x if that country receives more utility from f_{ix2} than from r_{ix2}. Country i balances these considerations and chooses the cost-minimizing value of r_{ix2}:[19]

$$r_{ix2}^{min} = \left(\frac{\alpha \gamma_x k_x}{\frac{\delta v_x}{\delta f_{ix2}}} - \frac{\alpha \beta_x k_x}{\frac{\delta v_i}{\delta s_{ix2}}} \right)^{\frac{1}{1-\alpha}}$$

Obviously, the larger is r_{ix2}^{min} the less additional resources will be needed in the form of f_{ix2} in order to make an offer incentive compatible for country x; the cost-minimizing value is denoted f_{ix2}^{min}.

Noting that $\frac{\delta v_i}{\delta s_{ix2}} < 0$, r_{ix2}^{min} is higher relative to f_{ix2}^{mIn} the higher the values of α, γ_x, k_x, and β_x and the lower the value of $\frac{\delta v_x}{\delta f_{ix2}}$. Higher values of γ_x and k_x increase the value to country x of each unit of r_{ix2}, decreasing the total amount of resources, $r_{ix2}^{min} + f_{ix2}^{min}$, needed to ensure incentive compatibility. Higher values of C_x will obviously increase the necessary compensation. Referring back to inequality 3.7, an offer is made by country i and accepted by country x if:

$$M_x \geq v_i(R_i - r_{ix1}) - v_i(R_i - r_{ix2}^{min} - f_{ix2}^{min}) - \beta_x k_x ([r_{ix2}^{min}]^\alpha - [r_{ix1}]^\alpha) \quad (3.9)$$

Higher values of M_x increase the likelihood of an offer. Additionally, inequality 3.9 is more likely to be satisfied when the total compensation ($r_{ix2}^{min} + f_{ix2}^{min}$) is lower and when a greater portion of this is made up of r_{ix2}^{min}; country x's incentive compatibility shows that these in turn are more likely for higher values of γ_x and k_x and lower values of C_x. Finally, directly from inequality 3.9 it can be seen that the inequality is more likely to hold, and a deal be offered, for higher values of β_x and k_x, which increase the benefit that country i receives from additional development in country x. On the other hand, the greater the opportunity cost of taking resources from $v_i(\cdot)$, including allocating away from country y (which depends on β_y and k_y), the less likely that inequality 3.9 will be satisfied.

Changes in the Value of M_x

A key component of Case 2 is that the industrialized state has full information and is able to offer the developing country exactly enough compensation to make it incentive compatible to provide M_x. Given this, in some cases the industrialized state is extracting a substantial surplus; for a given value of M_x the surplus is greater the higher are α, γ_x, k_x, and β_x and the lower is C_x. In other cases, particularly when C_x is high and α, γ_x, k_x, and β_x are low, the industrialized country may be operating quite close to its incentive compatibility constraint. It is instructive to envision what occurs when the value of M_x changes under these different scenarios. If country i is well inside its constraint then M_x can decrease a sizeable amount and not render the deal incompatible for country i. However, when country i is operating at or near its constraint, even small decreases in the value of M_x can lead to large changes in the resources devoted to country x by country i. If country i receives little utility from development in country x, or if the government of country x is unable or unwilling to devote resources received in exchange for providing M_x into enhancing development outcomes, then M_x may be providing the main basis for resource flows from country i to country x. In this case, a decrease in M_x that makes it not incentive compatible for country i to pursue M_x will result in a sizeable decrease in resource flows.

The thought experiment is helpful in understanding the impact of broad strategic shifts on relations between industrialized and developing countries, such as those that occurred with the end of the Cold War. As the bipolar power struggle ended, the value of non-development concessions granted by many developing countries in furtherance of Western aims in the Cold War decreased substantially almost overnight. This saw an overall decline in resource transfers, such as foreign aid.[20] Countries led by dictators in relatively remote areas that were not using funds for development were particularly hard-hit, as the example of Zaire, now the Democratic Republic of the Congo, demonstrates. As discussed in Chapter 2, the West viewed Mobutu Sese Seko, the authoritarian leader of Zaire, as an important ally in the attempt to contain the spread of communism in Africa during the Cold War. Unlike many dictators, Mobutu did not fall with the end of the Cold War; he remained in power until he was forced into exile in 1997. Following the Soviet collapse, his usefulness to the West was eliminated and donors had no taste for supporting corrupt, human-rights-abusing dictators who served no strategic purpose. Aid commitments from OECD donors to Zaire fell from $850 million in 1988 to $116 million in 1990, and remained at these lower levels throughout the remainder of Mobutu's time in power.[21]

With no strategic benefits left to offer, and a track record of using development assistance for purposes other than development, Mobutu's government found that industrialized states derived no utility from investing development resources in his country, and his resources shrank accordingly.

Key Insights from Case 2

- Development considerations influence the likelihood of reaching a deal in which a developing state provides a non-development concession to an industrialized state, even in situations in which the developing country is uniquely positioned to provide the concession.
- A deal for a non-development concession is more likely to be incentive compatible for both the industrialized and developing country the higher the value each places on development in the country (β_x and γ_x) and the higher the ability of the developing country to turn resources into development (k_x).
- As the value of the non-development concession (M_x) decreases, the likelihood that a deal remains incentive compatible for the industrialized state depends on the values both states place on development (β_x and γ_x) and the efficiency of the developing country in turning resources into development outcomes (k_x).

Case 3: Substitutes and Non-Development Interactions

This section takes up the scenario in which industrialized country i seeks a non-development concession that either country x or country y can provide. Examples in which the location of the concession is relatively unimportant include votes in international bodies or reduction of greenhouse gas emissions. In both of these cases it is likely that the industrialized state will seek to "buy" a favor from multiple countries. However, given scarce resources, it cannot purchase the concession from all countries. Therefore, it will look for the countries that provide the most benefit for the least cost. For the purpose of simplicity in modeling, it is easiest to collapse these different "types" of countries into two representative countries, x and y.

In deciding whether and where to make an offer, country i will compare its utility when country x provides the concession to its utility when country y provides the concession, and compare both to the utility in the baseline scenario, Case 1. As the concession is costly to the governments of developing countries (although not necessarily equally costly across developing countries), there is a constraint that the package offered to country x or country y must be incentive compatible, as was true in the last section for country x. For instance, reducing GHG emissions could increase the cost of short-term development, which the developing country government would not like. As above, if neither of the scenarios provides more utility to country i than Case 1, then country i does not make any offer and the game defaults to the outcome in Case 1.

It is useful to examine a situation in which both country x and country y are potential providers, which occurs if the industrialized country would receive higher utility from either one providing the concession than it receives if neither one provides it. In this case, each developing country views the other as a credible rival. Within this premise, I will denote the scenario in which country x provides the concession with the subscript 3 and the scenario in which country y provides the concession with the subscript 4. Country i will compare its maximum utility if x provides the concession to its maximum utility if y provides the concession; the value of the concession is M_x if country x provides it and M_y if country y provides it. Analogously with Case 2, the utility function for country i if country x is the provider is given by:

$$U_{i3} = M_x + \beta_x k_x [r_{ix3}]^\alpha + v_i (R_i - s_{ix3}) \tag{3.10}$$

where $s_{ix3} = r_{ix3} + f_{ix3}$. Differing from Case 2, if country x believes that country y will provide the concession if country x chooses not to, then x is faced with the choice between the utility it receives from providing the concession itself:

$$U_{x3} = \gamma_x k_x [r_{ix3}]^\alpha + v_x (R_x + f_{ix3}) - C_x \tag{3.11}$$

and its utility if country y provides the concession:

$$U_{x4} = \gamma_x k_x [r_{ix4}]^\alpha + v_x (R_x) \tag{3.12}$$

where $r_{ix4} < r_{ix1}$ and $U_{x4} < U_{x1}$ as long as C_y is positive, since some r_x will be diverted to y in exchange for providing M_y. Thus, the reservation utility for x should it reject i's offer is lower than in the situation it faced in Case 2 above. The incentive compatibility constraint for country x is given by:

$$\gamma_x k_x [r_{ix3}]^\alpha + v_x (R_x + f_{ix3}) - C_x \geq \gamma_x k_x [r_{ix4}]^\alpha + v_x (R_x) \tag{3.13}$$

Symmetrically, for the scenario in which country y provides the concession:

$$U_{i4} = M_y + \beta_y k_y [r_{iy4}]^\alpha + v_i (R_i - s_{iy4}) \tag{3.14}$$

where $s_{iy4} = r_{iy4} + f_{iy4}$. The incentive compatibility constraint for country y is given by:

$$\gamma_y k_y [r_{iy4}]^\alpha + v_y (R_y + f_{iy4}) - C_y \geq \gamma_y k_y [r_{iy3}]^\alpha + v_y (R_y) \tag{3.15}$$

Country i will offer the deal to country x if $U_{i3} > U_{i4}$. Rearranging terms, x is offered the deal when the following holds (with the superscript *min* denoting the value resulting from cost minimization):

$$M_x \geq M_y + \beta_y k_y [r_{iy4}^{min}]^\alpha - \beta_x k_x [r_{ix3}^{min}]^\alpha + [v_i(R_i - s_{iy4}^{min}) - v_i(R_i - s_{ix3}^{min})] \quad (3.16)$$

Inequality 3.16 shows that in order for country i to choose country x, the value of receiving the concession from country x (M_x) must be larger than the sum of the opportunity cost of receiving it from country y (M_y) plus the additional value the industrialized state receives from development if country y receives r_{iy4} for providing the concession, less the offsetting benefit of increased utility from enhanced development in country x,[22] plus any difference in $v_i(\cdot)$ between scenarios 4 and 3 (which will be negative if $s_{ix3} < s_{iy4}$)

Obviously the likelihood of being chosen to provide the concession increases in M and decreases in C, since higher M increases the value to country i and lower C decreases the amount of compensation needed to make an incentive compatible offer to the developing country. However, the decision of country i depends on the "net" cost of buying the concession, which is increasing in the use of resources, $s_i = r_i + f_i$, but partially offset by benefits from development that increase directly with higher values of β and/or k and indirectly with higher values of γ (which increases the value of development resources for the developing state and therefore the amount of compensation that is given through r_i, thus providing an offsetting development benefit to country i).

A key insight of the model is that, when faced with multiple potential providers of a concession, an industrialized state will be influenced by development considerations when choosing the provider of a non-development concession. It is unsurprising that the industrialized country's choice is influenced by the relative value of the benefits (M_x, M_y) and the costs it needs to compensate (C_x, C_y). What the model highlights is that the decision will also be influenced by the different values of $\beta_x, \beta_y, k_x, k_y, \gamma_x$, and γ_y. When differences between M_x and M_y and between C_x and C_y are not particularly large, the industrialized state is more likely to seek a non-development concession with a state when its own utility from development in the state (β) is higher, when the developing country is relatively efficient at turning resources into development (higher k), and/or when the developing country government places a higher value on compensation in the form of development resources (higher γ).

I have assumed full information for ease of exposition. In a more realistic situation in which the values of M_x, M_y, C_x, and C_y are not precisely known to the other parties, the values of the βs, γs, and ks help define the zone of possible agreements (if any) in negotiation, increasing or decreasing the likelihood that a deal can be reached. This more realistic scenario might allow the developing country to extract some surplus for itself, as country i doesn't know its true reservation value. This makes granting the concession valuable to the developing country, increasing its desire to "win" the deal over its potential rival provider.

Key Insights from Case 3

- When faced with multiple potential developing country providers of an outcome that it values (other than development), an industrialized state will be influenced by the relative benefit it receives from development outcomes in each potential provider (β), the relative efficiency at which each turns resources into development (k), and the relative value placed on development by the developing country governments (γ, which influences the value of "payment" offered in the form of development resources).
- This implies that development considerations influence the cross-national distribution of non-development interactions between industrialized and developing countries.

Case 4: International Institutions?

The model also provides insight into when industrialized states may prefer bilateral action rather than multilateral action coordinated through an international institution. Returning to Case 1, suppose there is a second industrialized state, country j, with preferences for development given by β_{jx} and β_{jy}. It is useful to rewrite country i's preferences as β_{ix} and β_{iy} to distinguish between the two industrialized states. Now the utility functions of the two states can be given as:

$$U_{i5} = \beta_{ix}k_x(r_{ix5} + r_{jx5})^\alpha + \beta_{iy}k_y(r_{iy5} + r_{jy5})^\alpha + v_i(R_i - g_{i5}) \qquad (3.17)$$

$$U_{j5} = \beta_{jx}k_x(r_{jx5} + r_{ix5})^\alpha + \beta_{jy}k_y(r_{jy5} + r_{iy5})^\alpha + v_j(R_j - g_{j5}) \qquad (3.18)$$

Given scarce resources and diminishing returns to each term in the utility function, country i will provide fewer resources to countries x and y if country j is also providing resources to these countries, and similar considerations guide the decisions of country j, producing the familiar result of free-riding and underprovision if the sum of the marginal benefits to countries i and j of pursuing development in countries x and y is greater than the marginal cost at the resulting level of provision. An international institution could lock in contributions at a level that increases total welfare of the industrialized states. However, if the industrialized states have divergent preferences for where resources should be spent, this can decrease the level of free-riding in the first place (reducing the potential benefits for an institution), and can lead to negotiation difficulties over the distribution of resources if an institution is contemplated.[23]

To illustrate the effect of divergent preferences, assume a situation in which country i receives significantly more utility from development in country x than in country y and country j has the opposite preferences, receiving more benefit from country y's development than from country x's development. In terms of the model, $\beta_{ix} \gg \beta_{iy}$ and $\beta_{jy} \gg \beta_{jx}$. In the absence of an institution, country i will invest most of its development resources in country x and country j will invest most of its development resources in country y. As country j is giving little to country x, there is not much ability for country i to free-ride on j's efforts (or lack thereof) in country x. The same is true for country j's ability to free-ride on the efforts of i in country y. In fact, because of diminishing returns to the benefits, it is even possible that the two industrialized states completely specialize, with country i giving all its development resources to country x and country j giving all its development resources to country y. With or without complete specialization, under divergent preferences free-riding is substantially reduced, although not necessarily eliminated. Country i may give country x more than it would have in Case 1 (when it gave more resources to country y), and both country i and country j (to a lesser extent) will benefit from this. However, country i may decrease development spending overall through cuts to y (relative to Case 1) as a result of country j also providing resources.

Even with complete specialization it is possible that the sum of the marginal benefit to countries i and j of an additional dollar spent on development will be higher than the marginal cost of providing it, meaning Pareto improvements exist. However, with complete specialization it is possible that $\frac{\delta U_{is}}{\delta r_{ixs}} > \frac{\delta U_{is}}{\delta r_{iys}}$ and $\frac{\delta U_{js}}{\delta r_{jys}} > \frac{\delta U_{js}}{\delta r_{jxs}}$; given specialization there is no expectation that the marginal utility for i (or j) of providing a dollar of development resources is equal across countries x and y. This means that if resources are increased through an institution, country i may prefer that additional money be spent in developing country x, while country j prefers that it be spent in developing country y, setting up a situation in which the countries would need to bargain to determine which of several Pareto improving points are chosen (assuming they can identify them), with distributional consequences for the amount that countries i and j benefit from the institution.[24] These distributional concerns increase the difficulty of the bargaining problem. That, coupled with the decline in free-riding that accompanies divergent preferences and the costs of maintaining an institution, may be enough to render an institution suboptimal.[25]

While this example has built on Case 1 for simplicity, it can easily be extended to Cases 2 and 3 in which development outcomes are only one consideration in determining resource allocation. Take, for example, funding for climate change mitigation by industrialized states in developing countries, which is often intended to contribute to development while mitigating climate change. An international institution might have a mandate to maximize GHG reduction to achieve the largest possible impact from funds on climate mitigation. However, countries *i* and *j* will want to maximize their own utility, which is increased both by climate mitigation and by development resulting from funding for climate mitigation. The preference for maximizing utility through both development and climate mitigation with the same funds will divert funds from their most efficient use for achieving mitigation (assuming the projects preferred for development reasons are not also the most efficient for climate mitigation). This will decrease the desirability of handing over control to an institution that will emphasize efficiency in climate mitigation. When countries *i* and *j* have divergent preferences regarding the location of development outcomes, the same difficulties observed in Case 4 with regard to development will manifest themselves in consideration of non-development coordination as well.

Key Insights from Case 4

- Divergent preferences regarding the cross-country allocation of development resources reduce the prevalence of free-riding but also increase the preference for bilateral, as opposed to multilateral, provision of development resources.
- When development considerations influence interactions in non-development issue areas, the preference for bilateral over multilateral provision in development will affect the likelihood of multilateral cooperation on the non-development issue as well.

Testing the Model

The model highlights the main aspects of the targeted development framework and provides observable implications for testing it across policy issue areas. In the model, industrialized states are assumed to make decisions in their own self-interest, including decisions to allocate resources for development promotion. This implies that resources are expended for development when and where it increases the industrialized country's utility, relative to using the same resources for other purposes. The value an industrialized state places on development (β) can vary over time. For instance, with increased interconnections between industrialized and developing states in recent decades, industrialized country governments will be more concerned with the impact of negative spillovers from underdevelopment and will increase the resources allocated to development promotion. The value placed on development by an industrialized state will also vary across developing countries. This leads to targeting: where this value is higher, more resources will be devoted to enhancing development.

The relative value placed on development is also a function of opportunity costs. Holding development preferences constant, when the utility associated with using resources for other purposes increases or decreases, there will be a reallocation of scarce resources to reflect changes in relative priorities (in the model, these other priorities are represented by M and the $v_i(\cdot)$ function). For instance, when the Cold War ended there was no longer a need to spend resources "containing" the spread of Soviet influence, which freed those resources for other purposes. This led to an increase in resources available for pursuing development.

The model also incorporates the varying abilities of developing countries to turn resources into development outcomes (modeled as k). An industrialized state using resources for development will receive higher utility for a given amount of resources the more development is actually produced. The implication follows that industrialized states will incorporate the abilities of targeted states when determining the amount of resources and type of development programs to pursue within a country. For instance, an industrialized country might alter the mix of foreign aid and trade concessions offered to different countries based on their quality of governance and ability to harness trade for growth.

Finally, the model produces specific observable implications across the issue areas examined in this book. Foreign aid, largely coopted for containment and other geostrategic purposes during the Cold War, should see a marked shift toward a targeted development focus due to both the collapse of the Soviet Union (which decreased the opportunity costs of using resources for development) and the rise in interconnections between industrialized and developing states (which increases the payoff to development). As the importance of development has increased, we should observe industrialized states incorporating concerns for development into other policy areas, such as trade. Increased access to markets can be a powerful development tool, but granting this access to their own markets can be politically challenging for governments in industrialized states that face protectionist pressures from domestic interest groups. When a government places high importance on development in particular countries and believes a trade agreement will further this goal, it will be more inclined to bear the costs associated with pursuing development through trade agreements. To be most effective at mitigating future climate change and helping countries adapt to current climate-related difficulties, climate finance should flow where it will be used most efficiently for adaptation and mitigation. The model suggests otherwise: given that climate finance is often simultaneously used for development purposes, an industrialized state pursuing targeted development will allocate climate finance where it provides the largest returns in utility for itself, summed across both climate and development outcomes. The remainder of this section draws more concrete expectations for each of the issue areas before turning to the empirical chapters.

Foreign Aid

Following a targeted development strategy, industrialized states will give aid disproportionately to countries from which they expect the largest potential effects from negative spillovers (in terms of the model, these developing countries will have higher values of β). These can include nearby states, states with large populations, and those tied to the donor through historical connections, migrant networks, or trade. The theory predicts systematic variation in cross-national allocation that is linked to these ties between donors and recipients; the empirical analysis examines whether such variation is observed. The theory also predicts that foreign aid will have become more development-focused over time, as targeted development gained in importance relative to geostrategic purposes for giving aid. Given the relatively long history of foreign aid programs and data availability, the empirical analysis is able to test whether there are changes over time in aid allocation that are consistent with a shift toward targeted development. Finally, the composition of aid flows is also examined, testing for evidence that donors systematically vary the basket of aid offered to account for differences in the capacity and/or willingness of governments across developing countries to produce development outcomes with aid (in terms of the model, this is testing donors' response to different values of k across developing countries). Industrialized states pursuing targeted development will take steps to craft a strategy that increases the likelihood and magnitude of development outcomes in targeted countries.

Trade Agreements

Granting preferential access to its own market is a powerful tool an industrialized country can use to spur growth in developing countries. It can also be politically costly, as domestic interest groups are likely to lobby for protection from increased competition associated with reduced barriers. A costly tool, such as a preferential trade agreement, is more likely to be used when the benefits of development promotion increase, suggesting an increase in preferential trade agreements between industrialized and developing countries as the desire to counter underdevelopment has increased. The theory also argues that these will be targeted. An industrialized state should seek a trade agreement with a developing country when the benefit to itself of development (β) is high and when the developing country has political and economic institutions and policies (k) that position it to benefit from increased access to an industrialized country market. Chapter 5 documents the rise in trade agreements between industrialized–developing country dyads since the end of the Cold War. It then tests whether there is a link between foreign aid and trade agreements, hypothesizing that these may act as complements for an industrialized country pursuing targeted development in particular states. The empirical analysis also examines the relationship between average income in a developing country and the likelihood of signing an agreement with an industrialized state. Development benefits of a trade agreement will most likely be highest for developing countries in the "middle of the pack" with regard to income. Those that are particularly underdeveloped likely lack the capacity to capitalize on a trade agreement to stimulate growth (lower k), while the richest of the developing countries are less in need of trade assistance (and likely create fewer spillovers, meaning benefits to the industrialized state of development in the countries (β) are lower). Existing explanations of the pattern of trade agreements largely ignore the benefits to the industrialized state of development abroad associated with these agreements; the chapter tests whether incorporating targeted development advances our understanding of the observed patterns.

Climate Finance

The stated purpose of climate finance is to mitigate future climate change and assist countries in adapting to circumstances related to climate change that is already under way. There is clearly a connection between development and climate change mitigation and adaptation. However, climate funds are supposed to focus on climate issues in developing countries while traditional aid focuses on development concerns; climate funds are to be "new and additional" to existing development aid. The model implies that when development considerations coexist with other priorities, as is true with climate finance, the desire to pursue targeted development will result in a less efficient use of resources for their stated purpose. The empirical analysis examines whether funding for climate change mitigation and adaptation in developing countries is skewed toward countries where the industrialized state places a higher value on development (higher β), with the intent to have the funds simultaneously improve development and address issues associated with climate change. The chapter also analyzes whether industrialized states prefer to allocate adaptation funds to developing countries where failure to adapt to climate change could lead to increased spillovers for themselves. This means the funding is more likely to be tracked to places that have higher benefit to the donor (higher β) and not necessarily to the countries most in need of adaptation assistance.

The next three chapters form the empirical portion of the book, testing the targeted development framework in the issue areas of foreign aid allocation, preferential trade agreements, and climate finance.

4

Reorienting Foreign Aid*

> One in five people in the world today, over 1 billion people, live in poverty on less than one dollar a day. In an increasingly inter-dependent world, many problems—like conflict, crime, pollution, and diseases such as HIV and AIDS—are caused or made worse by poverty.
> —United Kingdom's Mission Statement for the Department for International Development

> Humanitarian problems, such as extreme poverty, famine, refugee crises, and natural disasters, as well as global issues such as those related to the environment and water, are important issues that need to be addressed in order for the international community as a whole to achieve sustainable development. These problems are cross border issues that present a grave threat to each and every human being.
> —Japan's Official Development Assistance Charter, 2003.

By the end of 2009 the United Kingdom was experiencing its deepest recession since World War II, with unemployment rising and Fitch Ratings stating that to avoid a credit downgrade the country's government needed to "articulate more credible and stronger fiscal consolidation during the course of 2010 to underpin confidence in the sustainability of public finances."[1] Dissatisfaction with the handling of the crisis by the Labour government led to their loss in the May 2010 elections, and a coalition government of Conservatives and Liberal Democrats was formed. In October of that year the new government announced an austerity plan that the *Financial Times* called "the most drastic budget cuts in living memory," noting that they "far exceed anything contemplated in the US." To reduce the deficit the austerity plan aimed to cut defense spending by up to 8%; undertake large reductions in spending in areas such as welfare programs, local government, police budgets, and funding for the BBC; shrink the size of the public sector workforce; and increase the retirement age.[2] Notably, and controversially with the public, foreign aid was spared from cuts—in fact, it was scheduled to continue its pre-crisis projected increases to reach 0.7% of the country's gross national income by 2013 (up from 0.36% prior to the 2008 onset of the global financial crisis) a goal that was met on time.[3] In 2015, a year that would see another round of austerity measures causing thousands to protest in the streets of London, the 0.7% target for aid was enshrined into law under the Conservative government led by David Cameron, officially protecting it from current and future budget cuts.

Scholars who study foreign aid advance multiple, at times conflicting, explanations for the rationale underlying donor aid decisions. One set of studies argues that aid is a tool to advance geopolitical strategy, with development concerns subordinated to non-development priorities of the donor states.[4] Under this scenario, one might expect aid to follow military and diplomatic priorities, but would hardly expect the aid budget to continue rising while those for defense and the Foreign Office are cut, as was the case under the United Kingdom's austerity plan. Another line of research argues that foreign aid is an extension of the welfare state, favored by left-leaning governments as a way of promoting their worldview abroad.[5] This also does not offer much insight as to why a *conservative* government would increase foreign aid, or why *any* government would continue to increase aid while cutting welfare spending at home.

Leaders of the Conservative and Liberal Democrat parties in government offered a different explanation. Foreign aid, they argued, is needed to promote development abroad to advance the national interest of the United Kingdom. Aid is not simply a tool to pursue non-development interests, as had so often been the case during the Cold War. It is also not only about "doing good" abroad, although if development succeeds it will be good for both the aid recipients and the United Kingdom. Instead, development is a national security goal. David Cameron, prime minister of the United Kingdom from 2010 to 2016, noted that "helping those in need is not just about responding with our hearts. It's about our heads too ... if we invest in countries before they get broken, we might not end up spending so much on dealing with problems—whether that's immigration or new threats to our national security."[6] Nicholas Clegg, leader of the Liberal Democrat party and deputy prime minister in the coalition government, justified the increases in aid by arguing that "If you want to deal with terrorism, extremism, if you want to stop people upping sticks and moving across continents and coming to settle in Europe and here, you have got to make sure the circumstances are better for them."[7]

Targeted Development and Foreign Aid

The statements by Cameron and Clegg are consistent with a targeted development approach guiding foreign aid policy. The leaders note the consequences for their own country of continued underdevelopment abroad, arguing that development resources are needed to limit "problems" such as migration or extremist threats. If this rationale guides aid policy, then aid resources will be targeted most heavily toward the likely sources of these spillovers.

This chapter examines foreign aid allocation over four decades, from the Cold War through the war on terror. The empirical analysis covers aid from 23 donors to 156 recipients and follows in a long tradition of scholarly work that examines patterns in aid allocation to better understand donor motivations.[8] The emphasis is on analyzing the current period since 2001, with comparisons to the Cold War and the 1990s. This three-period categorization follows that used by Robert Fleck and Christopher Kilby,[9] and reflects an understanding in the aid community that the end of the Cold War and the terrorist attacks of September 11, 2001, mark logical breaks for considering potential changes in foreign aid policy.

The theory developed in the preceding chapters argues that industrialized states pursue development abroad in an effort to cut down on negative spillovers from underdevelopment that could adversely affect their own countries. To advance this goal, states focus their development efforts on countries from which the expected impact of spillovers on themselves is greatest. This pattern will have emerged over time, as industrialized states moved on from the geopolitics of the Cold War to confront an increasingly interconnected world. While the chapter will examine the role of targeted development in foreign aid in greater detail, it is helpful to highlight predictions from the theory at the outset. If a desire to pursue targeted development is influencing foreign aid policy, the study of aid allocation should reveal the following:

- Aid will be allocated disproportionately to countries from which the expected impact of spillovers from underdevelopment on the donor is greatest.
- To improve the likelihood that aid leads to improved development outcomes, donors will alter the composition of aid based on characteristics of the recipient country government.
- The allocation of foreign aid has shifted over time, from a pattern consistent with Cold War strategic priorities to a pattern that incorporates the desire of donors to promote targeted development.

Industrialized countries will invest development resources abroad when and where it serves their interest. This implies variation across countries and over time in the amount of foreign aid allocated, to reflect the rising importance of development as a foreign policy goal and the disproportionate effect on donors of underdevelopment in different recipients. Additionally, when donors prioritize development, they should care not only about the amount of aid, but about its effectiveness for achieving development outcomes. Aid will be both *targeted* and *development-oriented*. Targeting implies a cross-national allocation pattern in which a donor focuses aid on recipients from which the likely impact of spillovers is high. Development-oriented requires that donors take steps to craft an aid basket that is consistent with the needs and capabilities of a chosen recipient, in order to increase likely development outcomes. The theory requires both elements to hold. Showering corrupt dictators with infusions of fungible cash is not consistent with prioritizing development, no matter how likely the recipient is to inflict spillovers on the donor: if the cash will not be used for development, it cannot be part of a targeted development strategy and is more consistent with geopolitical influence over foreign aid. Targeting poor, well-governed states regardless of their likelihood of creating spillovers is also inconsistent with the theory, suggesting more of a role for humanitarian concerns in aid policy. The empirical analysis will examine both cross-national patterns of aid allocation and patterns of aid composition to determine if observed patterns match expectations derived from the targeted development framework.

The argument is that the desire to pursue targeted development has become a significant factor in determining aid allocation. This is not meant to suggest that it is the only consideration driving aid decisions. Aid is an important policy tool and there will be instances of geopolitical and humanitarian motivations, in addition to targeted development, in the current period. In fact, donors can increase resources for development priorities without necessarily detracting from their geostrategic goals vis-à-vis developing countries by increasing the amount of resources. The expectation is to observe a trend toward increasing importance for targeted development considerations in guiding allocation decisions. Additionally, it should be noted that pursuing targeted development can be a complement to, rather than a substitute for, other motivations for giving foreign aid. For instance, policymakers and scholars have argued that donors "brand" their aid to increase the sense of good feeling toward the donor.[10] Obviously donors can simultaneously pursue both the foreign policy goal of development and that of good will with the same foreign aid. Others have argued that domestic political factors influence legislative support for foreign aid[11] or that some industrialized states are motivated by welfare-state considerations.[12] The targeted development theory is agnostic regarding how governments gain domestic support for their aid budgets. Rather, it specifies how they will allocate the budgeted aid across recipient states.

Historical Perspective

Modern foreign aid programs to developing countries are most often traced to the 1949 decision by US President Harry Truman to create a program for sending technical assistance to developing states, part of which is quoted at the outset of this book. In 1961 members of the Organization for Economic Cooperation and Development (OECD) formed the Development Assistance Committee (DAC), which signified that development assistance was becoming an established policy area between industrialized and developing states. An important (and useful) component of DAC membership is data reporting: countries that join the DAC agree to report their foreign aid flows to the organization in a regular and standardized manner. By definition, flows counted as official development assistance and reported to the DAC do not include military aid.

Figure 4.1 shows aid commitments from DAC countries from 1970 to 2014 in constant dollars.[13] Total aid from DAC countries (including their contributions to multilateral institutions) as well as the bilateral component is shown, with additional lines showing these net of aid to Iraq and Afghanistan. There is an overall upward trend in the amount of flows, with DAC aid rising from around $50 billion in 1970 to more than $160 billion in 2014. Figure 4.2 shows net disbursements of foreign aid as a percent of gross national income for the DAC,

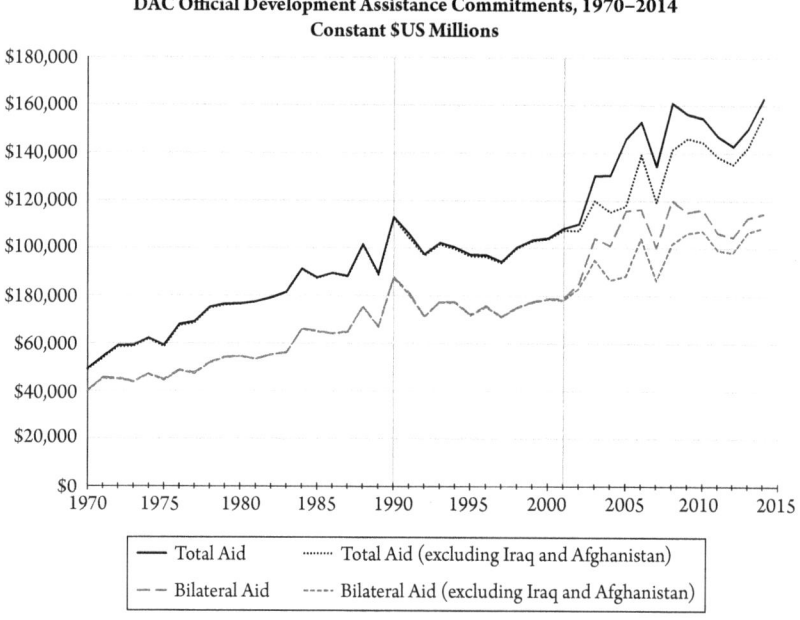

Source: Table DAC3a, available online at stats.oecd.org; extracted January 4, 2017. "Part 2" aid included for the 1993–2004 period from historical files to ensure comparability across time.

Figure 4.1 Official Development Assistance Commitments, 1970–2014 (Constant $Millions).

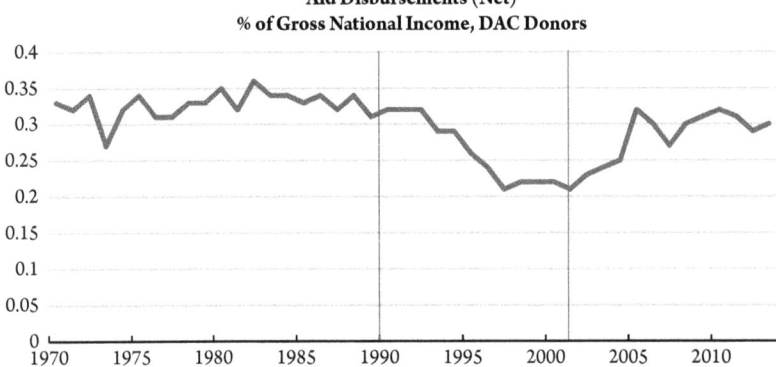

Figure 4.2 Official Development Assistance as a Percent of Gross National Income for DAC Donors, 1970–2013.

often considered a measure of aid "effort." The appendix to this chapter lists aid expenditures and percent of gross national income by donor for the year 2013.

Solid lines mark the years 1990 and 2001 in Figures 4.1 and 4.2, corresponding with the end of the Cold War and the start of the war on terror. The overall trend supports the importance of these as possible turning points in foreign aid policy. Figure 4.1 shows a general upward trend of aid during the Cold War and a short spike brought about by sudden aid flows to Eastern Europe as the Iron Curtain collapsed, followed by an end to the increases in aid spending throughout the 1990s. Aid effort, shown in Figure 4.2, declined markedly during the 1990s, as national income rose in donor states while aid flows remained stagnant. Since 2001, aid flows and effort have increased significantly, even excluding aid to Iraq and Afghanistan. The start of the global recession sent aid commitments on a roller-coaster ride, but by 2014 they were 50% above the level in 2000.[14] The remainder of this section reviews conclusions of scholars and policymakers regarding changes in aid objectives over time. The following sections apply the targeted development framework to aid allocation, differentiate it from existing explanations, and develop and test observable implications of the theory.

Evolving Aid Objectives

Empirical studies of aid allocation for the Cold War period conclude that aid was primarily a tool for advancing the political and economic interests of donor states.[15] Alfred Maizels and Machiko Nissanke note that if aid produced development, it was "an incidental effect."[16] Former British Development Minister Hilary Benn asserted that during the Cold War "aid was provided to dictators just because they were on 'our side.'"[17] The primacy of the strategic purposes for aid was reinforced by the decline of aid commitments when the Cold War ended.[18] Carol Lancaster, deputy administrator for USAID from 1993 to 1996, notes of US aid in the 1990s that "without the Cold War rationale, the priority of aid diminished considerably in the foreign policy community."[19] Jean-Claude Berthélemy and Ariane Tichit (2004) perform a number of statistical tests on differences in foreign aid between the 1980s and 1990s, concluding that "a major outcome of the end of the Cold War has been the strong decline in aid commitments of bilateral donors."[20]

Aid experts have argued that the decline in geopolitical purposes for aid in the 1990s was accompanied by a shift in aid priorities. Deborah Brautigam and Stephen Knack note the fall in aid to authoritarian regimes that had been strategically important during the Cold War.[21] Ngaire Woods argues that the focus of aid shifted to promoting human security in the 1990s.[22] David Bearce and Daniel Tirone show that aid in the 1990s differed from Cold War aid in that it was more likely to both induce economic reform in recipients and lead to economic growth.[23] Others demonstrate that aid is less likely to entrench authoritarian regimes in the post–Cold War period.[24]

Following the terrorist attacks of September 11, 2001, there was a widespread increase in foreign aid. Austria, Belgium, Finland, France, Ireland, Italy, the Netherlands, New Zealand, Spain, Sweden, the United Kingdom, and the United States all recorded aid increases of more than 50% between 2001 and 2006, with some (but not all) declining after the onset of the global financial crisis.[25] Activists and scholars have been skeptical of the development intent behind these increases in aid, arguing that with the emergence of terrorism as a new global threat aid will return to its Cold War pattern of advancing geostrategic goals at the expense of development priorities. An Action Aid report on foreign aid claims that "The war on terror is like a new Cold War where everything is subordinated to a single purpose."[26] Bearce and Tirone, whose analysis ends in 2001, offer the out-of-sample prediction for the war on terror that "as foreign aid once again becomes more useful for military-strategic purposes, it becomes less effective at promoting economic growth and development."[27] Ngaire Woods notes that, as a result of the war on terror, one concern is that "Donors may hijack foreign aid to pursue their own security objectives."[28] An Oxfam (UK) report claims that the war on terror will "weaken donors' commitment to poverty reduction."[29] The nongovernmental organization Christian Aid expressed a similar concern, publishing "The Politics of Poverty: Aid in the New Cold War" in 2004.[30]

To many observers, structural changes reinforce this view of the securitization of foreign aid. On coming to power in May 2010, the coalition government in the United Kingdom created a new security council to meet weekly; members included the Prime Minister, Foreign Secretary, Defense Secretary, and International Development Secretary, as well as other senior government ministers and officials.[31] In the United States, the Department of State and the Agency for

International Development issued a joint strategic plan for the first time in 2003. These joint plans continued under the administration of Barack Obama, which also implemented a Quadrennial Diplomacy and Development Review, issuing reports in 2010 and 2015 and further linking planning on development and broader foreign policy goals. In 2013, Australia's new conservative government under Prime Minister Abbott brought the Australian Aid Agency (AusAID), which had been independent of other government agencies, into the Department of Foreign Affairs and Trade. That same year, the Canadian government decided to align the Canadian International Development Agency (CIDA) more closely with the Department of Foreign Affairs, folding it into a new Department of Foreign Affairs, Trade and Development (renamed Global Affairs Canada after the 2015 elections).

A Targeted Development Explanation

The argument that aid in the post-2001 period will resemble Cold War aid assumes (implicitly) that the importance of development has remained constant. If increasing concerns for the impact of underdevelopment on donor well-being influence donor preferences, then there is no particular reason to expect a return to Cold War aid patterns, when development was seen as a relatively unimportant goal, simply because geopolitical concerns increase. Targeted development suggests a more development-oriented, although not humanitarian-motivated, explanation for the recent increases in foreign aid as well as the closer alignment between aid agencies and broader foreign policy and security institutions. Connections between industrialized and developing countries have deepened in recent decades. Wealthy countries are less able to insulate their populations from problems associated with underdevelopment abroad than they were historically. To combat these problems, wealthy states will pursue a strategy of targeted development.

Donors pursuing targeted development with foreign aid will give aid disproportionately to the countries where development will provide the most benefit for themselves, and will take steps to increase the likelihood that aid actually results in development. The increased importance placed on development promotion abroad suggests a closer working relationship between development agencies and the foreign policy apparatus to determine where development will be most beneficial for the donor state. The result of pursuing targeted development with foreign aid will be more development-oriented than often feared by those who lamented the closer association between aid agencies and the foreign policy and security arms in government. At the same time, development will be pursued to advance the self-interest of the donor rather than responding to objective measures of humanitarian need.

The following two sections apply the theory to the areas of cross-national aid allocation and aid composition, deriving testable implications and presenting the results of the empirical analysis.

Cross-National Aid Allocation Patterns

It is important to distinguish non-development self-interest pursued with aid from self-interest pursued through development. Non-development self-interest consists of buying/rewarding military support or votes in international bodies, propping up friendly governments, rewarding countries that open up to donor exports, or more generally "buying" favors from the recipient government in exchange for aid. The intended outcome can be achieved even if no additional development occurs. This is what has traditionally been meant by donor interest, and such factors have been found to influence the allocation of foreign aid.

Interest pursued through development generates different predictions regarding aid allocation. According to the theory of targeted development, substantial portions of aid are targeted to promote development in the best interest of the donor. This implies a cross-national allocation pattern in which a donor focuses aid on recipients from which the likely impact of spillovers from underdevelopment is high. This section generates expectations for the cross-national allocation of aid under a targeted development strategy, and distinguishes this from traditional accounts based on the expectation that donors pursue their non-development strategic interests with aid funds.

The expectation is not that in any period donors exclusively pursue either self-interested development or geopolitical concerns with foreign aid; obviously, donors can pursue multiple goals at one time. Neither do I want to argue that humanitarian concerns never play a role in aid decisions—there are certainly instances in any period that cannot be easily explained without some regard for humanitarian motivations. Rather, the point is that the relative importance of motivations has shifted over time, from a dominant role for geopolitical concerns during the Cold War to an increasing role for promoting self-interested development in the current period.

It is useful to lay out the different predictions between a geopolitics-based model and a targeted-development–based model with regard to variables that can be used to analyze donor intent. Table 4.1 presents expectations for key variables under both scenarios, with the former predicted to be stronger during the Cold War and the latter stronger during the post-2001 period. The variables in the first set are often associated with geopolitical explanations but are not particularly relevant for pursuing targeted development. These include measures of military importance, such as the amount of military assistance provided by

Table 4.1 **Predicted Association Between Explanatory Variables and Aid Allocation**

	Geopolitics	Targeted Development
US Military Assistance	positive	diminishing/none
Donor–Recipient Arms Transfers	positive	diminishing/none
Security Council Membership	positive	diminishing/none
UN Vote Distance	ambiguous	diminishing/none
Former Colony	positive	positive
Donor Exports	positive	positive
Population	ambiguous	positive
Income	ambiguous	negative
Distance	ambiguous	negative
Migration	none	positive
Donor Imports	none	positive
Natural Disaster	none	positive

the United States (the only donor to publish these data) to a developing country and arms transfers between a donor and recipient. Scholars have also argued that donors may use aid to buy influence with countries occupying one of the rotating seats on the UN Security Council,[32] and multiple studies argue that foreign aid may be used to influence voting in the UN General Assembly, although the exact relationship between UN votes and aid is not straightforward.[33] These geopolitical variables are expected to be important predictors of aid during the Cold War, with diminishing importance in the post-2001 period.

Measures in the second set, relating to former colonial status and donor exports, are predicted to have the same relationship with foreign aid under both scenarios: although the explanations differ, the anticipated statistical relationships are in the same direction. From a geopolitical rationale, former colonies will receive more aid as colonial powers seek to maintain their sphere of influence after independence. Donors can use aid as leverage in international trade negotiations, pushing aid recipients to be more open to their exports; they can also tie aid directly to the purchase of exports. Neither of these explanations requires development to occur for donor interest to be met. Targeted development goes a step further and argues that donors seek to promote development in their former colonies because the historical ties that bind them together can also serve as transmission vehicles for negative spillovers (e.g., unwanted migration, spread of disease through travel, instability that draws in the former colonial power).

Likewise, targeted development is consistent with increasing development in export markets, to further boost demand (relative to forced opening without development). While the similar predictions across theories mean that these variables are not well suited for differentiating between them, both variables form an important part of the overall pattern expected across variables under each scenario.

The variables in the final set have clear predictions under a targeted development framework but ambiguous or no expectations from a geopolitical standpoint. The impact of unwanted spillovers is likely higher from nearby, populous, and poorer countries than from those that are more distant, less populous, and wealthier, generating clear predictions of a positive relationship between aid and population and a negative relationship between aid and both distance and income under the targeted development framework. For geopolitical explanations the relationships for these variables are less clear. For instance, aid used to buy geopolitical favors is consistent with a negative coefficient on both population and income, as these favors may be cheaper to buy from small, poor states.[34] On the other hand, it might be more valuable to buy influence in larger, slightly better-off countries that perhaps command a more prominent place on the world stage, suggesting a positive relationship is possible. A geopolitical explanation can be formed for any relationship between aid and distance: if donors give aid where it best suits their interest on other measures, then no relationship will be observed; if donors use aid to project power outside their immediate spheres of influence, a positive relationship between aid and distance may exist; and if donors use aid to solidify influence in their own neighborhoods, it will generate a negative correlation between aid and distance. Of course, donors may use aid for all three, suggesting that perhaps the most likely outcome is noise if geopolitical considerations are driving the relationship between aid and distance. Few previous studies have controlled for distance, and none have tested whether the relationship between distance and aid varies over time.[35]

Geopolitical, non-development, explanations do not generate predictions between aid allocation and the last three variables listed in Table 4.1: migration, donor imports, and natural disasters. As previous migration is a predictor of future migration,[36] donors wishing to promote development and decrease the push factors for migration will focus aid disproportionately on those countries that have sent them migrants in the past;[37] the potential relationship between aid and migration was overlooked for decades in empirical studies of foreign aid, perhaps due to low data availability in earlier periods. While the link between donor exports or total trade between a donor–recipient pair and aid allocation is well studied,[38] there has been little attention paid to potential links between donor imports from a developing country and aid to that country.[39] There are multiple reasons that donors may favor development in recipients from which they receive higher imports. First, they may wish to invest in increasing the quality of the imports. Second, since wages are higher in more developed countries, promoting development can eventually raise the wages in the source country, decreasing the difference between domestic and foreign wages in the long run. Finally, in countries targeted for development promotion, donors may pursue this through both foreign aid and increased openness to the recipient country's imports, an issue explored more fully in Chapter 5. While it is difficult to disentangle the motivations surrounding the links between donor exports and aid flows, examining links between donor imports and aid flows offers an important test for the targeted development explanation. Concern regarding the potential for negative spillovers in the aftermath of a disaster can lead to increased aid, although humanitarian motivations may operate in such cases as well.

The possibility that donors may be driven by humanitarian concerns offers a plausible alternative interpretation for the hypothesized relationship between aid commitments and the variables income, population, and natural disasters. While the relationship between these variables and aid would be the same under either a targeted development or humanitarian explanation, the patterns on other variables differ across these explanations. If humanitarian concerns are the primary motivating force for aid, then aid flows should go where the need is greatest. Instead, targeted development predicts that aid will flow disproportionately to developing countries where connections with the donor increase the likelihood of spillovers, such as nearby states and those where the donor has ties through migration or trade that could serve as transmission mechanisms. Examining empirical results across multiple variables helps disentangle the explanatory power of targeted development relative to both geopolitical and more purely humanitarian agendas.

Change over Time

The expectation is that the importance of targeted development has grown over time, particularly since 2001. There are surprisingly few empirical analyses that examine the post-2001 period separately from the broader post–Cold War timeframe. Those that exist, while offering important insights, are limited in terms of the countries covered and variables whose impact is modeled as changing over time. Todd Moss, David Roodman, and Scott Standley compare aid from the United States in the 1990s with the post-2001 period and argue that most countries did not see a change in aid allocation post-2001; change occurred on the front lines of the war on terror, but not at the expense of the rest because aid budgets increased.[40] Robert Fleck and Christopher Kilby analyze US aid across the Cold War, 1990s, and post-2001 periods; they find variations in the impact of recipient income on aid allocation but do not examine changes in the relationship between other variables and aid flows over time.[41] Paul Clist examines changes in the responsiveness to recipient income and governance in aid allocation for seven bilateral donors, finding increasing sensitivity to poverty but not governance; this study also does not test for differences in donor interest variables across periods.[42] The analysis in this chapter helps fill the gap in knowledge regarding aid flows post-2001, while comparing this to earlier periods.

Data

The dataset includes yearly, dyadic data on aid commitments from 23 OECD donors to 156 recipients for the period 1973–2012. The starting point for this database is a list of all members of the Development Assistance Committee (DAC) of the OECD for all years that they were members of DAC.[43] The list of donor-years was then crossed with a list of all potential recipients for all years in which they were eligible to receive aid. Only independent states are counted, as aid to territories might be expected to follow different patterns than aid to sovereign parties. In the dataset, a country is deemed eligible to receive aid for all years post-independence, unless it crosses the high-income threshold and graduates from aid eligibility. According to OECD reporting rules, countries graduate from eligibility for official development assistance after two years classified as "high income"; after this point no data on aid receipts are collected for these states by the OECD and they are not counted in the analysis.

Dependent Variable

I follow the general trend in the literature studying aid allocation by using data on aid commitments, rather than disbursements, as the latter may lag the original policy decision by several years. The dependent variable is the natural log of (one plus) aid commitments from a donor to a recipient in a given year.[44] Data are from the OECD's International Development Statistics online database.[45]

Explanatory Variables

Explanatory variables can be categorized as recipient-level or dyad-level. Recipient-level variables include *Income* and *Population* drawn from the World Bank's *World Development Indicators*.[46] Income is measured in constant dollars and both variables are logged. *Disaster* is the natural log of (one plus) the sum of the total number of people affected or killed as a result of natural disasters in a country in a given year.[47] *Civil War* equals one if a recipient experienced one or more civil wars in a given year[48] and zero otherwise. *Democracy* is the average of a recipient's values on the civil liberties and political rights variables published by Freedom House; this scale ranges from zero to seven and is inverted so that higher scores reflect greater democracy.[49] *US Military Assistance* is the log of (one plus) the reported constant-dollar value of military aid received by the recipient from the United States in a given year.[50] This is included for all dyads (not just those where the industrialized state is the United States) as individual donor data on military assistance are not available and as military assistance from the United States may serve as a proxy of general military importance to itself and its allies, particularly during the Cold War. *Security Council Member* is an indicator variable that equals one if a recipient held a rotating seat on the UN Security Council in year *t* and zero otherwise.[51]

Dyadic measures capture donor–recipient relationships. *Distance* records the log of distance between donor and recipient.[52] The log of (one plus) the dollar value of arms transfers from donor to recipient is included *(SIPRI Arms Transfers)*.[53] *UN Vote Distance* measures the absolute value of the difference between donor and recipient ideal point estimates for UN General Assembly votes.[54] *Donor Exports* and *Donor Imports* are from the International Monetary Fund's *Direction of Trade Statistics* and are converted to constant dollars and logged.[55] *Former Colony* equals one if the recipient was ever a colony of the donor and zero otherwise.[56] *Migration* is the log of migrant flows from the recipient to the donor.[57]

Analysis

As in all dyadic studies of aid allocation, the dependent variable has multiple zero values: 28% of the observations in the post-2001 period and 41% in the Cold War period are zeros. There is no consensus in the aid literature regarding the appropriate way to model these. I follow studies that specify a Tobit model with left-censoring at zero.[58] Results are reported separately for the Cold War and post-2001 periods. A separate set of models is estimated for the entire 1973–2012 timeframe in which all explanatory variables are interacted with period indicator variables. Results from the interaction models facilitate comparison of coefficients across the Cold War, 1990s, and post-2001 periods, but the interpretation of the impact of individual variables on aid allocation in any period other than the base period is not straightforward.[59] This periodization provides insight as to whether variables appear to be reverting from a pro-development pattern in the 1990s to a more geostrategic pattern, similar to the Cold War, in the post-2001 period.

Fixed effects for year and donor are included in all models.[60] Recipient fixed effects are not included. The hypotheses concern donor intent, and the interpretation of results on dyadic variables is inconsistent with the theory when recipient fixed effects are included. For instance, with recipient (rather than donor) fixed effects, a negative coefficient on distance would signal that recipients receive more aid from donors that are closer (the variation would hold recipient fixed but vary the distance to donors), but would not tell us whether donors give more aid to recipients that are closer to themselves. Analogous problems with interpretation apply to other dyadic measures once recipient fixed effects are included. The theoretical expectation is that variation across recipients is more important than variation within a recipient, particularly for variables that change slowly over time within a country. One of the main arguments for including fixed effects is to control for recipient-specific, time-invariant omitted variables that may be correlated with included variables of interest. A key test of the theory examines changes over time; to the extent that change over time is observed, it is unlikely to be driven by unmodeled, time-invariant factors.

Variables are lagged by one period unless there is a theoretical reason to suppose that aid commitments may respond within the same year to situations captured by those explanatory variables. For instance, when a natural disaster occurs, aid commitments increase in the same year. Similarly, if a state sees a spike in its military importance or becomes a member of the UN Security Council it is likely to receive increases in aid commitments while it holds geopolitical significance, rather than with a lag. Other variables such as income, which should be measured prior to aid commitments, are lagged. As a practical matter, choosing to lag any variable or not does not change any conclusions. Standard errors are clustered on dyad to address concerns of heteroskedasticity.

Table 4.2 reports results of the analysis of dyadic aid allocation separately for the periods 1973–1988 (Cold War) and 2002–2012 (post-2001). Models 1 and 2 use all available data for each period. Model 3 presents the analysis for the post-2001 period restricted to dyads present in both periods, to ensure that any observed differences are not due to changes over time in donors and recipients, or in countries/dyads with data availability. For each set of models, the p-values associated with post-estimation t-tests for a significant difference in coefficients across models are reported. While the results of Tobit models are reported, there are no substantive changes to the conclusions if the models are estimated using Ordinary Least Squares (OLS) rather than Tobit.

The results in Table 4.2 are consistent with a shifting donor focus toward pursuing a strategy of targeted development: coefficients have the signs predicted by the targeted development theory in the post-2001 period and the differences across time periods are striking. During the Cold War (Model 1) donors gave more aid, on average, to recipients that were poor (lower income), strategically important (higher US military assistance, higher arms transfers, and rotating members of the UN Security Council), and trade partners (higher exports and imports), but did not privilege larger or nearby states. In the post-2001 period

Table 4.2 **Determinants of Dyadic Aid Allocation**

	All Available Data			Same Dyads Only	
	1973–1988	2002–2012	Test for Difference Across Periods	2002–2012	Test for Difference Across Periods
	Model 1	Model 2		Model 3	
Distance	−0.357	−2.364***	p=0.000	−1.772***	p=0.000
	(0.36)	(0.00)		(0.00)	
Population (lagged)	−0.213	0.851***	p=0.000	0.870***	p=0.000
	(0.19)	(0.00)		(0.00)	
US Military Assistance	0.111***	0.035**	p=0.004	0.041**	p=0.012
	(0.00)	(0.03)		(0.05)	
SIPRI Arms Transfers	0.068***	−0.020	p=0.002	−0.025	p=0.002
	(0.01)	(0.24)		(0.24)	
UN Vote Distance	−0.951**	−0.174	p=0.052	−0.660***	p=0.481
	(0.01)	(0.30)		(0.01)	
Security Council Member	0.862***	0.236	p=0.065	−0.202	p=0.003
	(0.00)	(0.14)		(0.33)	
Former Colony	5.185***	4.491***	p=0.386	2.996***	p=0.004
	(0.00)	(0.00)		(0.00)	
Donor Exports (lagged)	0.438***	0.371***	p=0.364	0.244***	p=0.028
	(0.00)	(0.00)		(0.00)	
Donor Imports (lagged)	0.145***	0.223***	p=0.065	0.338***	p=0.000
	(0.00)	(0.00)		(0.00)	
Income (lagged)	−3.576***	−2.232***	p=0.000	−2.345***	p=0.000
	(0.00)	(0.00)		(0.00)	
Disaster	0.158***	0.105***	p=0.027	0.088***	p=0.006
	(0.00)	(0.00)		(0.00)	
Civil War (lagged)	0.364	0.201	p=0.678	−0.146	p=0.211
	(0.32)	(0.27)		(0.54)	
Democracy (lagged)	0.578***	0.333***	p=0.044	0.213**	p=0.006
	(0.00)	(0.00)		(0.02)	
Donor fixed effects	yes	yes		yes	
Year fixed effects	yes	yes		yes	

Continued

Table 4.2 **Continued**

	All Available Data			*Same Dyads Only*	
	1973–1988	2002–2012	*Test for Difference Across Periods*	2002–2012	*Test for Difference Across Periods*
	Model 1	*Model 2*		*Model 3*	
Constant	20.023***	18.491***		15.231***	
	(0.00)	(0.00)		(0.00)	
Sigma	8.589***	6.241***		5.987***	
Observations	20,275	32,533		16,014	
Censored	8,342	8,948		4,036	
Uncensored	11,933	23,585		11,978	
Dyads	1,614	3,533		1,614	
Recipients	111	156		111	
Donors	15	23		15	
Migration (lagged)		0.676***		0.730***	
		(0.00)		(0.00)	

Dependent variable is the log of (one plus) aid from donor to recipient in year *t*. Tobit models with standard errors clustered on dyad; p-values in parentheses. All variables except Civil War, Former Colony, Democracy, UN Vote Distance, and Security Council Member are measured in natural logs.
*p < 0.10; **p < 0.05; ***p < 0.01.

(Model 2) donors gave more aid to recipients that were poor, populous, and proximate to themselves. The coefficient on distance becomes negative and significant in the post-2001 period and the coefficient on population is positive and significant in the later period.

There is a significant decrease in the value of coefficients on *US Military Assistance, SIPRI Arms Transfers,* and *Security Council Member,* and the latter two variables are not significant in the post-2001 period.[61] Trade remains positively correlated with aid allocation, with donor imports gaining in importance relative to donor exports.[62] Since data on *Migration* are available for the post-2001 period only, Models 2 and 3 are also estimated separately including *Migration* and the resulting coefficient is reported at the bottom of the results in Table 4.2; as hypothesized, it is positive and significant.

Status as a former colony of the donor retains a significant relationship with aid flows in the post-2001 period, although its importance may have declined over time. The change over time for the coefficient on income is consistent with an interpretation that donors were more concerned with poverty in the Cold War. However, the results are also consistent with an alternative interpretation based on using aid to buy influence in the Cold War.[63] To determine whether the results are driven by any particular region, the models were re-estimated dropping each region in turn, and the main conclusions hold.

An alternative to the separate-period analyses is the interaction framework discussed above. The models in Table 4.3 cover the full period from 1973 to 2012. Two indicator variables are added: *Period 2* takes the value of one for observations in the years 1990–2001, while *Period 3* takes the value of one for observations in years 2002–2012. The omitted category is the Cold War (1973–1989). Every variable from Table 4.2 is entered into the models on its own and interacted with both *Period 2* and *Period 3*.[64] In addition to providing an alternative specification, the inclusion of all three periods facilitates analysis of any possible "reversion" of aid to its Cold War pattern in the post-2001 period.

In Table 4.3 the coefficient on each non-interacted substantive variable can be interpreted as its value during the Cold War (omitted period). The coefficients on the interaction terms measure differences from the omitted period. For example, the coefficient on *Population* represents the relationship between population and aid allocation during the Cold War. The positive, significant coefficient on the interaction term *Population*Period 2* shows that the coefficient in period 2 (1990–2001) has shifted significantly in a positive direction compared to its value in the Cold War, while the positive, significant coefficient on *Population*Period 3* is also interpreted relative to the Cold War. For any variable, the effect in *Period 2* or *Period 3* is the sum of the coefficient on the base term and the coefficient on the appropriate interaction term. Overall, the interaction terms between substantive variables and *Period 3* demonstrate the same shifts over time observed in Table 4.2.

The results in Table 4.3 show no evidence of reversion to a Cold War pattern for aid allocation. In many cases comparing the coefficient for a variable interacted with *Period 3* with the same variable interacted with *Period 2* suggests that aid may be moving even further from its Cold War pattern in the post-2001 period. For instance, for both *Distance* and *Population* interaction with *Period 3* produces coefficients of larger magnitude than interaction with *Period 2*, and the impact of *US Military Assistance* does not appear to have fallen for *Period 2* but does decrease significantly from its Cold War value in the post-2001 period.

Table 4.3 **Determinants of Dyadic Aid Allocation, Period Interactions**

	All Available	Same Dyads
	Model 4	Model 5
Period 2 (1990–2001)	−6.460	−8.786**
Period 3 (2002–2012)	0.852	−2.429
Distance	−0.265	−0.259
Distance*Period 2	−0.942***	−0.341
Distance*Period 3	−2.211***	−1.623***
Population (lagged)	−0.160	−0.161
Population*Period 2	0.720***	0.601***
Population*Period 3	1.047***	1.082***
US Military Assistance	0.106***	0.105***
US Military*Period 2	0.015	0.012
US Military*Period 3	−0.070***	−0.062**
SIPRI Arms Transfer	0.065***	0.066***
SIPRI*Period 2	−0.097***	−0.100***
SIPRI*Period 3	−0.089***	−0.094***
UN Vote Distance (lagged)	−0.833**	−0.842**
UN Vote*Period 2	1.832***	0.994***
UN Vote*Period 3	0.640*	0.127
Security Council Member	0.827***	0.836***
Security Council*Period 2	−0.959**	−1.055**
Security Council*Period 3	−0.578*	−1.049***
Former Colony	4.962***	4.955***
Colony*Period 2	−0.510	−2.234***
Colony*Period 3	−0.357	−1.896***
Donor Exports (lagged)	0.412***	0.412***
Exports*Period 2	−0.017	0.071
Exports*Period 3	−0.018	−0.157*
Donor Imports (lagged)	0.134***	0.133***
Imports*Period 2	0.070*	0.103**
Imports*Period 3	0.102**	0.230***
Income (lagged)	−3.330***	−3.333***

Continued

Table 4.3 **Continued**

	All Available	Same Dyads
	Model 4	Model 5
Income*Period 2	0.753***	0.442**
Income*Period 3	0.987***	0.853***
Disaster	0.138***	0.138***
Disaster*Period 2	−0.002	0.044*
Disaster*Period 3	−0.029	−0.047*
Civil War (lagged)	0.519	0.532
Civil War*Period 2	−0.331	−0.218
Civil War*Period 3	−0.332	−0.717*
Democracy (lagged)	0.539***	0.542***
Democracy*Period 2	−0.060	−0.136
Democracy*Period 3	−0.193*	−0.318**

Dependent variable is the log of (one plus) aid from donor to recipient in year t. Tobit models with standard errors clustered on dyad. All variables except Period 2, Period 3, Civil War, Former Colony, Democracy, UN Vote Distance, and Security Council Member are measured in natural logs. *p < 0.10; ** p < 0.05; ***p < 0.01.

Table 4.4 shows results from models analogous to Models 1 and 2 from Table 4.2 for each donor with data available for both periods. The results provide additional evidence consistent with movement toward targeted development and demonstrate that changes over time are observed widely across donors. Of the sixteen donors with data available in both periods,[65] the results for fifteen show a coefficient on *Population* that changes from insignificant or negative in the Cold War to significant and positive in the post-2001 period. For *Distance*, ten of sixteen donors change from an insignificant or positive coefficient in the Cold War to a significant, negative coefficient in the post-2001 period. The coefficient on *US Military Assistance* is positive and significant for twelve donors during the Cold War and only five donors in the post-2001 period. The importance of *SIPRI Arms Transfers* also declines as does the number of donors for which *Donor Exports* are important, while the number of donors with a positive, significant coefficient for *Donor Imports* increases from three to eight. For these donors, thirteen have sufficient data on migrant flows to include this in the analysis for the post-2001 period without drastically reducing the number of observations; of these, nine show a significant and positive association between migrant flows from the recipient to the donor and aid allocation from the donor to the recipient.[66]

Table 4.4 **Determinants of Aid Allocation by Donor**

	Australia		Austria		Canada	
	Cold War	2002–2012	Cold War	2002–2012	Cold War	2002–2012
Income (lag)	−5.337***	−1.661***	−1.676**	−1.863***	−3.670***	−2.026***
Population (lag)	−1.338**	0.735*	1.466**	1.278***	−0.157	0.712**
Disaster	0.073	−0.023	0.170**	0.019	0.092*	0.105**
Distance	−10.350***	−13.167***	−0.981	−1.407***	−0.784	−2.398***
US Military	−0.110	0.006	0.188**	−0.031	0.128**	0.124**
SIPRI Arms Transfers	−0.009	−0.220*	0.075	0.094**	0.065	−0.056
Exports (lag)	0.721***	0.280	0.245**	0.584***	−0.011	0.055
Imports (lag)	0.273**	0.194	0.072	0.218**	−0.011	0.200**
Civil War (lag)	−0.664	3.428***	−0.209	−0.386	0.117	0.270
Former Colony	−12.082***	−7.575***				
Democracy (lag)	1.853***	1.159***	0.446	0.028	0.748**	0.641***
UN Vote Distance	1.000	3.082***	0.232	−1.364**	−0.667	1.605**
Security Council Member	1.183	0.310	1.008	0.264	0.886	0.568
Migration (lag)		1.211***		0.605***		−0.063
	Denmark		Finland		France	
	Cold War	2002–2012	Cold War	2002–2012	Cold War	2002–2012
Income (lag)	−9.964***	−5.369***	−5.375***	−2.221***	−2.267***	−0.638***
Population (lag)	−0.163	2.132**	1.131	1.240***	−0.214	0.356*
Disaster	0.084	0.035	0.087	0.114*	0.058	0.024
Distance	5.247**	−3.704***	6.770***	−1.141*	1.445	−0.315
US Military	0.211	0.175	0.239*	0.084	0.021	0.027
SIPRI Arms Transfers	0.619	−0.280		0.022	0.114**	−0.027
Exports (lag)	2.101***	0.547	0.712***	0.270*	0.923***	0.695***
Imports (lag)	−0.308	0.512***	0.285	0.220***	−0.056	0.068

Continued

Table 4.4 **Continued**

	Denmark		Finland		France	
	Cold War	2002–2012	Cold War	2002–2012	Cold War	2002–2012
Civil War (lag)	0.941	−0.563	1.761	0.237	0.532	−0.511*
Former Colony					7.849***	1.782***
Democracy (lag)	1.098*	0.653	1.086**	−0.117	0.273	−0.054
UN Vote Distance	−0.151	0.381	4.756***	−0.285	−0.311	0.016
Security Council Member	1.254	−2.226	−0.294	0.158	0.900	0.107
Migration (lag)		1.400**		0.263		0.285***

	Germany		Italy		Japan	
	Cold War	2002–2012	Cold War	2002–2012	Cold War	2002–2012
Income (lag)	−1.511***	−0.785***	−1.837***	−2.426***	−1.046***	−0.592***
Population (lag)	0.103	1.238***	0.916	1.080**	0.248	0.439***
Disaster	−0.016	−0.015	0.041	0.261***	0.108***	0.042***
Distance	1.160	−0.987***	−0.843	−2.284***	−0.305	−1.601***
US Military	0.197***	0.048**	0.172***	0.100	0.133***	0.061***
SIPRI Arms Transfers	−0.002	−0.042*	0.045	−0.068	0.039	0.000
Exports (lag)	0.178	0.229	0.397	0.447	0.393**	−0.068
Imports (lag)	0.084	0.086	0.123	0.262	0.118*	0.099***
Civil War (lag)	−0.421	−0.791***	0.164	−0.705	−0.899	−0.209
Former Colony				2.018		−0.410
Democracy (lag)	0.193	0.074	−0.425	0.198	0.085	0.270***
UN Vote Distance			−2.077*	1.134*	−2.568***	0.355*
Security Council Member	0.809*	0.068	0.802	0.391	1.058**	0.262
Migration (lag)		0.078				0.519***

Continued

Table 4.4 **Continued**

	Netherlands		New Zealand		Norway	
	Cold War	2002–2012	Cold War	2002–2012	Cold War	2002–2012
Income (lag)	−2.532***	−2.530***	−4.159***	−2.399***	−5.951***	−2.775***
Population (lag)	−0.251	2.509***	−0.496	0.756*	0.544	1.812***
Disaster	0.036	0.139*	0.158	0.082	0.234**	−0.010
Distance	2.167***	−4.336***	−18.629***	−17.773***	6.774***	−0.498
US Military	0.135**	0.115	0.292**	0.086	0.232**	0.090
SIPRI Arms Transfers	0.018	−0.123	0.894***	−0.076	0.732***	0.056
Exports (lag)	0.550***	0.149	0.409**	0.277	0.767***	0.069
Imports (lag)	0.068	0.029	0.607***	0.191	−0.002	0.172*
Civil War (lag)	0.326	0.269	1.440	1.678	−0.432	−0.451
Former Colony	2.374	10.556*	−2.317	−5.132**		
Democracy (lag)	0.515***	0.648*	1.252**	1.360***	0.784*	−0.437
UN Vote Distance	−1.093	0.725	3.967**	4.787***	4.570***	−1.533*
Security Council Member	0.595	0.225	2.266	−0.080	1.276	0.278
Migration (lag)		1.714***		0.923***		0.988***

	Sweden		Switzerland	
	Cold War	2002–2012	Cold War	2002–2012
Income (lag)	−5.728***	−3.659***	−4.650***	−2.176***
Population (lag)	0.057	1.341***	0.379	2.397***
Disaster	0.472***	0.066	0.204**	0.064
Distance	3.988	−1.571**	−0.384	−3.169***
US Military	0.085	0.086	0.321***	0.036
SIPRI Arms Transfers	−0.023	−0.026	0.135	−0.148
Exports (lag)	0.718*	0.467*	0.138	−0.068
Imports (lag)	0.367	0.343***	0.011	0.079
Civil War (lag)	0.661	−0.162	1.832	−1.111
Former Colony				
Democracy (lag)	1.137	−0.103	−0.343	0.131
UN Vote Distance	7.982***	−2.493***		
Security Council Member	0.856	0.293	1.528	0.643
Migration (lag)		0.861***		

Continued

Table 4.4 **Continued**

	United Kingdom		United States	
	Cold War	2002–2012	Cold War	2002–2012
Income (lag)	−3.173***	−2.029***	−4.461***	−0.881***
Population (lag)	−0.858**	1.013***	−1.488**	1.278***
Disaster	0.047	0.040	0.121**	0.038
Distance	2.118*	−0.852	2.153*	−0.543
US Military	0.183***	0.129**	0.412***	0.141***
SIPRI Arms Transfers	0.063	−0.062	0.066	−0.001
Exports (lag)	0.989***	−0.148	0.560***	−0.212
Imports (lag)	0.043	0.559***	−0.143**	0.027
Civil War (lag)	−1.062	−0.180	1.294	−0.367
Former Colony	1.877*	3.462***	−1.409	2.457
Democracy (lag)	0.647***	0.038	0.200	−0.100
UN Vote Distance	−0.615	−1.165*	−2.697***	−1.278***
Security Council Member	0.241	0.580	0.408	−0.197
Migration (lag)				0.121

*p < 0.10; **p < 0.05; *** p < 0.01.

Both the pooled dyadic and the by-donor analyses show convincing evidence of a change in the determinants of aid allocation over time. During the Cold War the evidence suggests donors were pursuing non-development, geopolitical goals with their foreign aid. In the post-2001 period, the evidence is consistent with donors following a strategy of targeting aid toward countries where development may decrease the potential for negative spillovers that affect the donor. I now turn to a brief look at the relationship between governance in the recipient and cross-national allocation before analyzing patterns of aid composition across recipient states.

Recipient Governance and Cross-National Allocation

Scholars have attempted to ascertain donors' commitment to development by examining the link between recipient governance and the amount of aid received. The premise is that, since aid is more likely to promote growth in better-governed countries,[67] we will observe higher aid flows to well-governed states if donors are using aid to promote development. Most scholars analyzing the link between aid and quality of recipient governance find little evidence of donor selectivity with regard to governance. While a few studies argue that bilateral aid has become more selective with respect to governance over time,[68] most studies find no link between governance and bilateral aid flows,[69] or no change over time in the relationship.[70] Some even argue that poorly governed countries receive more aid,[71] or that bilateral donors have become less selective with regard to quality of governance over time.[72]

A problem with inferring donor intentions regarding development from the relationship (or lack thereof) between recipient governance and the amount of aid allocated to a country arises in that governance is simultaneously a signal of capacity and need. While well-governed countries may have higher capacity to turn aid into development, they may also have less need for aid. Well-governed countries can be thought of as more efficient, producing more development per aid dollar. On the other hand, poorly governed states are more likely to create negative spillovers. In terms of the effects on a donor's attempt to maximize utility, the price for a unit of development is lower in well-governed states, but so is the marginal utility of development for the donor (measured by the number of prevented spillovers). This suggests that the overall relationship between governance and the amount of aid received is ambiguous when donors use aid to maximize utility by pursuing targeted development abroad. As will be seen in the next section, the ambiguity disappears when hypothesizing links between quality of governance and the composition of aid received.

While the need and capacity simultaneously signaled by governance quality result in ambiguous predictions regarding the direct impact of governance on the amount of aid allocated, it is likely that a donor is particularly concerned with the increased need associated with poor governance if it occurs in states more likely to create spillovers for itself. This suggests an interaction between quality of governance and other determinants of targeted development assistance: when the likelihood of spillovers is high independent of recipient governance, a donor will respond to poorer governance with more aid. From Table 4.1, the most plausible variable to test this interaction is *Distance*. Other variables associated with targeted development can also be seen as a result of governance (e.g., better governance may lead to fewer migrants and more donor imports), whereas distance from the donor cannot be caused by recipient governance. The expectation is that poorer governance will result in more aid for recipients that are proximate to the donor.

A measure of governance is constructed from the Worldwide Governance Indicators (*WGI*) dataset for each recipient-year and reflects average value on five measures: political stability, government effectiveness, regulatory quality, rule of law, and control of corruption.[73] Rather than using raw scores on this average variable, a yearly rank is created with a value of 1 assigned to the country with the worst average governance for the year in this dataset, ranging up to a maximum of 162 for the country with the best governance average in the year with the highest country coverage. The rank is created because various scholars have questioned the usefulness of the raw scores in cross-national, time-series analyses.[74] However, criteria similar to rank are explicitly used by aid agencies, such as the Millennium Challenge Corporation (MCC), for making aid decisions based on measures from the WGI.[75] This variable is then logged and used for the analysis. In practice, no conclusions change if the raw average score or non-logged rank is used instead. The WGI measure is used because it offers broader country coverage than other governance indicators, with each recipient receiving a score for at least part of the time period. If a measure drawn from the International Country Risk Guide (described in the next section) is used in place of the WGI measure, the results are similar, but the country coverage decreases by about one-third.

To examine the relationship between governance and cross-national aid allocation in the post-2001 period, the measure of governance rank (*WGI*) is added to Model 2 from Table 4.2. This measure was not included in the analysis for that table due to lack of data on governance for the earlier period, but including it does not detract from the findings on other variables for the post-2001 period.[76] The coefficient on this variable is insignificant (−0.127; p=0.32). It appears that there is no direct effect of recipient governance on the amount of aid received. Alternatively, adding the *WGI* governance variable and its interaction with *Distance* to Model 2 from Table 4.2 results in negative, significant coefficients on *WGI* and *Distance* and a positive, significant coefficient on the interaction. Figure 4.3 depicts the relationship between distance and

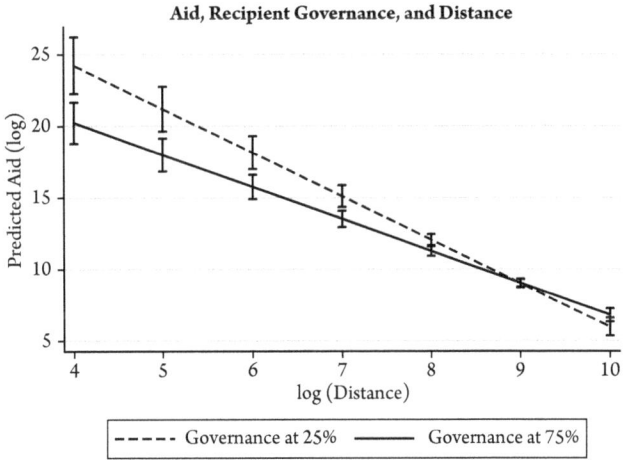

Figure 4.3 Predicted Aid, Recipient Governance, and Distance in the Post-2001 Period. Vertical bars represent 95% confidence intervals.

aid for a relatively poorly governed country (*WGI* set to its value at the 25th percentile) and a relatively well-governed country (*WGI* set to its value at the 75th percentile), with other variables held at their mean values. In both cases, aid decreases with distance. However, for recipients in the neighborhood of the donor, the poorly governed state receives significantly more aid than the better-governed state. This difference declines as distance increases.[77] It appears that donors are particularly concerned with providing aid to poorly governed recipients when they are also nearby and therefore more likely to generate spillovers that reach the donor.

The Composition of Foreign Aid

While governance does not play a direct role in determining the amount of aid received, under a targeted development framework it should play a role in determining the composition of aid. Donors may at times have an interest in promoting development in poorly governed countries, but they will need to craft a different basket of aid and pursue different within-country objectives than in a well-governed recipient if aid is to be effective. Incorporating the heterogeneity of aid offers a step forward in disentangling donor responses to both the need and capacity signaled by recipient governance quality. In recent work scholars have shown that donors alter the composition of aid[78] or the delivery mechanism[79] in response to quality of governance in the recipient. This section tests whether donors respond to variations in recipient governance by altering the composition of aid in the post-2001 era. Proponents of the view that aid is reverting to a Cold War paradigm would expect little impact of governance on composition in this period.

Variations in governance quality represent different ability and/or willingness of the recipient government to use aid for development. Donors pursuing development—targeted or otherwise—should account for this when determining the type of aid to allocate to a country. Concerns for effectiveness should lead them to favor sectors with relatively high government involvement in well-governed recipients, and focus on sectors with more limited government involvement in poorly governed recipients. Altering the composition of aid away from sectors with high public sector involvement allows donors to continue engaging poorly governed recipients while attenuating the negative effects of poor governance on aid outcomes.

The analysis of aid composition for the post-2001 period uses data from the OECD's online Credit Reporting System (CRS) database. Data are more sparsely available for earlier periods. The analysis uses the breakdown of aid by sector, and results are reported here for General Budget Support, Economic

Infrastructure, Production Sectors, Social Sectors, and Humanitarian Assistance. "General Budget Support" consists of "unearmarked contributions to the government budget" and "support for the implementation of macroeconomic reforms (structural adjustment programmes, poverty reduction strategies)." "Economic Infrastructure" aid is mainly used in transportation, communications, energy, banking and finance, and business services. "Production sectors" include agriculture, forestry, fishing, industry, mining, construction, trade, and tourism. The "Social Infrastructure and Services" (Social Sector) classification includes funds for education, health, population, water, and government and civil society. "Humanitarian Relief" is meant to include help rendered for a situation that is the result of a manmade or natural disaster.[80]

Involvement of the recipient government varies based on the sector to which aid is given. The OECD includes another categorization, channel of aid delivery, which captures whether aid is delivered through the public sector, nongovernmental organizations, or multilateral organizations. Unfortunately, data for this classification are limited over time, making it problematic for general analysis. Nevertheless, variations in channel of delivery in the available data support the idea that government involvement differs by sector. Using data for 2012, of the aid categorized by channel, the percent channeled through the public sector is 96% for General Budget Support, 88% for Economic Infrastructure, 58% for Production Sectors, 58% for Social Sectors, and 10% for Humanitarian Assistance. In each case the vast majority of remaining aid is channeled through nongovernmental organizations or multilateral organizations.[81]

The unit of analysis in this section is the recipient-year. A dyadic approach to sector-level analysis could be misleading, as donor specialization across sectors is encouraged under guidelines for aid effectiveness. Here I examine whether the composition of aid summed for all bilateral OECD donors varies across recipients based on quality of governance. For the post-2001 period, the main measure of governance is the *WGI* measure, described above. Every potential recipient has a value for this variable in at least some years. A drawback is that coverage begins in 1996. To allow for comparison with the Cold War, as an alternate measure I use an average of a recipient's score on two components of the International Country Risk Guide (*ICRG*) ratings, Control of Corruption and Rule of Law, rescaled to lie on the interval $[0,1]$ with higher levels representing better governance. While this measure is available since 1984, its country coverage is smaller: for the 126 recipients with a measure of governance from the WGI in 2012, only 78 (62%) have a value reported for the *ICRG* measure.

Equations for all sectors are specified in a multi-equation system using a seemingly unrelated Tobit framework with left-censoring at zero and standard errors clustered on recipient. In one set of models the dependent variables are the percent of total OECD aid committed to a recipient in year t that is allocated to a given sector (logged).[82] Another set of models uses the log of (one plus) aid commitments to each sector from OECD donors as dependent variables.

Table 4.5 reports coefficients on governance variables (*WGI* or *ICRG*) across sectors. Full regression results are not reported to conserve space; each model includes controls for *Democracy, Income, Population, Disaster,* and *Civil War.* Panel A of Table 4.5 reports the coefficients on the *WGI* measure when the dependent variable is the percent of total OECD aid allocated to the indicated sector, and provides strong support for the hypothesis that donors vary the composition of aid to reflect the quality of governance in recipients. Based on models including year fixed effects, the first row of coefficients shows that, in a given year, countries that rank higher on the *WGI* measure receive a larger percentage of their aid allocated to Budget Support, Economic Infrastructure, and Production Sectors, while the percent of aid allocated for Humanitarian Relief declines as governance improves. In the second row, results from models including recipient fixed effects show that within a recipient the percent of aid allocated by sector responds similarly to changes in governance rank. Panel B of Table 4.5 shows the coefficients on *WGI* when the dependent variable is the log of the amount of aid allocated to the sector indicated, and similar patterns are observed.

The final portion of Table 4.5, Panel C, shows results from models using the *ICRG* measure. For the post-2001 period, variation across sectors in the relationship between governance and aid is again observed. The last row in Table 4.5 reports coefficients on the *ICRG* variable for the period 1984 (first year the measure is available) to 1988. The results from this period should be interpreted with care and are, at most, suggestive. Donors were less likely to report aid by sector in this earlier period; for 1988, 73% of aid is classified by sector, compared with 98% for 2012.[83] Nevertheless, it is interesting that no pattern for governance emerges across sectors in the earlier period.

Industrialized states do not necessarily alter the amount of aid given to a recipient based on quality of governance, but they do adjust aid composition. Poorly governed states receive a different basket of aid than well-governed states, and their aid is skewed toward sectors with a more limited role for government. This is consistent with donors responding to the nuances of recipient countries in an attempt to improve the development outcomes associated with aid expenditures. Evidence suggests that this variation based on quality of governance may be a relatively new development. If so, this is consistent with a growing desire to advance development in chosen recipients.

Table 4.5 Governance and Aid by Sector

Panel A: Percent of Total Aid by Sector (WGI)

Measure	Time Period	Fixed Effects	Budget Support	Economic Infrastructure	Production Sectors	Social Sectors	Humanitarian Relief
WGI	2002–2012	Year	0.796***	0.480***	0.263***	0.012	−0.428***
			(0.00)	(0.00)	(0.00)	(0.80)	(0.00)
WGI	2002–2012	Recipient	0.665***	0.366***	0.319***	0.021	−0.567***
			(0.01)	(0.00)	(0.00)	(0.72)	(0.00)

Panel B: Amount of Aid by Sector (WGI)

Measure	Time Period	Fixed Effects	Budget Support	Economic Infrastructure	Production Sectors	Social Sectors	Humanitarian Relief
WGI	2002–2012	Year	4.361***	0.897***	0.355	−0.017	−0.641*
			(0.00)	(0.00)	(0.14)	(0.91)	(0.08)
WGI	2002–2012	Recipient	6.025***	1.042***	0.767***	0.122*	−1.102***
			(0.00)	(0.00)	(0.00)	(0.08)	(0.01)

Panel C: Percent of Total Aid by Sector (ICRG)

Measure	Time Period	Fixed Effects	Budget Support	Economic Infrastructure	Production Sectors	Social Sectors	Humanitarian Relief
ICRG	2002–2012	Year	4.094***	2.191***	−0.199	−0.035	−1.304**
			(0.00)	(0.00)	(0.67)	(0.89)	(0.04)
ICRG	1984–1988	Year	1.197	−0.005	−0.209	−0.192	−0.575
			(0.44)	(0.99)	(0.72)	(0.78)	(0.33)

Estimated using a seemingly unrelated Tobit framework with errors clustered on recipient; p-values in parentheses. Controls: Democracy, Income, Population, Disaster, Civil War. * p < 0.10; ** p < 0.05; *** p < 0.01.

A Note on Aid Effectiveness

While this chapter focuses on understanding donor intent, changes in intent over time can have important implications for studying aid effectiveness. Shifts in motivation in favor of development suggest that past performance on development outcomes is not necessarily a good predictor of future results. Aid critics decry the ineffectiveness—even harmfulness—of foreign aid. William Easterly, for instance, writes of "the tragedy in which the West spent $2.3 trillion on foreign aid over the last five decades and still had not managed to get twelve-cent medicines to children to prevent half of all malaria deaths. The West spent $2.3 trillion and still had not managed to get four-dollar bed nets to poor families."[84] If aid was motivated for those five decades by a desire to provide medicine and bed nets, then its failure to do so is cause for extreme pessimism regarding the likelihood of aid effectiveness in the future. However, if aid was motivated by different reasons in the past, and motivation shifts in favor of the medicines and bed nets, then the picture looks less bleak. Of course aid still may prove ineffective. Donors may not be competent at spurring development and aid agencies developed during the Cold War may have difficulty adapting to new priorities. Yet with changes in intent we cannot infer effectiveness from past results and must examine outcomes separately by period to better measure the impacts of aid.

Discussion

The targeted development framework posits that industrialized countries will pursue development abroad in order to decrease the impact on themselves from spillovers associated with underdevelopment. The attention to development will vary across developing countries and over time to reflect differences in the anticipated effects due to underdevelopment. Results from the examination of aid allocation patterns strongly support the conclusion that current patterns align with expectations from the targeted development framework. Donors focus aid on countries that are poor, large, and proximate, and that have existing ties to the donor through trade, migration, or colonial history. There have been changes in the determinants of aid allocation over time, with geopolitical factors playing a significantly stronger role in determining aid flows historically and targeted development considerations gaining explanatory power in recent years. Variations in aid composition suggest that donors consider recipient government capacity for development when determining the types of aid, which also appears to be a break from previous patterns.

While the patterns uncovered in this chapter are consistent with a targeted development approach, this book argues that targeted development has become a major foreign policy objective for industrialized states. If true, this would affect policy across multiple issue areas, not only in the obvious development realm of foreign aid. This is particularly true where foreign aid can be expected to have a relatively small impact, such as in middle-income countries where aid represents only a small percent of national income. In these cases, a commitment to further development will require increased trade and investment to help countries capitalize on the development they have already achieved. There is still a role for foreign aid, but to have an impact it must be coupled with other policies for increased economic engagement. The next chapter turns to the issue of preferential trade agreements, to see if this pattern observed in foreign aid can be seen in the politically sensitive area of trade as well.

Chapter 4 Appendix

Table A4.1 **Official Development Assistance by OECD Donor, 2013**

Donor	Aid ($ millions)	Donor	Aid % of Gross National Income
United States	31,545	Norway	1.07
United Kingdom	17,881	Sweden	1.02
Germany	14,059	Luxembourg	1.00
Japan	11,786	Denmark	0.85
France	11,376	United Kingdom	0.72
Sweden	5,831	Netherlands	0.67
Norway	5,581	Finland	0.55
Netherlands	5,435	Switzerland	0.47
Canada	4,911	Belgium	0.45
Australia	4,851	Ireland	0.45
Italy	3,253	France	0.41
Switzerland	3,198	Germany	0.38
Denmark	2,928	Australia	0.34
Belgium	2,281	Austria	0.28
Spain	2,199	Canada	0.27
Korea*	1,744	New Zealand	0.26
Finland	1,435	Iceland*	0.26
Austria	1,172	Japan	0.23
Ireland	822	Portugal	0.23
Portugal	484	United States	0.19
Poland*	474	Spain	0.16
New Zealand	461	Italy	0.16
Luxembourg	431	Korea*	0.13
Greece	305	Slovenia*	0.13
Czech Republic*	212	Greece	0.13
Slovak Republic*	85	Czech Republic*	0.11
Slovenia*	60	Poland*	0.10
Iceland*	35	Slovak Republic*	0.09

*Country joined DAC since 2013 and is not included in the main analysis in Chapter 4.

5

Preferential Trade Agreements as Development Policy

> While CAFTA is the right thing to do for democracy, it is also the smart thing to do for U.S. security. We do not live in isolation from what happens in Central America. Criminal gangs, trafficking in drugs, even trafficking in persons, create dangerous transnational networks. When there is instability and poverty in our neighborhood, it is common sense to help our neighbors address those problems at home rather than import them into our own country.
> —Robert Zoellick, Deputy Secretary of State, May 24, 2005[1]

At 12:03 a.m. on July 28, 2005, the US House of Representatives passed the Dominican Republic-Central America-United States preferential trade agreement Implementation Act, paving the way for President George W. Bush to sign into law the trade agreement commonly known as CAFTA-DR. The vote on the bill was 217 in favor and 215 opposed. Heading into voting, supporters did not know if they had the votes they needed. George W. Bush, Vice President Dick Cheney, and numerous high-ranking members of their administration visited Capitol Hill in the days leading up to the vote in an attempt to gain enough support for passage.[2] Even with this full-court press, House leadership had to keep voting open well beyond usual time limits to secure the last needed votes. They traded promises of transportation projects and passage of a bill authorizing new tariffs on Chinese goods for votes in favor of CAFTA-DR.[3] This was a fairly extraordinary effort to secure passage of a trade agreement with a group of countries that, collectively, had an economy in the years leading up to the vote slightly smaller than that of Pittsburgh, Pennsylvania.[4]

The signing of CAFTA-DR is part of a broader trend in trade agreements between industrialized and developing countries. Virtually nonexistent before 1990, trade agreements between a wealthy state and one or more developing states now play a key role in defining relationships between these groups. Figure 5.1 shows the growth in the number of dyads consisting of a high-income

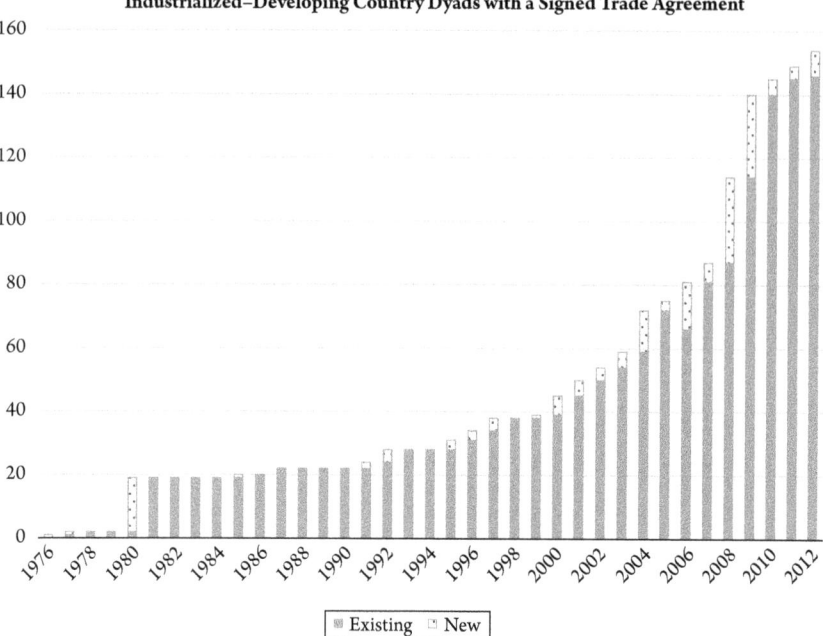

Figure 5.1 Count of Industrialized–Developing Dyads in a PTA. European Union members combined. Number of existing dyads fluctuates with EU enlargement and developing country graduation to "high income" status, creating some dips (such as 2006). Coding of agreements is based on the Regional Trade Agreements database from the World Trade Organization.

OECD country and a developing country covered by a preferential trade agreement (PTA); the top segment shows new pairs entering into an agreement that year, while the full bar shows the cumulative effect. In 1990, twenty-two industrialized–developing country dyads, constituting just over 1% of the total number of dyads from that year that will be examined in this chapter, were covered by a PTA.[5] By 2012, 154 dyads, 11% of the total for that year, had a PTA in effect.

This growth in agreements has occurred while multilateral efforts to forge agreement between developed and developing countries through the World Trade Organization have been marked by a significant lack of success, most notably the apparent failure of the Doha Round after fourteen years of negotiations in December 2015. Sharp disagreements between industrialized and developing countries were instrumental in the lack of progress and eventual collapse of the trade round. The contrast between the success of these countries in negotiating PTAs and the failure of the WTO round focusing on development is stark.

This chapter employs the targeted development framework to advance and test explanations for the growth in PTAs between industrialized and developing countries. The actions of industrialized states in these situations cannot be understood by reference to standard trade theory alone. Instead, incorporating concerns for development and potential spillovers helps explain the pattern of trade agreements that has emerged. After laying out the theory, the chapter examines it through a case study of CAFTA-DR followed by a dyadic time-series analysis.

Targeted Development and PTAs

Industrialized states pursuing a strategy of targeted development will seek to increase their own utility through development promotion abroad by employing multiple policy tools, including trade agreements. As a long-run vehicle for sustainable growth, trade offers significant potential for developing countries, arguably much more so than foreign aid. If industrialized country governments are seeking to promote development abroad in a targeted manner, they will naturally look to trade as a vehicle for achieving this goal. Yet not all countries are well positioned to harness the potential of a trade agreement; some lack the infrastructure and policies to capitalize on preferential market access to spur domestic growth.

Industrialized states seeking to promote targeted development will use foreign aid and trade agreements as complements. Seeking to prevent the negative effects of spillovers on themselves, on average industrialized countries will provide more foreign aid to, and be more willing to pursue trade agreements with, those countries where spillovers are expected to have the largest impact on themselves. The theory therefore predicts that developing countries that receive more aid from a specific industrialized state are, on average, also more likely to be offered a PTA with that state.

The distribution of trade agreements, however, will not depend only on where development is most important to a wealthy state. It will also reflect the perceived usefulness of a trade agreement for achieving development outcomes. Offering a trade agreement to a country that is not capable of using it to increase growth will not further a targeted development agenda. Additionally, given the limited capacity of industrialized countries to expend the resources and political capital negotiating and approving agreements, they are likely to be reserved for developing countries where aid itself is less likely to have a sizeable development impact.

Operating under these constraints, industrialized states will view countries near the middle of developing country incomes as good candidates for trade agreements. They are relatively wealthier than the poorest states, meaning that a given amount of foreign aid is likely to be a much smaller percentage of national income and therefore have limited ability, on its own, to push development to the next level. These countries are also more likely than their lower-income counterparts to have reached a point in their development progress where they are well positioned to capitalize on preferential market access to promote growth. Existing infrastructure, government capacity regarding trade, and existing trade patterns will position these countries to benefit from such agreements more than the poorest states.

The theory predicts that the wealthiest of developing states are less likely to be targeted for a trade agreement based on development concerns. This category of countries is less likely to create negative spillovers and more likely to be able to achieve development benefits associated with trade without outside assistance. That is not to say industrialized states do not pursue agreements with these countries. Rather, when they pursue such agreements it is more likely to be consistent with standard motivations based on mutual gains from trade and less likely to have development considerations as the primary motivating factor.

When a developing state signs a trade agreement with an industrialized state, the wealthier country will align its foreign aid priorities to assist the developing country in gaining benefits from increased trade. Thus a trade agreement will not be seen as a substitute for aid, as well-specified aid programs can increase the impact of trade agreements by building infrastructure to facilitate trade, offering technical assistance related to trade, and pursuing other forms of trade capacity building. Industrialized countries target states for development and then craft a strategy that reflects the various needs and capabilities of targeted states. Where states are not well positioned to benefit from a trade agreement, such as in low-income countries, foreign aid will be the primary tool. When a trade agreement is seen as a viable vehicle for growth, industrialized states will pursue this option and use foreign aid to increase the impact of the agreement.

It is useful to summarize the testable implications of using trade agreements to pursue targeted development. The following will be examined in this chapter, through the in-depth study of CAFTA-DR and dyadic time-series analysis:

- Receiving a larger portion of an industrialized country's foreign aid will be associated with an increased likelihood of also signing a trade agreement with that industrialized state, reflecting the multi-policy approach used to pursue a targeted development agenda.
- Developing countries in the "middle of the pack" with regard to income are more likely to sign a trade agreement with an industrialized state compared to both poorer and wealthier developing countries.

- When an industrialized country signs a trade agreement with a developing state, it will use its foreign aid to increase the development benefits of signing the agreement.

Understanding the development aspects helps explain the motivations of an industrialized state in pursuing agreements with small-market, developing countries. Trade agreements are a potentially powerful development tool, but they are also a politically challenging tool to use for promoting development abroad. In an industrialized country there will be domestic constituencies, in particular import-competing groups, that are opposed to trade liberalization. Given the small market size of many developing countries, the potential economic gains to an industrialized state of increased trade with these countries is small. This leads to a situation in which powerful groups can oppose a deal and there is no strong constituency in the industrialized state lobbying in favor of the deal. It is only when development concerns—or other concerns not directly related to domestic trade lobbies—loom large that the government of an industrialized state will seek to overcome organized interests supporting trade protection in order to pursue a trade agreement with a small, developing country market promising few direct economic returns via trade. The flip side of this argument is that it is difficult to explain the political capital expended by governments in industrialized countries to ensure domestic passage of these agreements based solely on a traditional "gains from trade" logic.

Existing Theories of Trade Agreements

There is a well-developed literature examining the formation of PTAs generally, and a growing literature specifically addressing the recent emergence of multiple agreements between industrialized and developing states. The argument advanced here builds on two strands from the general literature. The first advances domestic political economy explanations for the emergence of PTAs.[6] The insights coming from this branch of literature are well suited for explaining the decision of developing country governments to pursue agreements with large, wealthy markets. It is, however, difficult to rely solely on standard domestic political economy explanations to understand the actions of an industrialized country government pursuing a trade deal with much smaller, poorer markets. A more complete picture is drawn by also incorporating the possibility that these agreements create positive externalities for the industrialized country outside the standard trade calculus. While the externality discussed here is development, it is similar to arguments advanced by scholars regarding security externalities and the signing of trade agreements.[7]

Before drawing insights from existing theories, it is worthwhile to note that negotiating a PTA between an industrialized and developing country pair differs from negotiations that occur between countries at more similar levels of development. An obvious difference is the power asymmetry during negotiations, which has led some scholars to argue that industrialized states gain an advantage in bilateral negotiations while developing states may benefit from a multilateral framework.[8] Another important difference is that when an industrialized–developing country pair considers forming a PTA, they are often not contemplating the difference between forming the agreement and having no agreement, but the difference between an already existing nonreciprocal agreement and a proposed reciprocal agreement.[9] The Generalized System of Preferences (GSP), allowed under the "Enabling Clause" of the GATT, permits industrialized states to offer better than most favored nation (MFN) treatment to developing states in a non-reciprocal manner. Thus goods from developing states covered under a GSP agreement face lower barriers to entry into an industrialized state than do goods from countries not covered under a GSP agreement with that industrialized state. Given the unilateral and discretionary nature of these agreements, including the ability of the industrialized state to alter them at will, many scholars question their effectiveness at increasing developing country trade, a point to which I return below.

Domestic Political Economy

With this backdrop, it is useful to determine which aspects of trade agreements between industrialized and developing countries are well explained by theories of trade agreement formation more broadly. Focusing on the domestic politics of trade agreements and drawing attention to the role played by both free-trade–oriented and protectionist interest groups, Gene Grossman and Elhanan Helpman note that "governments ... respond to political pressures from industry special interests but also pay some heed to the plight of the average voter."[10] The idea that governments seek to balance demands (and contributions) from special interests with social welfare (and votes) is a common theme in domestic political economy models of trade agreements. When deciding whether to pursue an agreement, the government considers gains to special interest groups (export-oriented sectors, importers of intermediate goods), losses to special interest groups (particularly import-competing sectors), general welfare gains (if trade creating) or losses (if trade diverting), and transaction costs of negotiating, designing, and securing domestic passage of an agreement. As Edward Mansfield and Helen Milner note, in order for an agreement to be pursued "the governments involved must decide that the benefits from concluding the agreement will exceed the associated costs."[11] In the current context, this must hold for both the developing and industrialized states involved in order for an agreement to be formed.

Developing Countries

On the surface, developing states appear to gain little, if anything, in moving from a non-reciprocal to a reciprocal trade agreement. Under GSP arrangements, developing countries gain some preferential access to markets in industrialized countries without any concessions on their part. However, the unilateral nature of the preferences limits their usefulness: many sensitive sectors in the industrialized state are excluded from GSP preferences, and the preferences that are given unilaterally under GSP may also be withdrawn unilaterally.[12] If GSP has the intended effect of increasing exports, a developing country may lose eligibility for products that become too successful, as the preference will no longer be deemed necessary; to avoid this the developing state may hold back on exports to the industrialized country, thus not fully realizing gains that would accrue with more stable market access. Similarly, many GSP arrangements are income-based; if investing in trade increases a country's income it may "graduate" from eligibility. An example of this is the Everything But Arms (EBA) arrangement under which the European Union grants duty-free and quota-free access to all exports, with the exception of weapons, from least developed countries. Once a country is no longer considered "least developed" it becomes ineligible for EBA after a three-year transition period. The uncertain future of the preferences makes it difficult for them to help attract investment; if investments succeed in increasing trade under the preference arrangement, the preferences may be ended and the profitability of the investment threatened—a fact known to potential investors. Mark Manger and Kenneth Shadlen argue that the propensity of a developing country to pursue a reciprocal agreement with an industrialized state is determined by its dependence on unilateral, removable preferences, with higher levels of what they term "political trade dependence" increasing the likelihood of signing a reciprocal trade agreement.[13]

Successfully concluding a reciprocal agreement with an industrialized state will reduce uncertainty and should lead to increased investment. Tim Büthe and Helen Milner argue that reciprocal trade agreements also reassure investors regarding political risk from the developing country government associated with their investment. The trade agreement may contain clauses prohibiting expropriation, establishing dispute settlement mechanisms, or incorporating language governing the treatment of foreign investment; including these in an international agreement serves as a commitment device for the developing country government that can reassure foreign investors.[14]

From a domestic political economy standpoint, exporters in the developing state should favor a PTA with an industrialized state, which provides a large and wealthy market for their goods. Although unilateral schemes already granting access for exports may be argued to dampen the motivation of exporters to pursue a reciprocal agreement,[15] the possibility of reducing uncertainty and attracting investment through a reciprocal agreement makes it highly likely that exporters will be organized and motivated to lobby in favor of its negotiation and passage.[16] Moving from a unilateral to a reciprocal agreement will harm firms in the developing country that will now face stronger competition from imports, giving them an incentive to lobby against the agreement. Outside of the interest groups, the general public (voters) are likely to benefit from lower-priced imports and the boost to the economy from expanding exports. It is not difficult to envision scenarios in which the government finds it worthwhile to side with export lobbies and general welfare over the protest of import-competing groups, and therefore seek to negotiate and implement a PTA with an industrialized state.

Industrialized Countries

For the wealthier countries in industrialized–developing country dyads the situation is different and depends on the size of the developing country market and its relative wealth. Obviously, industrialized states do not need to sign an agreement with a developing country to attract investment or signal credibility. When considering an agreement with a large-market developing country or a relatively well-off developing country, exporters and importers of intermediate goods in the industrialized state may be motivated by potentially sizeable gains to organize and lobby the government for passage of the agreement. Mark Manger argues that multinational firms in an industrialized state lobby their government to establish trade agreements with developing countries to facilitate vertical fragmentation of production by lowering barriers to intra-industry trade.[17] According to Manger, the observed pattern of industrialized–developing country agreements is the result of "a contest between major economic powers to gain access to emerging markets and important production locations, to impede such access for competitors, and to restore it when others have moved first."[18]

It is unclear how or whether this logic extends to smaller developing countries in addition to "emerging markets and important production locations." Manger conducts case studies of trade agreements with Mexico, Thailand, Malaysia, and Chile; while possibly representative of emerging markets, results from this group cannot be assumed to explain signing agreements with smaller developing countries. To put this in perspective, the analysis in this chapter contains 128 developing countries in 2012; the 4 developing states examined by Manger rank in the top 13 in this group in terms of overall economic size measured by

GDP (and Chile has since graduated to "high income" status, so is no longer a "developing" country).

PTAs between industrialized and developing states are not confined to large markets such as these. Developing countries as large as or larger than Chile when it signed the trade agreement with Japan examined by Manger (the smallest economy of the cases he includes) had signed PTAs with industrialized countries covering 30 dyads by 2012; for smaller developing economies, such agreements covered 164 dyads.[19] While multinational corporations may indeed have incentives to lobby for preferential access to Mexico, Thailand, or Chile, are there really no substitutes for Cambodia, Cameroon, Nicaragua, or Peru? This is not to argue that the incentives of multinational firms do not drive trade agreements with large developing states; rather, the point is that what applies for large markets may not have the same explanatory power for the signing of agreements with small developing states.

When the potential partner is both developing and small, the domestic political economy justifications for signing an agreement fall short. The amount of trade—intra-industry or otherwise—is low. Exporters from the industrialized state likely do not gain much through better market access to a small, developing market. On the other hand, these small markets will have a comparative advantage at producing some goods and trade will lead to specialization in these areas, increasing production in the developing country and exports to the industrialized state. The industrialized country market is large, so domestic producers of import-competing goods stand to lose significantly by trade openness—arguably much more than exporters will gain by preferential access to much smaller markets. If lobbying is proportional to potential benefits, import-competing firms should lobby more extensively than export-oriented firms. Added to this is the possibility that firms facing potential losses will be more motivated than those facing potential gains,[20] further tipping the balance toward import-competing firms that risk losses from developing country competition.

In addition to having stronger motivation, import-competing firms in the industrialized state are also better organized. The existence of unilateral preferences prior to a reciprocal agreement creates a situation in which many gains from protection for domestic firms in the industrialized state can only be realized in the future and domestic firms are organized to protect these potential future gains. When a unilateral arrangement is in place the developing country already receives preferential access to the industrialized country market. However, preferences for individual products can end if imports become a threat to domestic industry, and industrialized partners such as the United States and the European Union have mechanisms by which domestic groups can advocate for their removal. This potential to ask for an end to preferences has created an incentive for import-competing industries in the preference-granting state to closely monitor trade in these areas and remain prepared to lobby the government for protection when circumstances make this a viable option.[21]

That industries monitor the unilateral agreement so closely suggests that a high expected value is attached to these (future) benefits and that they will fight hard to keep them. As Çağlar Özden and Eric Reinhardt argue, "the ease of altering unilateral (as opposed to GATT-bound reciprocal) commitments skews protectionist pressures within the donor state towards the GSP instrument."[22] Furthermore, the fact that import-competing firms are already organized will lower the cost of collective action and make them more likely to engage in lobbying efforts,[23] including attempts to thwart the move to a reciprocal agreement. It also means the government can expect future contributions from protectionist special interests as long as the possibility of lifting preferences remains; enshrining these preferences in a reciprocal agreement will result in the government forgoing these future benefits from the interest groups.

A standard domestic political economy framework cannot fully explain the motivations of an industrialized country government in pursuing an agreement with a much smaller, poorer state. The small market size limits potential gains to exporters and consumers, while import-competing firms are motivated and organized to oppose such agreements. The government will only risk the wrath of, and forgo the potential contributions from, protectionist groups if there is an additional benefit to doing so.

Development Externalities from Trade

Decreasing negative spillovers by promoting development in partner states increases the payoff to an industrialized state of signing agreements with small, relatively poor developing countries. This is similar to the argument advanced by Joanne Gowa[24] and Gowa and Edward Mansfield[25] regarding trade agreements and security externalities. They argue that signing a trade agreement can increase the well-being of the trade partner, allowing additional resources to be spent on military purposes; this creates a positive security externality when signing an agreement with an ally and a negative externality when signing with a potential enemy. Here, I argue that when signing with a developing country, the agreement can create positive development externalities if the industrialized state is likely to feel negative effects from spillovers that will be decreased by development brought about through increased trade.

By locking in preferences through a reciprocal agreement, the government of an industrialized state is tying its hands with regard to future protection and thus forgoing potential gains from special interests that would lobby for removal of preferences in the future if the unilateral agreement remained in force. Given the domestic political economy situation, an industrialized country government will only seek to move from a unilateral to a reciprocal agreement with a small developing country when the gains brought about by externalities are enough to compensate for the loss of support from domestic interest groups. In the absence of an agreement, the government in the industrialized state faces a problem of time inconsistency since it cannot credibly commit to deny protectionist demands in the future.[26] Yet this very knowledge is what prevents the unilateral agreements from having a positive impact on exports and development in the developing country, since investors want to be assured that preferences will not vanish as production in the developing country increases. When sufficient development externalities are anticipated, the government of the industrialized state is willing to give up policy flexibility in the future in order to gain the benefit of increased development in the developing state.

Incorporating development externalities into an explanation of trade agreements between industrialized and developing states should be seen as a complement to, rather than a substitute for, existing explanations. In some cases, particularly for large developing states, a standard—or slightly augmented—political economy model may explain passage of the agreement. In other cases, such as the US agreement with Israel in 1985, geopolitics may play the decisive role. Similarly, development concerns can play a secondary role in garnering support for agreements that can be justified on economic grounds even without considering externalities; Manger acknowledges concerns for stability and immigration as reasons behind the North American Free Trade Agreement (NAFTA), in addition to the main rationale he raises regarding investment and vertical trade.[27]

In some cases development concerns can tip the balance, causing industrialized countries to sign agreements they would be unlikely to seek under standard political economy models. This will happen when the trade agreement is likely to promote development in the developing country and when the industrialized state is likely to benefit from this increased development. These instances are most likely with developing states at the "middle of the pack" with regard to income: those developed enough to benefit from an agreement yet poor enough that further development brought about by preferential treatment is likely to decrease negative spillovers. Even in these situations domestic political economy will matter: to gain support for the agreement, the government will turn to groups that will benefit from it but may have been insufficiently motivated to lobby (expend resources) to bring it about.

Development Impasse at the WTO

The importance of development externalities in the calculus of industrialized states provides an explanation for why pursuing development goals through trade is more likely to be adopted at a bilateral level than through the WTO. Negotiating reciprocal market access through the WTO requires lowering barriers to all countries to comply with MFN treatment. Yet for many developing country markets, the industrialized state will prefer to maintain policy flexibility in the future rather than lose the benefit of support from protectionist groups. It is only when development externalities are present and sufficiently large that the industrialized country government will determine that locking in access for the developing country is preferable to maintaining flexibility. Industrialized states will therefore wish to target their trade agreements toward particular developing countries where the gains outweigh the costs, rather than negotiate universal agreements under the WTO. In discussing the difficulty of reaching agreement at the WTO, Edward Mansfield and Eric Reinhardt point to the growth in membership and participation in trade disputes to explain the move toward bilateral agreements.[28] When it comes to negotiating on development, another impediment may be that industrialized states simply benefit more by locking in preferences with developing states where trade will provide a positive externality to themselves, while maintaining flexibility with other trade partners.

The remainder of this chapter looks in more detail at the example of CAFTA-DR raised at the outset and then proceeds to a cross-national empirical analysis of the pattern of trade agreements between industrialized and developing countries.

CAFTA-DR

The United States signed the trade agreement commonly known as CAFTA-DR with Costa Rica, El Salvador, Guatemala, Honduras, Nicaragua, and the Dominican Republic in 2004; entry into force began in 2006 and the agreement was in force for all members by 2009. This was the first reciprocal PTA between the United States and a group of developing countries. Unlike NAFTA, which the United States signed with Canada and Mexico (currently the two largest export markets for US goods), the justification for the United States to pursue CAFTA-DR based on a desire to gain from its own increased trade is suspect. Following its passage, *The Economist* described CAFTA as "a modest agreement between a whale (the United States) and six minnows (five nations of Central America—Guatemala, Honduras, El Salvador, Nicaragua and Costa Rica—plus the Dominican Republic)."[29]

Developing Countries

The stakes were quite large for the Central American economies negotiating CAFTA-DR. In 2000, the region sent 73% of its exports to the United States and received 55% of its imports from the United States.[30] However, since the signing of NAFTA between the United States, Canada, and Mexico, Central American exporters to the US market feared losing ground to competitors in Mexico; they were also under increasing pressure from low-cost Chinese manufacturing.[31] With the initial entry into force of NAFTA in 1994, Central American and Caribbean countries (including all eventual members of CAFTA-DR) lost advantages they had enjoyed over Mexico for access to the US market under the Caribbean Basin Initiative (CBI).[32] The CBI countries had enjoyed broader trade preferences for entry into the US market than had Mexico under GSP. The implementation of NAFTA removed this competitive advantage and Mexican exports in sensitive products received more competitive access (after a phase-in period). This was particularly hard on textile-producing firms in the Caribbean, as they saw investment and jobs relocated to Mexico.[33] These countries appealed for NAFTA parity, which was introduced in the US Congress for several years before eventually passing in 2000 over the objections of the domestic textile industry in the United States.[34] The desire to enshrine these preferences in a reciprocal PTA played a key role in garnering support for the deal on the part of the developing countries. They also believed CAFTA-DR would lead to increased foreign investment and promote enhanced cooperation between the Central American members of the agreement.[35]

Within Central American countries a fairly traditional political economy scenario separated supporters from opponents and determined the relative ease with which the agreement was approved across the developing country members. Diego Sánchez-Ancochea notes that passage and entry into force was relatively quick in El Salvador, Guatemala, Honduras, and Nicaragua because in these countries "social movements and trade unions are relatively weak and domestic capital is highly influential and dependent on the U.S. market."[36] In the Dominican Republic there was more of a political struggle to ratify the agreement. Andrew Schrank argues that traditionally export-oriented areas of the country favored CAFTA-DR, while relatively noncompetitive import-competing firms that had benefitted from import substitution industrialization (ISI) policies opposed the agreement because it would open markets and expose them to competitive pressures with which they were ill equipped to cope.[37]

Costa Rica was the last signatory to gain domestic approval for CAFTA-DR and the only one to hold a referendum in which the general public could vote for or against the trade agreement. The campaign leading up to the referendum was fiercely fought, with the "for" vote narrowly winning. Recently elected Costa Rican President Oscar Arias supported ratification, and Costa Ricans living in export-oriented areas of the country as well as highly educated voters were disproportionately in favor of the agreement.[38] Opponents, led by former presidential candidate and Arias rival Otton Solis, had support from domestic unions[39] and from low-skilled workers.[40] Pro-ratification campaigners were also likely helped by the greater experience and organization of their side compared to the relatively new apparatus supporting the anti-ratification side.[41] In each of the Central American countries traditional domestic political economy arguments based on the power of winners and losers from free trade appear to provide reasonable explanations for the negotiation and passage of CAFTA-DR.

United States

In the United States, a justification for the resources expended by the George W. Bush administration to gain support for CAFTA-DR based solely on direct economic gains from the agreement for domestic interest groups and voters is less clear. The website of the US Trade Representative (USTR) states that, as a group, the members of CAFTA-DR were the sixteenth largest goods trading partner for the United States in 2015.[42] Furthermore, they are—again as a group—a smaller US export market in the region than either Mexico or Brazil. Except for the fact that they are located in the same region and all signed the same trade agreement, there is no reason to group them when counting market size. They differ on multiple dimensions, including income: the wealthiest country, Costa Rica, has a per capita income more than four times that of the poorest country, Nicaragua; Costa Rica's trade with the United States is almost five times greater than trade between Nicaragua and the United States. Yet, even considered as a whole, this disparate group accounted for less than 2% of US trade in goods prior to and since signing CAFTA-DR.[43] Considered individually, none of these countries rank in the top thirty trade partners for the United States.

Commentators at the time recognized the small direct stakes for the US economy of passing CAFTA-DR. *The New York Times* wrote that "the economic impact on the United States would be trivial."[44] *The Economist* argued that "[i]n economic terms it is hard to see what all the fuss is about. Although CAFTA is important for Central Americans, whose main hope is for increased American investment, it will have only a small effect on America's economy."[45] Alexandra Guisinger has found that CAFTA-DR had very little salience with the average voter in the United States.[46] Yet in placing CAFTA as his "top trade priority," President George W. Bush ended up only narrowly avoiding a political embarrassment that would have made him the first US president in decades to have negotiated a trade agreement that was later denied by Congress.[47] Additionally, the controversy surrounding CAFTA-DR risked jeopardizing other trade negotiations on his agenda. If Bush could not deliver Congressional approval on CAFTA-DR, it would hurt the credibility of his administration when negotiating in the Doha Round at the WTO, which was at a critical point in 2005.[48]

The prospect of only small potential economic benefit for some domestic groups in the United States was coupled with a steep backlash from powerful protectionist special interest groups. The sugar industry was strongly opposed to CAFTA-DR. Members of Congress from sugar-producing areas, even Republicans who would generally support both free trade and a Republican president, faced intense pressure to vote against passage.[49] The actual value of additional sugar imports into the United States from CAFTA-DR countries is small, but the industry feared a precedent of decreased protection for sugar.[50] The powerful textile industry, which had only a few years previously opposed the granting of NAFTA parity to these same countries as members of the CBI (and succeeded in delaying it by several years),[51] initially opposed CAFTA-DR as well. However, as concern grew regarding low-cost imports from China in 2005, the portion of the textile industry that produces yarn, fabric, and other inputs endorsed CAFTA-DR once they were assured that many of the finished products from member countries would be required to use US inputs to receive preferential access to the US market. Members of Congress representing districts heavy in production of finished textile products still opposed CAFTA-DR.[52] Labor unions more generally organized opposition to CAFTA-DR, arguing that US jobs would be lost to the other CAFTA-DR countries in part due to the low level of protections for workers and the environment in the developing country member states. When presidents of the Central American countries and the Dominican Republic visited the United States to help garner support for the deal, the AFL-CIO organized cross-country protests using the slogan "Cafta We Don't Hafta."[53]

Although business groups such as the National Association of Manufacturers, the Chamber of Commerce, and the American Farm Bureau Federation supported CAFTA-DR,[54] their support alone was not enough to combat what *The New York Times* called "the political clout of vocal protectionist interest groups."[55] The administration had to strike deals with multiple individual lawmakers or small groups to gain their support. Those representing districts facing increasing pressure from Chinese products were promised the support of House leadership and the Bush administration for restrictions on Chinese imports and a tougher stance against Chinese currency manipulation.[56] To assuage fears regarding lack of protections for labor and the environment in CAFTA-DR countries, the administration promised to spend $40 million per year helping these countries enforce their existing laws.[57] Deals even became quite specific, with the White House promising that any trousers imported to the United States duty free from CAFTA-DR countries would need to be made with pockets and linings from US companies.[58] And the votes of some House members were likely brought around by the hope—and fear—of the impact their CAFTA-DR vote would have on the distribution of projects as part of the $286 billion transportation bill, including many projects earmarked for particular Congressional districts, that was simultaneously being negotiated in Congress.[59]

While standard horse trading consistent with a political economy framework can be used to explain how the Bush adminstration finally managed to get CAFTA-DR approval in Congress, a political economy explanation falls short in providing insight as to why the administration wanted the deal at all. Faced with small economic benefits for domestic groups and concentrated interests opposed to the deal, it is necessary to look beyond the economics of trade interest groups to understand the administration's rationale. A powerful motive was the desire to work toward a broader Free Trade Agreement of the Americas (FTAA), of which a Central American deal could be a key step.[60] An additional geopolitical consideration was the desire to provide an alternative path to growth from that being championed by Venezuelan President Hugo Chávez as part of his "revolution" for Latin America, financed by a surge in oil revenues. If the United States could increase its trade ties with Central America and promote development in the region, countries would be less likely to turn toward Chávez and Cuban President Fidel Castro for assistance.[61] This highlights growing links between development and geopolitics. Unlike policies in the Cold War, in which development resources were often coopted to pursue non-development-related geopolitical goals, the policy pursued by the United States in Central America from 2002 onward represents an instance in which promoting development simultaneously fulfills other foreign policy goals—but success relies on development actually increasing.

The Bush administration further made clear that the goals of CAFTA-DR went beyond trade promotion and embraced development. In an effort to garner support for passage of CAFTA-DR, Bush argued,

> If you're concerned about immigration to this country, then you must understand that CAFTA and the benefits of CAFTA will help create new opportunity in Central American countries, which will mean someone will be able to find good work at home, somebody will be able to provide for their family at home, as opposed to having to make the long trip to the United States. CAFTA is good immigration policy, as well as good trade policy . . . By transforming our hemisphere into a powerful trading area, CAFTA will help promote democracy, security and prosperity.[62]

In the lead-up to Congressional voting, Deputy Secretary of State Robert Zoellick wrote an opinion piece in *The Washington Post*, part of which is quoted at the opening of this chapter, highlighting the link between CAFTA-DR, development in Central America, and US security concerns.[63] Presidents from all six of the developing country partners in CAFTA-DR traveled to the United States in May 2005 to meet with leaders of the Bush administration, including President Bush, in an effort to increase Congressional support for CAFTA-DR. One of the meetings was with US Secretary of Defense Donald Rumsfeld, whose press release at the time argued that:

> "Economic progress and security are interdependent... Today, the threat to Central American and Caribbean security comes from an anti-social combination of gangs, drug traffickers, smugglers, hostage takers, and terrorists. It is increasingly clear that they can be effectively combated—and are being combated—only by close cooperation among nations. This trade agreement could help usher in a new era of cooperation between our countries and enhanced prosperity in the region.[64]

Following the vote on CAFTA-DR in the House of Representatives, House Majority Leader Tom DeLay noted that tying the agreement to national security may have gained the administration votes from some Republican members.[65]

Complementary Engagement in the Region

The likelihood that one of the key goals of the Bush administration in pursuing CAFTA-DR was increased development in the region is increased by the targeting of foreign aid to the developing country member states. Even as CAFTA-DR was encountering steep resistance in the US Congress in the spring and summer of 2005, the newly created Millennium Challenge Corporation (MCC) was negotiating compacts with CAFTA-DR countries. Honduras signed a $215 million compact with the MCC on June 15, 2005, becoming only the second country to do so. A compact for $175 million was signed between the MCC and Nicaragua the following month.[66] A compact with El Salvador worth $461 million followed in 2006. The remaining CAFTA-DR countries did not meet eligibility criteria for the MCC in 2005–2006: Costa Rica had a per capita income above the threshold for eligibility; Guatemala and the Dominican Republic met income eligibility requirements but did not at the time score highly enough on the indicators used by the MCC to be deemed eligible for a compact. Given their ineligibility for MCC funding, the administration in 2007 authorized an additional $10 million per year to address rural development needs in Guatemala and the Dominican Republic for up to five years "or until the two countries sign compacts."[67]

The increase in foreign aid from the United States to the developing country members of CAFTA-DR since the beginning of negotiations in 2002 can be seen in Figure 5.2. The first set of bars represents the average annual aid commitment

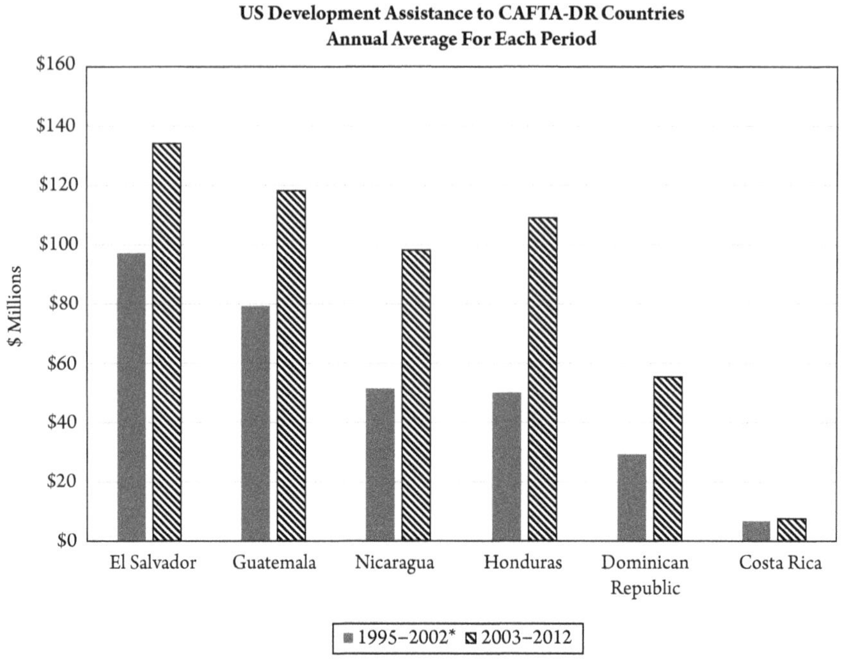

US Development Assistance to CAFTA-DR Countries
Annual Average For Each Period

Figure 5.2 US FOREIGN AID TO CAFTA-DR COUNTRIES. Data are for total commitments from the United States to each of the countries represented (Constant $millions), from the OECD DAC3a database available at stats.oecd.org. The average of the annual amounts for each period is reported. *Excludes 1999 due to the one-time surge in foreign aid as a direct response to Hurricane Mitch, which was catastrophic for Central America.

from the United States to each country for the period 1995–2002. This captures the time once the immediate aftermath of the Cold War had subsided but before CAFTA-DR negotiations were at an advanced stage.[68] The second set of bars shows the average annual aid commitment for the period following the commencement of negotiations on CAFTA-DR and through its initial years of implementation, 2003–2012. Except in Costa Rica, where the high level of development resulted in little foreign aid in either period, there was a marked increase in aid from the United States to each country in CAFTA-DR. The decision by the United States to pursue CAFTA-DR affected not only the amount but the composition of foreign aid as well. From the beginning there was a realization that in order to capitalize on trade to enhance development, assistance was needed in building trade capacity. CAFTA-DR was the first trade agreement to include a Committee on Trade Capacity Building (Chapter 19, Section B). The compacts negotiated between the MCC and Honduras, Nicaragua, and El Salvador at this time included projects specifically targeting trade facilitation. Each of the compacts included substantial funding for building roads to increase connectivity to rural areas within countries and facilitate transportation between Central American countries. They also each had a focus on increasing agricultural productivity and investing in higher-value crops.

I had the opportunity to conduct interviews with multiple aid agencies in Nicaragua and Honduras in the spring of 2006, within months of the entry into force of CAFTA-DR in these countries on April 1, 2006.[69] The shift toward trade capacity building was evident in multiple meetings and conversations, with some officials even worrying that aid was shifting "too far" toward facilitating growth through trade rather than providing more basic services. There was additional evidence that the United States was interested in boosting regional trade within Central America, not only trade between Central American countries and itself. For instance, one project I visited in Nicaragua was funded by USAID and implemented by Michigan State University. It helped farmers organize to achieve sufficient scale to compete in a regional market, offered advice regarding which crops to plant to increase returns as well as training and capital to make crop-switching a realistic option, and provided expertise for negotiating and signing contracts with regional (Central American) grocery chains. The program was meant to provide the opportunity for increased productivity and income for the farmers and growth for the economies, but had no direct impact on the United States through trade.[70] More broadly in my interviews it became clear that every aid agency—not just those from the United States—discussed ways in which aid could be used to help the countries benefit from CAFTA-DR. Thus the signing of the agreement appears to have more broadly shifted the dialogue in Central America toward pursuing development through building trade capacity.

Early Results

CAFTA-DR has been in effect for ten years and from a development standpoint the results are mixed. From the US perspective, negative spillovers from the region, such as violence, drug trafficking, and human smuggling, continue to affect its own well-being. While it is not possible to know the exact impact of the trade agreement on various outcomes, this section reviews developments over the past ten years that are relevant in thinking about CAFTA-DR and development in Central America.

One of the key reasons for developing countries to sign trade agreements is to increase foreign investment. Figure 5.3 shows the stock of foreign direct investment (FDI) in each of the developing country members of CAFTA-DR for the period 1990–2014.[71] For each country the actual yearly values (in constant dollars) are plotted, as well as a trend line that is based on the observed values for 1990–2002 (the year CAFTA-DR negotiations were announced), projected

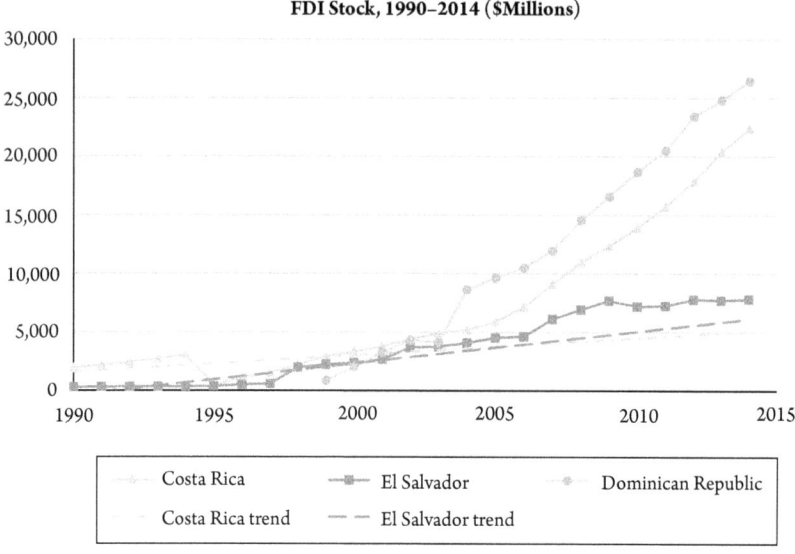

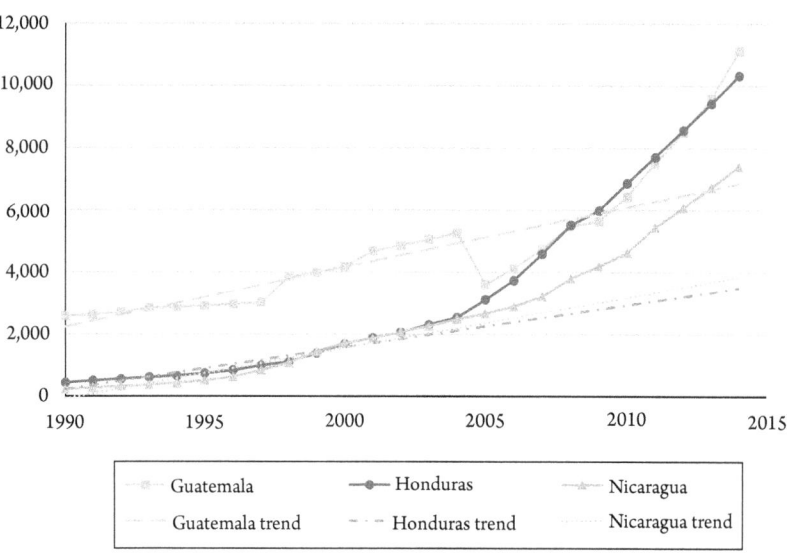

Figure 5.3 FDI Stock for Members of CAFTA-DR, 1990–2014. Data from UNCTAD, converted to constant $US using the BEA GDP deflator. Trend lines are generated assuming a linear trend for the period based on 1990–2002 data for each country; as data for the Dominican Republic are not available for many years in the 1990s, no trend is calculated for that country.

forward through 2014.[72] In every case the stock of FDI has grown faster since 2002 than the trend line for the country, suggesting that the prospect and then reality of CAFTA-DR were helpful in attracting investors.

Figure 5.4 performs the same analysis for income per capita, for which the results are more mixed. Costa Rica, the Dominican Republic, Honduras, and possibly Nicaragua appear to have achieved higher growth than would have been projected based on their 1990–2002 trend. El Salvador, however, has fared worse than the trend line, and Guatemala has grown almost exactly as would be expected based on the pre-CAFTA years. Both of these countries, along with Honduras, have seen significant increases in violence in recent years, which undoubtedly affect growth. It is not possible to know if growth would have been even worse without CAFTA-DR or if there has been no positive effect of CAFTA-DR in these countries (e.g., perhaps violence prevents these countries from realizing the potential development gains from trade).

The developing country members of CAFTA-DR have become less dependent on bilateral trade with the United States; exports to the United States fell from 73% of total exports from the region in 2000 to 43% in 2010, while the percent of total imports to the region originating in the United States fell from 55% to 46% for the same time period.[73] Intra-regional trade and trade with Mexico has increased, in part due to incentives for regional integration of supply chains within CAFTA-DR and a related PTA signed between the Central American members and Mexico.[74] Costa Rica has transitioned toward the production of higher-skilled exports for the technology sector, the Dominican Republic has increased its production of medical equipment and other manufactured goods, and Nicaragua has decreased its reliance on agriculture and increased its production of apparel and low-skill manufactured goods.[75] In contrast, the members of the Northern Triangle—Guatemala, El Salvador, and Honduras—have seen serious increases in violence that most likely have a negative impact on their ability to diversify their economies.

From the perspective of the United States and its desire to use CAFTA-DR to decrease migration and spillovers from Central America, the agreement has not been an unqualified success. This is particularly true with regard to the three Northern Triangle countries. Drug trafficking through the region into the United States has increased significantly in recent years.[76] The Migration Policy Institute notes that migration from Central America into the United States increased by 56% from 2000 to 2013.[77] Recent years have seen a surge in unaccompanied minors entering the United States from Central America over the US–Mexican border, with estimates of almost 100,000 arriving from Northern Triangle countries between October 2013 and July 2015.[78] This increase is tied to extreme violence in these nations; according to the United Nations Office on Drugs and Crime, Honduras and El Salvador had the highest homicide rates in the world in 2014, with Guatemala also on the list of the top 10 most violent countries (74.6, 64.2, and 31.2 homicides per 100,000 population, respectively),[79] while initial reports show an increase in El Salvador to 90

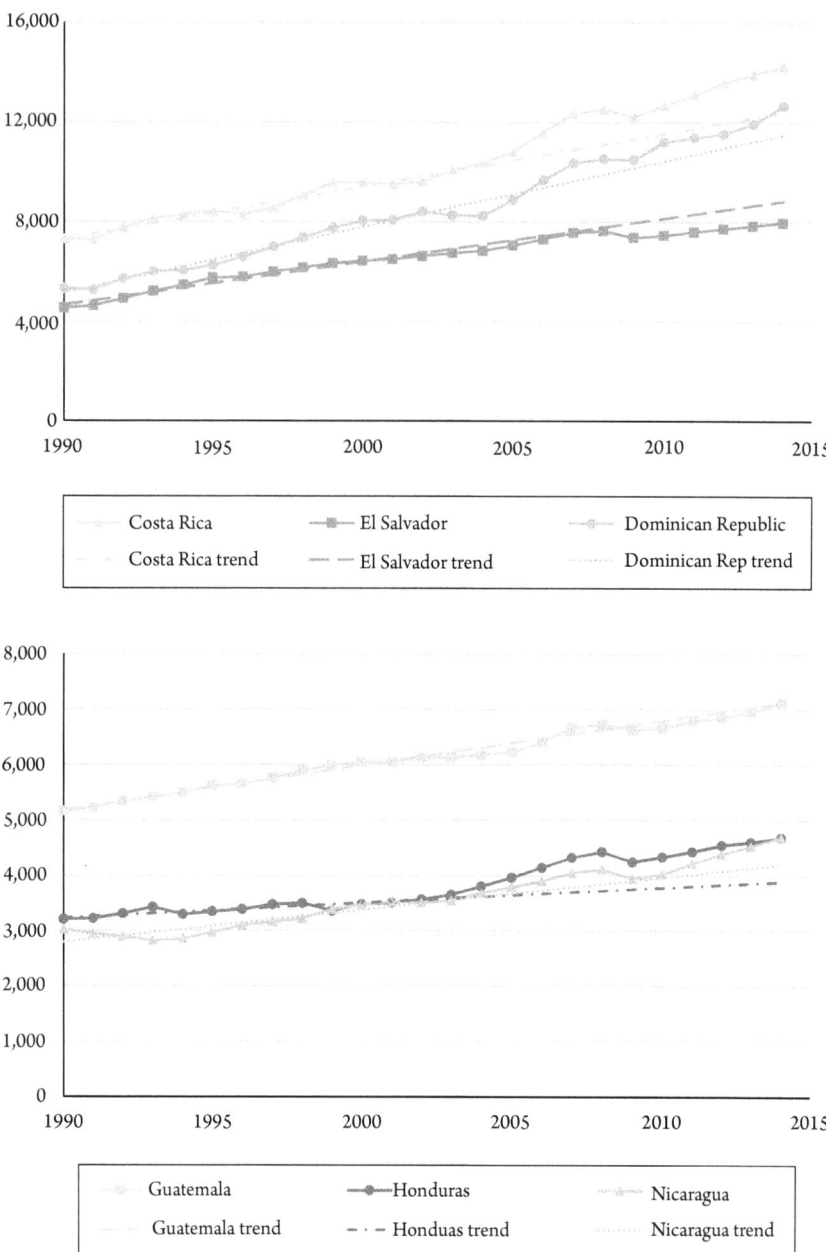

Figure 5.4 GDP per Capita for Members of CAFTA-DR, 1990–2014. Data are from the World Development Indicators and are measured in constant 2011 purchasing power parity dollars. Trend lines are generated assuming a linear trend for the period based on 1990–2002 data for each country.

homicides per 100,000 population in 2015.[80] In addition to the homicide rate, extortion and threats from gangs in these countries increase fear and insecurity, making migration more attractive. The increase in those fleeing violence, as opposed to earlier waves of more traditional economic migrants arriving in the United States, has taxed the resources of asylum processing on the US southern border of the United States and increased the likelihood of granting refugee status to those arriving.[81] The Obama administration responded with increased development and security aid to the region in recent years, an issue to which I return in Chapter 7.

Showing an opposite trend, migrants arriving in the United States from Costa Rica and Nicaragua declined from 2010 to 2013,[82] which likely reflects low violence and improving economic conditions in these countries as well as the relative ease with which Nicaraguan migrants can reach their much wealthier neighbor, Costa Rica, compared with the dangerous journey to the more distant United States.[83] Overall, in the decade since the implementation of CAFTA-DR, FDI and regional integration in Central America have increased significantly, and some countries in the region have translated this into growth. For those countries plagued by extreme violence, however, it appears that there are significant limits to the positive impact of signing a trade agreement, both for themselves and for industrialized states affected by underdevelopment from these countries.

Dyadic Analysis

The example of CAFTA-DR provides detailed insight that sheds light on the reasons states have for pursuing industrialized–developing country trade agreements. This section takes a different perspective, examining broader patterns that determine which dyads are likely to sign these agreements. Although, as shown earlier in Figure 5.1, the number of PTAs between industrialized and developing states has grown considerably over the last two decades, currently almost 90% of industrialized–developing country dyads are not covered by a PTA. As seen with CAFTA-DR, trade negotiations are costly, requiring significant use of resources during negotiations and drawing on political capital to gain passage once signed. Governments have a finite capacity to undertake these endeavors; each negotiation therefore has the associated opportunity cost of alternative plans not pursued. Given this, it is possible to interpret relative priorities of governments based on their choice of trade agreement partners.

This section examines the probability of a particular industrialized–developing country dyad signing a reciprocal PTA in a given year in the post-1991 period. The focus is on explaining the motivations of the industrialized states. The targeted development framework suggests that industrialized states will pursue agreements with developing countries where development increases the well-being of the industrialized state *and* where the trade agreement is likely to have a positive impact on development. Explanatory variables cover characteristics of the dyad and the developing state, but not those particular to the industrialized state. Only dyads that do not have a reciprocal trade agreement in force are included. Once a dyad signs a PTA it is excluded from the analysis for subsequent years. The list of industrialized–developing country dyads is generated in the same manner as that for aid in Chapter 4. A country is considered "developing" if it is independent and aid-eligible (although it need not actually be receiving aid) in a given year. Territories are excluded, as are countries for any years after they graduate from aid status by crossing the high-income threshold. High-income members of the OECD are used to create the list of "industrialized" countries for the dyads. The European Union is included as a single industrialized "country" entity, rather than including each member separately, since the members negotiate trade agreements jointly. Countries that joined the EU since 1991 are included as separate states for the time prior to joining the EU.

Dependent Variable

The dependent variable takes the value of one if a PTA between the dyad members was signed in a given year and zero otherwise. Data on PTAs come from the World Trade Organization's Regional Trade Agreements database. I include reciprocal agreements only; non-reciprocal preferential arrangements are not included.

It is rare (in the data) for an industrialized–developing country dyad to sign a free-trade agreement. For the 20,941 dyad-years included in the analysis, in only 125 cases is an agreement signed. However, the rarity reflects dyads leaving the dataset once an agreement is signed. In 2012 there are 1,400 industrialized–developing country dyads, but 146 of them signed an agreement prior to 2012, leaving 1,254 in the dataset to potentially sign agreements at a later time. A list of all industrialized–developing country dyads that concluded a preferential trade agreement by the end of 2012, as well as the year of signing, is included in the appendix at the end of this chapter.

Foreign Aid Variables

The analysis includes two measures related to foreign aid. For each industrialized–developing country dyad-year, the percent of the industrialized country's total aid commitment portfolio accounted for by aid to the developing country in that year is calculated (*Aid Share*). This captures the importance of the developing country as an aid recipient to the industrialized member of the dyad. As the empirical analysis in Chapter 4 demonstrates, aid is targeted toward developing countries from which the industrialized state can reasonably expect to receive negative spillovers from underdevelopment. If the industrialized country is using both trade agreements and foreign aid to boost development prospects in targeted countries, then the importance of a recipient in the donor's portfolio should be positively related to the likelihood of signing a trade agreement. This should be true even when other determinants of aid, such as distance, are included in the analysis.

The second aid variable measures total aid from all donors to the developing country as a percent of the developing country's GDP (*Aid % GDP*) in a given year. This captures overall aid dependence and should be negatively associated with the likelihood of signing a PTA. As noted above, some countries may not be in a position from which they can reasonably be expected to generate development from a trade agreement. This might include very poor countries, countries in conflict, or those with some level of state failure. High levels of overall aid dependence may be associated with these other conditions, signaling lack of readiness for a trade agreement. Data on foreign aid commitments are from the OECD's DAC3a online database.[84] To the best of my knowledge, neither of these variables has been included in analyses of the determinants of trade agreements.

Income

Industrialized countries seeking to use trade agreements as part of a targeted development strategy will focus on countries in the "middle of the pack" with regard to development: those developed enough to gain from increased opportunities for trade, but where underdevelopment still creates the potential for significant, cross-border, negative externalities. This differentiates a targeted development strategy from one based on maximizing direct gains from trade; this latter strategy would favor wealthier developing states that present more attractive markets for the industrialized country. Targeted development, on the other hand, implies a focus on positive development externalities for the industrialized state from signing trade agreements with developing countries. The wealthiest of developing states are unlikely to create negative spillovers to begin with, so there is limited potential for decreasing them through trade agreements. The poorest states are unlikely to be in a position to capitalize on a trade agreement to increase development. Targeted development suggests a focus on developing countries in the middle of the income range. To capture this, the analysis includes both the natural log of *Income*, measured as GDP per capita,[85] and its square; the former is expected to have a positive relationship with the likelihood of signing an agreement, while the latter should have a negative coefficient if the relationship is nonlinear. While scholars such as Manger and Shadlen control for the income of the developing state,[86] I am not aware of studies allowing for a nonlinear relationship between income in the developing state and trade agreements.

Control Variables

Multiple studies conducted by Mansfield, Milner, and co-authors have shown the importance of regime type and number of government veto players in studying ratification of trade agreements.[87] I control for level of *Democracy* in the developing country using the average of the country's values on the civil liberties and political rights variables published by Freedom House; this scale ranges from zero to seven and is inverted so that higher scores reflect greater democracy.[88] To control for veto points, I use the developing country's value on the variable *Checks* from the Database of Political Institutions.[89] Following the work of Gowa[90] and Gowa and Mansfield,[91] the analysis includes a measure of *Alliance* that is coded one if there is any type of alliance between the two dyad members.[92] Because larger (potential) trade partners may be more likely to sign an agreement even absent development externalities, measures for *Bilateral Trade* and the developing country's *GDP* are included. Data on trade flows are from the International Monetary Fund's Direction of Trade Statistics and include the sum of exports from and imports to the industrialized state from the developing state, converted to constant dollars using the US GDP deflator.[93] Data for GDP are from the World Development Indicators, measured in constant dollars. The natural log of both variables is used in the analysis. Following other work on trade, I control for the log of *Distance* between members of the dyad.[94] I also control for former colonial status with an indicator variable *Colony* that equals one if the developing country was ever a colony of the industrialized state and zero otherwise.[95]

European Union

When the industrialized member of a dyad is the EU, dyadic variable values are aggregated across EU members. *Aid Share* is the percent of total bilateral aid from EU members made up of aid to the developing country. *Bilateral Trade* with the developing country is summed across EU members. *Distance* is the average distance between the developing country and EU members. *Colony* takes the value of one if the developing country was ever a colony of any EU member; *Alliance* takes a value of one if the developing country has an alliance with any EU member state.

The analysis approximates a hazard model using a Logit model with variables capturing duration, duration-squared, and duration-cubed.[96] Duration is measured as number of years since 1980 (or since independence if post-1980). Time-varying independent variables are lagged two years to avoid concerns that signing, or anticipation of signing, the agreement is causing changes in the independent variable. Standard errors are clustered on dyads. Country fixed effects are not included due to the binary nature of the dependent variable; including country fixed effects in this setting induces separation, causing any countries that never experience a change on the dependent variable to be dropped from the analysis.[97]

Models are presented either controlling for market size using the natural log of GDP (preferred) or controlling for the natural log of bilateral trade. Given the high correlation between the two variables (corr=0.58) I chose not to include both in the same model.[98] GDP is the preferred measure because, while bilateral trade is a standard variable to include when analyzing the likelihood of signing an PTA, it is problematic in this situation. Prior to signing an agreement, unilateral preferences granted by the industrialized state are usually in place. As the industrialized state has significant discretion over these preferences, they may be targeting them toward particular states even prior to signing a reciprocal agreement; preferences granted under the CBI to countries that went on to join CAFTA-DR are a case in point. As another example, US preferences should be ended once imports from a country reach a certain level, but the president can waive this requirement and allow them to continue. These waivers may be more likely to occur if the industrialized state is benefitting from development externalities caused by trade with the developing country. Given this, development targeting may influence the level of bilateral trade prior to the signing of an agreement, making it impossible to disentangle the economic motivations related to trade from development motivations that might already influence trade patterns between industrialized and developing countries.

Results

Results from the analysis are presented in Table 5.1. Models 1, 2, and 3 control for market size using the natural log of GDP; Models 4 and 5 include the natural log of bilateral trade in place of GDP. In each case results are reported both excluding and including the squared term for *Income*.

The results are consistent with industrialized states pursuing targeted development through PTAs with developing countries. The relationship between aid and the likelihood of signing an agreement supports this hypothesis. Chapter 4 demonstrates that industrialized states give more aid to developing countries

Table 5.1 **Probability of Signing a Preferential Trade Agreement, 1992–2012**

	Model 1	Model 2	Model 3	Model 4	Model 5
Aid Share	0.064***	0.062***	0.152**	0.054**	0.051**
	(0.002)	(0.002)	(0.018)	(0.025)	(0.033)
Aid % GDP	−7.124***	−4.670***	−3.900**	−7.310***	−4.818***
	(0.000)	(0.007)	(0.029)	(0.000)	(0.004)
Income	0.061	4.323***	4.638***	0.050	4.365***
	(0.551)	(0.001)	(0.001)	(0.614)	(0.001)
Income Squared		−0.265***	−0.281***		−0.268***
		(0.002)	(0.001)		(0.002)
GDP	0.164***	0.164***	0.161***		
	(0.007)	(0.006)	(0.009)		
Bilateral Trade				0.146***	0.147***
				(0.001)	(0.001)
Distance	−0.985***	−1.010***	−0.988***	−0.915***	−0.939***
	(0.000)	(0.000)	(0.000)	(0.000)	(0.000)
Colony	1.069***	1.150***	1.193***	0.592**	0.666***
	(0.000)	(0.000)	(0.000)	(0.020)	(0.007)
Democracy	0.240***	0.223***	0.242***	0.235***	0.216***
	(0.000)	(0.001)	(0.000)	(0.000)	(0.000)
Checks	−0.139*	−0.139	−0.239***	−0.126	−0.125
	(0.096)	(0.122)	(0.004)	(0.115)	(0.147)
Alliance	−0.011	−0.088	−0.024	−0.286	−0.372
	(0.972)	(0.768)	(0.937)	(0.343)	(0.205)
Duration	−0.349*	−0.336*	−0.331*	−0.441**	−0.420**
	(0.052)	(0.061)	(0.067)	(0.024)	(0.030)
Duration-squared	0.031***	0.031***	0.031***	0.036***	0.035***
	(0.005)	(0.005)	(0.005)	(0.003)	(0.002)
Duration-cubed	−0.001***	−0.001***	−0.001***	−0.001***	−0.001***
	(0.005)	(0.003)	(0.004)	(0.002)	(0.002)
Constant	−2.521	−19.278***	−20.801***	−1.235	−18.277***
	(0.320)	(0.000)	(0.000)	(0.569)	(0.001)
Observations	20,941	20,941	20,731	20,741	20,741
Dyads	1,664	1,664	1,659	1,654	1,654
Industrialized Countries	12	12	12	12	12
Developing Countries	148	148	148	148	148

Dependent variable equals 1 if the industrial–developing dyad signed a reciprocal trade agreement in year t, zero otherwise. Logit models. Standard errors clustered on dyad (not shown); p-values in parentheses. *Significant at the 10% level; **Significant at the 5% level; ***Significant at the 1% level.

that are likely to transmit negative spillovers from underdevelopment to the industrialized state. As the results in Table 5.1 show, these same states—those that receive a higher share of the industrialized country's aid budget—are also more likely to sign a trade agreement. The coefficient on *Aid Share* is consistently positive and significant. To determine whether this is driven by outliers, Model 3 re-estimates Model 2 but excludes observations whose value on *Aid Share* is in the top 1%; the variable remains significant. Using Model 3, Figure 5.5 plots the predicted probability of signing a PTA at different levels of *Aid Share* with other variables held constant at their means. Given the relatively rare occurrence of signing in the data, the predicted probabilities are low but increase as the developing country's share of aid from the industrialized state grows.

While importance to an individual industrialized country increases the likelihood of a developing country signing an agreement, overall aid dependence has the opposite effect. The coefficient *Aid % GDP*, which captures total aid received from all donors as a percent of the developing country's GDP, is consistently negative and significant. The differences on the coefficients for *Aid Share* and *Aid % GDP* demonstrate the complex relationship between foreign aid and trade agreements as tools for development. When an industrialized state targets a particular country for development promotion, the country is likely to receive more aid and is more likely to conclude a trade agreement

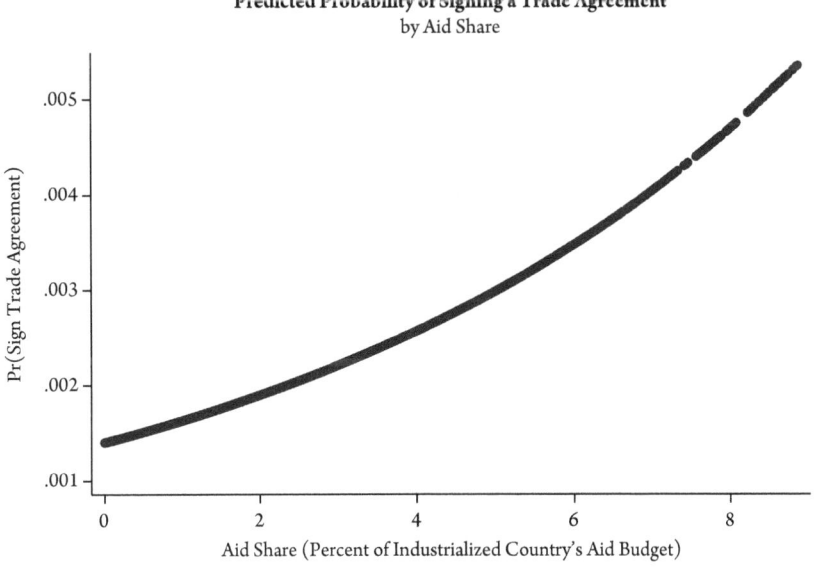

Figure 5.5 Predicted Probability of Signing a Trade Agreement, by Aid Share.

with the industrialized state, *ceteris paribus*. However, countries that are highly dependent on the international community (not necessarily on any particular donor) for aid are usually experiencing problems—conflict, poor governance, extreme poverty, natural disaster, or others—that limit the potential usefulness of a trade agreement. Thus there are some countries where aid is deemed to be a more effective tool; these countries may receive a large amount of aid as a percent of their total income but be deemed poor targets for a PTA.

Models 1 and 4 in Table 5.1, which exclude the term for *Income Squared*, show no evidence of a direct relationship between income of the developing country and the likelihood that it will sign a PTA with an industrialized state. The coefficients on both *Income* and *Income Squared* in the remaining models demonstrate the nonlinear relationship between income and likelihood of signing an agreement for developing countries. The results are consistent with industrialized states pursuing trade agreements with developing countries in the "middle of the pack." Figure 5.6 shows this relationship between probability of signing and income graphically, based on Model 2 with other variables held constant at their mean values. Vertical lines have been added to represent the $1.25/day World Bank cutoff for extreme poverty ($456 annually), the dividing line between low-income and lower-middle income ($875), between lower-middle income and upper-middle income ($3,465), and between upper-middle income and

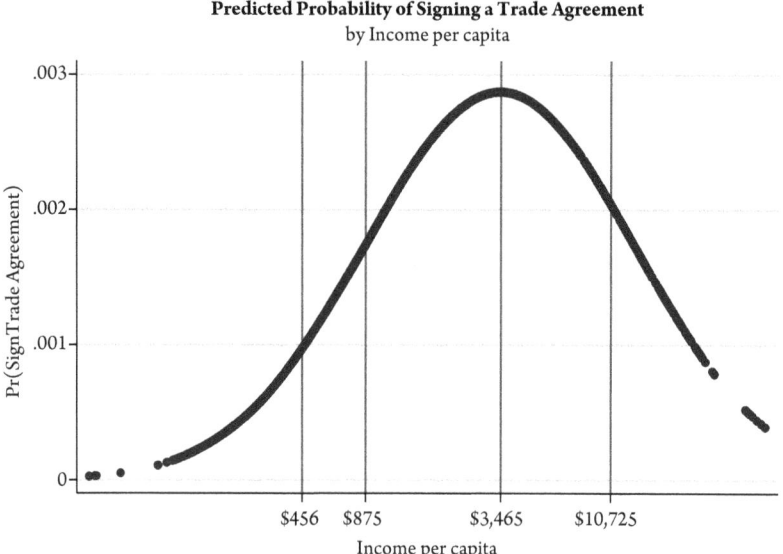

Figure 5.6 Predicted Probability of Signing a Trade Agreement, by Income per Capita.

high-income ($10,725) based on World Bank classifications.[99] The highest probability of signing is in the top portion of the lower-middle income and bottom portion of the upper-middle income groups, with the peak occurring close to the cutoff point between these two classifications. Of the remaining variables, in some cases the relationships are similar to what would be expected from studies of trade agreements more broadly, while in others it appears that there are some differences when restricting the analysis to industrialized–developing country dyads. The coefficients on both *GDP* and *Bilateral Trade* have the expected signs and significance. It is perhaps interesting that in models including *Bilateral Trade* instead of *GDP* the coefficient on *Aid Share* decreases in both magnitude and significance, suggesting that *Bilateral Trade* may be picking up existing preferences based on the developing country's importance to the industrialized state, which also resulted in higher aid. This is not the only possible interpretation of this pattern, but it is suggestive and invites caution when interpreting trade flows as a predictor of the likelihood of signing an agreement: the same underlying factors may increase initial trade flows and increase the likelihood of an agreement. The coefficient on *Distance* is consistent with the established finding that closer countries are more likely to sign agreements.

If the developing country is a former colony of the industrialized state, the dyad is more likely to sign an agreement; this finding is consistent with that of Manger and Shadlen,[100] which focuses on industrialized–developing country agreements, but differs from Mansfield and Milner,[101] which finds a negative relationship between colonial status and likelihood of signing an agreement when examining the broader universe of dyads eligible to sign trade agreements. As found by Mansfield and Milner,[102] when the developing country is a democracy, the dyad is more likely to sign a PTA (all the industrialized states in the analysis are democracies). Their finding regarding veto points appears less robust when the analysis is confined to industrialized–developing country dyads: although always negative, the coefficient on *Checks* is not always significant and is sensitive to the countries included, jumping in both size and significance in Model 3 when aid outliers are omitted. There appears to be no relationship between having an alliance and signing a trade agreement among these dyads, contrary to the findings regarding the broader universe of agreements as demonstrated by Gowa[103] and Gowa and Mansfield[104] and more recently confirmed by Mansfield and Milner;[105] this lack of a relationship when confined to industrialized–developing country dyads was also found by Manger and Shadlen.[106]

Discussion

Industrialized states pursuing a targeted development strategy through trade agreements will seek to sign these agreements with developing states where development will increase their own well-being and where the developing country is likely to capitalize on the agreement to improve its development outcomes. At times predictions from the targeted development framework run contrary to existing expectations regarding the likelihood of signing trade agreements more broadly. The discussion of CAFTA-DR and the results of the dyadic statistical analysis are consistent with an important role for targeted development in guiding the decision by an industrialized state to pursue a trade agreement with a developing state. Contrary to standard political economy models, the Bush administration expended considerable political capital and went against the wishes of powerful lobbies to sign and ratify a trade agreement with six countries from Central America and the Caribbean that represent a tiny market for US producers. In doing so, the administration touted the benefits to the United States of increased development in the region. It also took concrete steps, through increased foreign aid focused on building trade capacity, to promote development through trade in member states.

The dyadic analysis confirms that industrialized states more generally are likely to sign agreements with developing countries where the development outcomes are most important to themselves, as indicated by the positive association between the share of its aid budget devoted to a particular developing country and the likelihood of signing an agreement with that same state. As demonstrated in the CAFTA-DR case, aid and trade agreements can serve as complements in the multi-tool approach to pursuing a targeted development strategy. However, as they do when differentiating the composition of foreign aid based on the different capabilities and needs of recipients, industrialized states also recognize the varying ability of developing states to benefit from PTAs. Those states least likely to turn a trade agreement into better development outcomes, such as least developed countries and/or those with high overall aid dependence, are less likely to sign trade agreements with industrialized states. Taken together with the results regarding foreign aid from Chapter 4, this suggests that targeted development informs policy in multiple issue areas and is carried out in a manner that considers the relative capabilities of targeted states.

Chapter 5 Appendix

Table A5.1 **Industrialized–Developing Dyads Signing PTAs**

Industrialized Country	Developing Country	Year Signed
Australia	Papua New Guinea	1976
EU	Syria	1977
Australia	Fiji	1980
Australia	Kiribati	1980
Australia	Nauru	1980
Australia	Samoa	1980
Australia	Solomon Islands	1980
Australia	Tonga	1980
Australia	Tuvalu	1980
Australia	Vanuatu	1980
New Zealand	Fiji	1980
New Zealand	Kiribati	1980
New Zealand	Nauru	1980
New Zealand	Papua New Guinea	1980
New Zealand	Samoa	1980
New Zealand	Solomon Islands	1980
New Zealand	Tonga	1980
New Zealand	Tuvalu	1980
New Zealand	Vanuatu	1980
US	Israel	1985
Norway	Turkey	1991
Switzerland	Turkey	1991
Canada	Mexico	1992
Norway	Israel	1992
Switzerland	Israel	1992
US	Mexico	1992
EU	Israel	1995
EU	Tunisia	1995
EU	Turkey	1995
Canada	Chile	1996
Canada	Israel	1996
EU	Morocco	1996

Continued

Table A5.1 **Continued**

Industrialized Country	Developing Country	Year Signed
EU	Jordan	1997
EU	Mexico	1997
Norway	Morocco	1997
Switzerland	Morocco	1997
EU	South Africa	1999
New Zealand	Singapore	2000
Norway	Macedonia, FYR	2000
Norway	Mexico	2000
Switzerland	Macedonia, FYR	2000
Switzerland	Mexico	2000
US	Jordan	2000
Canada	Costa Rica	2001
EU	Egypt	2001
EU	Macedonia, FYR	2001
Norway	Jordan	2001
Switzerland	Jordan	2001
EU	Algeria	2002
EU	Chile	2002
EU	Lebanon	2002
Japan	Singapore	2002
Australia	Singapore	2003
Norway	Chile	2003
Switzerland	Chile	2003
US	Chile	2003
US	Singapore	2003
Australia	Thailand	2004
Japan	Mexico	2004
Norway	Lebanon	2004
Norway	Tunisia	2004
Switzerland	Lebanon	2004
Switzerland	Tunisia	2004
US	Costa Rica	2004
US	Dominican Republic	2004

Continued

Table A5.1 **Continued**

Industrialized Country	Developing Country	Year Signed
US	El Salvador	2004
US	Guatemala	2004
US	Honduras	2004
US	Morocco	2004
US	Nicaragua	2004
Japan	Malaysia	2005
New Zealand	Chile	2005
New Zealand	Thailand	2005
EU	Albania	2006
Japan	Philippines	2006
Norway	Botswana	2006
Norway	Lesotho	2006
Norway	Namibia	2006
Norway	South Africa	2006
Norway	Swaziland	2006
Switzerland	Botswana	2006
Switzerland	Lesotho	2006
Switzerland	Namibia	2006
Switzerland	South Africa	2006
Switzerland	Swaziland	2006
US	Colombia	2006
US	Oman	2006
US	Peru	2006
Japan	Chile	2007
Japan	Indonesia	2007
Japan	Thailand	2007
Norway	Egypt	2007
Switzerland	Egypt	2007
US	Panama	2007
Australia	Chile	2008
Canada	Colombia	2008
Canada	Peru	2008
EU	Antigua and Barbuda	2008

Continued

Table A5.1 **Continued**

Industrialized Country	Developing Country	Year Signed
EU	Barbados	2008
EU	Belize	2008
EU	Bosnia-Herzegovina	2008
EU	Côte d'Ivoire	2008
EU	Dominica	2008
EU	Dominican Republic	2008
EU	Grenada	2008
EU	Guyana	2008
EU	Jamaica	2008
EU	Montenegro	2008
EU	Serbia	2008
EU	St. Kitts and Nevis	2008
EU	St. Lucia	2008
EU	St. Vincent and Grenadines	2008
EU	Suriname	2008
EU	Trinidad and Tobago	2008
Japan	Cambodia	2008
Japan	Laos	2008
Japan	Myanmar	2008
Japan	Vietnam	2008
New Zealand	China	2008
Norway	Colombia	2008
Switzerland	Colombia	2008
Australia	Cambodia	2009
Australia	Indonesia	2009
Australia	Laos	2009
Australia	Malaysia	2009
Australia	Myanmar	2009
Australia	Philippines	2009
Australia	Vietnam	2009
Canada	Jordan	2009
EU	Cameroon	2009
EU	Fiji	2009

Continued

Table A5.1 **Continued**

Industrialized Country	Developing Country	Year Signed
EU	Madagascar	2009
EU	Mauritius	2009
EU	Papua New Guinea	2009
EU	Seychelles	2009
EU	Zimbabwe	2009
New Zealand	Cambodia	2009
New Zealand	Indonesia	2009
New Zealand	Laos	2009
New Zealand	Malaysia	2009
New Zealand	Myanmar	2009
New Zealand	Philippines	2009
New Zealand	Vietnam	2009
Norway	Albania	2009
Norway	Serbia	2009
Switzerland	Albania	2009
Switzerland	Serbia	2009
Canada	Panama	2010
Norway	Peru	2010
Norway	Ukraine	2010
Switzerland	Peru	2010
Switzerland	Ukraine	2010
Japan	India	2011
Japan	Peru	2011
Norway	Montenegro	2011
Switzerland	Montenegro	2011
EU	Colombia	2012
EU	Costa Rica	2012
EU	El Salvador	2012
EU	Guatemala	2012
EU	Honduras	2012
EU	Nicaragua	2012
EU	Panama	2012
EU	Peru	2012

6

Climate Finance for Developing Countries

> Accelerating climate change has caused serious impacts. Higher temperatures and extreme weather events are damaging food production, rising sea levels and more damaging storms are putting our coastal cities increasingly at risk and the impacts of climate change are already harming economies around the world, including those of the United States and China. These developments urgently require enhanced actions to tackle the challenge.
> —US—China Joint Announcement on Climate Change, November 12, 2014

The promise by industrialized countries to contribute significant amounts of funding for climate change adaptation and mitigation in developing countries was hailed as one of the few successes of a disappointing fifteenth meeting of the Conference of the Parties (COP 15) to the United Nations Framework Convention on Climate Change (UNFCCC). In the 2009 Copenhagen Accord, developed states made a commitment to provide $30 billion for the period 2010–2012, scaling up to $100 billion per year by 2020. This funding was to be "new and additional" to existing aid, with a "significant portion" flowing through a newly created Green Climate Fund.[1] The Accord provided no breakdown of contributions by donor, nor did it earmark a particular portion for either adaptation or mitigation or provide details as to where the money would be spent.

For many developing states, adapting to current problems associated with the changing climate is more important than mitigating future climate change. The benefits of successful adaptation projects can be location-specific and enjoyed immediately; the benefits of mitigation programs are diffuse and realized in the future. It is easy to understand why resource-strapped developing countries facing drought, storms, loss of land to sea level rise, and other immediate problems place significantly more weight on receiving adaptation funding. Added to this is the call for adaptation aid based on arguments of justice and historical fairness: experts estimate that 79% of global carbon emissions between 1850 and 2011 were produced by today's industrialized states, while the costs of climate change currently and in the future are disproportionately borne by developing countries.[2] Despite the documented need for adaptation assistance,[3] funding has been slow to materialize.[4] The United Nations Environment Program (UNEP) notes a significant finance gap between the amount needed for adaptation and that being spent.[5]

The majority of climate finance flowing from industrialized to developing countries has targeted mitigation rather than adaptation programs.[6] An explanation for this stems from a traditional understanding of adaptation finance as providing a private benefit for recipient countries while mitigation programs can create a public good enjoyed by all countries, including the donor. Climate change is a "global public bad"; reducing emissions anywhere benefits all countries. While the majority of accumulated greenhouse gases (GHGs) in the atmosphere originated in today's industrialized states, developing countries account for 63% of annual emissions currently.[7] It is essential that strategies designed to limit climate change include plans to reduce GHG emissions in developing countries. Given this, it is perhaps not surprising that to date industrialized countries have favored using more of their climate financing to further this goal rather than respond to calls for increased adaptation assistance.

There are signs that the balance in importance between mitigation and adaptation may be shifting. The Paris Agreement on climate change negotiated at the twenty-first meeting of the Conference of the Parties to the UNFCCC (COP 21) in December 2015 called for increased funding for adaptation and more balance between funding for mitigation and adaptation.[8] The targeted development framework suggests that the focus on adaptation will continue to increase. As climatic changes progress and increase the likelihood of spillovers from developing states affecting the well-being of industrialized countries, a greater emphasis on adaptation will emerge.

Targeted Development and Climate Finance

The targeted development framework generates predictions regarding the cross-national distribution of climate funding. Projects funded to address climate change adaptation or mitigation often contain both climate-related and development goals. For example, the 2015 Paris Agreement calls for "making finance flows consistent with a pathway towards low greenhouse gas emissions and climate-resilient development" (Article 2.1(c)). Thus industrialized states can often use the same funds to simultaneously pursue desired outcomes regarding both development and climate. According to the model developed in Chapter 3, when an industrialized state uses the same funds for development and other purposes it will seek to maximize the total benefit to itself, summed across development and other outcomes. In this case, benefits include both development and climate change adaptation or mitigation. The simultaneous use of "climate" funds for both development and climate will skew them away from the most efficient allocation for achieving climate goals. There is also an additional concern that failure to adapt to climatic changes will increase spillovers from affected states. Anticipating this, an industrialized state should be most interested in funding adaptation projects in countries from which spillovers, should they occur, would have adverse impacts on itself.

This chapter analyzes cross-national allocation of funding for climate change adaptation and mitigation for the period 2010–2012 from 23 industrialized countries to 123 developing countries. To summarize the main expectation, if climate finance decisions fit within the targeted development framework, then the analysis should reveal the following:

- Funding for both mitigation and adaptation will be skewed away from its most efficient use to address climate-related problems and will be at least partially guided by the same self-interested factors that determine foreign aid allocation more generally.
- Climate adaptation funding should disproportionately respond to climate-related changes in countries from which spillovers to the industrialized state from those changes are expected to be greatest, which include those closest to the industrialized state.

Serious attention to the importance of tracking climate finance only emerged following the signing of the 2009 Copenhagen Accords. The relatively new and evolving nature of climate finance presents both challenges and opportunities for analysis. On the challenges side, data are limited and donors themselves may still be determining their ideal strategies for using climate financing; they are also new to the idea of cataloging funding for climate purposes. Data limitations and the possibility of changes in donor behavior as they adjust to the new realities of large-scale climate finance mean that conclusions are more tentative than in established policy areas, and more apt to change going forward. However, this also presents an opportunity to test the theory put forth in this book in a new and evolving setting—to see if there is evidence that a desire to promote targeted development can explain government actions even as policy rolls out in a relatively new issue area. Additionally, the theory provides insights into how policy may evolve in the future, which can be useful to analysts attempting to understand new policies and forecast trends.

The remainder of this section further probes expectations for adaptation and mitigation financing if industrialized states are motivated by a targeted development strategy.

Adaptation

There is clearly a link between the negative impacts on a country due to climatic changes and broader development concerns. Multiple studies have argued that environmental changes are likely to have negative effects on output and economic growth.[9] Analysis by Frances Moore and Delavane Diaz shows that the negative impact of climate change on development may be much larger than previously estimated.[10] Robert McLeman notes that environmental impacts interact with other factors to drive migration outcomes.[11] Others argue that the impacts of climate change can exacerbate conflict.[12]

Industrialized states will be concerned with spillovers from developing countries due to climate change in the same way they are concerned with development-related spillovers more generally. The allocation of adaptation resources will be skewed to meet an industrialized state's broader development goals, rather than responding to relative need for adaptation assistance across developing countries. This implies that, in general, the allocation of funds for climate adaptation will be similar to the allocation of development assistance more broadly, a claim that is tested below. However, when a climate shock occurs that increases the likely impact of spillovers on an industrialized state, the state should respond with increased funding for adaptation. This suggests that an industrialized state will increase adaptation assistance to countries that experience negative climatic shocks, but only (or at least disproportionately) in states from which it fears spillovers. This is similar to the way in which aid donors are shown to respond to poor governance in Chapter 4, increasing aid in poorly governed, nearby states to mitigate spillovers related to poor governance. The empirical analysis tests whether an industrialized state responds differently to climate shocks in a country based on proximity to itself.

Mitigation

Limiting GHG production is a global public good. Reductions of emissions anywhere, financed by anyone, will have the same effect on limiting global warming. The option to fund programs in developing countries that will decrease future GHG emissions is attractive in that the same amount of emission reductions is generally less expensive in these states. Industrialized countries have well-established infrastructures that may be costly to change; where cost-effective, many of these states have already been implementing policy changes that have stabilized or reduced their gas GHG. As a result, there is less "low-hanging fruit" in industrialized states for emissions reductions. Developing countries, on the other hand, currently produce the majority of emissions and their emissions are still rising. They are also still rolling out infrastructure and can face choices between high-emissions and low-emissions technologies as they move forward. Installing or switching to technologies that produce fewer emissions may be prohibitively costly for many developing states to undertake on their own, but may also represent the most cost-effective way of reducing emissions from a global social welfare perspective. Thus outside financing for climate mitigation in developing countries can play an important role in achieving global emissions reduction targets.

The public good nature of the climate change problem creates an incentive for free-riding,[13] with each nation seeking to shoulder as little of the emissions reduction burden as possible while still achieving the desired goal of minimizing climate change. However, if each nation acts accordingly the problem will not be adequately addressed and—from a socially optimal perspective—too much climate change will occur. In situations in which countries might each have an incentive to underprovide, but where underprovision by all is worse for each than collective provision, countries might form an international institution to coordinate their actions and monitor shirking.[14]

While emission reductions represent a global public good, the total effects of climate finance ostensibly used for mitigation may also include other benefits. Finance for climate change can be used to pursue multiple goals of the funding state in the recipient state. In particular, industrialized states can use the same funds to simultaneously pursue development and climate mitigation.

An industrialized state seeking to promote climate change mitigation and development with the same funds will target these funds to maximize the benefits to itself summed across both goals. As a result, funding to pursue climate change mitigation through programs in developing countries will be skewed toward those countries where the funds can also provide other benefits, including through development promotion, to the funding state. For example, an industrialized state may be deciding between funding a development-oriented climate mitigation program in Country A or using the same resources to fund a development-oriented climate mitigation program in Country B. Country A is particularly efficient at using climate mitigation finance and the program in Country A yields the highest return in terms of emissions reductions. Country B is somewhat less efficient in emissions reductions, but a dollar spent there provides the industrialized country funder with other, non-climate, benefits (such as reduced spillovers from underdevelopment) in addition to the reduced emissions. If the sum of emissions benefits and non-emissions benefits to the industrialized country is higher when funds are spent in Country B, then the industrialized country will divert funds from the more efficient state (from a climate mitigation perspective) to Country B.

As a result of simultaneously pursuing multiple objectives with funds designated for climate mitigation, industrialized states will not maximize emissions reductions per dollar spent, except in the extremely unlikely scenarios that emissions reductions and private benefits are maximized through the same allocation pattern, or that potential non-emission benefits to the industrialized state from climate mitigation funds are zero. This is not to say that efficiency in producing results for climate change mitigation is not important in driving funds. Rather, the argument is that this is not the sole driver: funding patterns will also reflect attempts to increase donor utility through development (or other private benefits). If true, the empirical analysis should uncover evidence that the cross-national allocation of funding for climate change mitigation is partly driven by the same considerations that motivate development assistance more generally. In this case, attempts to mitigate climate change through funding projects in developing countries will suffer from inefficient provision—from the point of view of climate change mitigation—as funds are used not to provide the maximum impact in terms of climate mitigation but to provide the largest benefits to funding states. However, the presence of other benefits should also decrease the incentives to free-ride that are usually put forth to explain lack of contributions for financing public goods.

Institutions for Climate Funding

The discussion of climate finance so far suggests that the prospect of a coordinated international response to climate change adaptation and mitigation through international institutions will have only limited appeal for industrialized states. Funding states will prefer to target adaptation assistance where it will provide the most benefit to themselves in terms of reduced spillovers. They will prefer to target mitigation assistance to countries where the funds can produce benefits in addition to the public good of reduced emissions. The amount and location of non-climate benefits will differ across industrialized states based on the extent of their interactions with various developing countries, leading to divergent preferences for the allocation of climate funding.

In spite of this, multiple international institutions have been set up to finance climate change adaptation and mitigation projects in developing countries. Some funds, such as the Carbon Fund at the World Bank, represent new initiatives undertaken by established institutions. In other cases, such as with the Green Climate Fund, new institutions have been created by the UNFCCC to assist with the flow of climate change–related resources across countries. Their existence could provide evidence against the preference by donors for a bilateral response.

However, on examination, both the structure of the institutions and the low financial commitments made by donors suggest that they do not represent an example of funders relinquishing control over resources, as they might do if they were motivated to maximize the global efficiency of resources for the purposes of adaptation and mitigation.

Climate finance institutions have been created with internal structures that often duplicate, rather than sidestep, the posturing by donors that would be present in broader negotiations. To date they are not well funded and have been slow to approve projects and get funding to potential recipients. Jonah Busch of the Center for Global Development notes the slow process for obtaining funding through the Carbon Fund, which was set up to pay countries for avoiding deforestation. Busch notes that after "eight years writing a charter, negotiating a rulebook, and vetting proposals" the Fund has finally granted provisional approval to two country programs. The process through the approval pipeline is slow, in part because proposals must "please 11 donors plus the World Bank at every stage."[15] The Green Climate Fund was established following the signing of the Copenhagen Accord in 2009 and a "significant portion" of funding promised by industrialized states—which has a goal of reaching $100 billion annually by 2020—is meant to be tracked through this fund. As of the end of 2015 the fund had received a total of $1.6 billion in funding, had approved only eight projects worth a total of only $168 million, and had yet to actually disburse *any* project funds.[16]

Funding Patterns for Adaptation and Mitigation

The models estimated in this chapter build off of those estimated in Chapter 4 for the cross-country allocation of aid commitments. Each set of results presented in this section—unlike in Chapter 4—includes models in which the dependent variable is confined to aid specifically designated by the donor as targeting climate adaptation or mitigation. All models also include key independent variables related to the need for adaptation or mitigation assistance. The goal is to assess the importance of non-climate concerns in dictating donor allocation patterns as well as the impact of climate-related variables in determining aid flows. All results are reported first for adaptation or mitigation aid and then for total aid commitments. The results for total aid are important to determine whether any observed relationships between climate variables and climate aid correspond to changes in overall aid levels or are associated with diversion of aid from other purposes with little effect on aggregate aid amounts.

The analysis covers the period from 2010 to 2012. The first reporting year for foreign aid following the signing of the Copenhagen Accord, in which wealthy donors pledged to increase aid specifically for the purposes of addressing climate change adaptation and mitigation needs in developing countries, is 2010. Going along with this, 2010 is also the first year that donors had the option of "marking" their aid commitments as focusing on climate change adaptation and/or mitigation projects when reporting to the OECD. Thus, from 2010 to 2012 it is possible to look at the relationship between variables of interest and aid specifically marked for climate-related purposes; data on some key independent variables are only available through 2012.

Data

The data on aid for climate adaptation and mitigation are potentially more problematic than data on overall aid commitments. While marking of records is encouraged, donors are not required to tag their aid spending by climate change purpose. Historically, it has taken at least a few years for all donors to begin reporting consistently when new categorizations for aid are introduced. Thus the data now are likely an incomplete picture of all projects that can be linked to adaptation and/or mitigation purposes. To smooth these data, rather than conducting the analysis annually I collapse the period 2010–2012 into a single cross-section of all dyads. In doing this measures of aid, migrants, military assistance, arms transfers, and number of people affected by a natural disaster are summed across the three years, *Security Council Member* equals one if the recipient was a member of the UN Security Council for any time between 2010 and 2012, and other variables that change over time are averaged over the period. This section describes variables introduced here for the first time; sources and details for control variables will be the same as in Chapter 4 and are not repeated in detail here.

Aid Variables

Three different dependent variables are used in the analysis. Tables 6.1 and 6.2 include models in which the dependent variable is the log of (one plus) aid designated by the donor as financing adaptation to climate change in the recipient. Table 6.3 includes models using the log of (one plus) aid marked by the donor for use in climate mitigation. Aid totals for these variables are calculated from the OECD DAC/CRS "Rio Markers entire dataset."[17] Commitments are summed by donor-recipient-year for all projects in which the "climateAdaptation" marker was set to "1" for adaptation aid or the "climateMitigation" marker was set to "1" for mitigation aid. They are then summed to create a value for each donor–recipient pair for the period 2010–2012 for both adaptation and mitigation, which is then logged for the analysis. All tables also include analogous models in which the dependent variable is the natural log of total aid commitments; these data are taken from Table DAC3a as described in Chapter 4.

Adaptation Relevant Variables

Climate-related shocks provide a measure of potential need for adaptation assistance. Two climate shock variables, one measuring increased temperature in an already hot country (*Hot Shock*) and one measuring decreased precipitation in an already dry country (*Dry Shock*), are included in the analysis. Data on average annual temperature and total annual precipitation from the Climatic Research Unit were used to construct these measures.[18] Each shock variable is constructed to capture two components: baseline values and change. Both are important in that the impact of a change in temperature or precipitation likely depends on the baseline values for these variables: an increase in temperature is more likely to create problems if the country is already relatively hot and decreased precipitation should have a larger negative impact in a country if it is already relatively dry.

The *Hot Shock* variable is constructed as follows. First, for each country-year two variables based on rolling averages are produced: one is the annual temperature averaged over the previous five years (t-1 through t-5) and the other is the annual temperature averaged over the five-year period preceding that (t-6 through t-10). Since the analysis is a cross-section of the period 2010–2012, these are then averaged within a country for these three years. *Hot Shock* is coded as one if both of the following hold: (1) the average temperature for the period t-6 through t-10 is in the top 10% of values for this variable in the data and (2) the average temperature measured over the period t-1 through t-5 is hotter than the value for the period t-6 through t-10. *Hot Shock* is coded zero otherwise. Thus to be coded as "1" on this variable a country must have had an average annual temperature in the top 10% of all countries in the earlier period (t-6 through t-10) and also have experienced an increase in average temperature since that period. *Dry Shock* is coded similarly: to be coded as a "1" on this variable, a country must have had annual precipitation in the lowest 10% in the first period (t-6 through t-10) and must have experienced a decrease in annual precipitation from the period t-6 through t-10 to the period t-1 through t-5. Approximately 3.7% of observations are coded as one for *Hot Shock* and 5.9% of observations are coded as one for *Dry Shock*.

Mitigation Relevant Variables

Given that the location of emissions is irrelevant for their impact on climate change, a distribution of mitigation finance that is efficient from a climate change perspective should privilege those areas where the most mitigation—either from current or expected future emissions under business as usual—can be achieved for the least cost. There is no direct measure of this, but there are several available measures that should be associated with increased mitigation finance if donors are seeking to get the most mitigation per dollar spent. Countries where development and emissions increases are occurring rapidly should be likely candidates for mitigation programs that can be used to help the rapid development proceed in a manner that produces fewer emissions. Two measures of GHG emissions are used, both from the World Bank's World Development Indicators.[19] The first is the log of total GHG emissions (in kilotons) produced by the developing country for each year; when collapsed for the 2010–2012 period the maximum value for the three years is used. The second is the percent change in the developing country's GHG emissions in year t relative to 1990; again, when the data are collapsed the maximum value recorded for the years 2010–2012 is used. Total GHG emissions and/or the growth in emissions should be positively associated with mitigation aid if donors are targeting the aid to maximize impact on GHG emissions. Also included from the World Development Indicators are measures of growth in GDP per capita (*Income Growth*) and growth in urban population (*Urban Growth*) to determine whether mitigation assistance is related to broader measures of growth and urbanization.[20]

Adaptation Results

When donors are pursuing targeted development with climate funding, the expectation is that the funds will not necessarily flow to where they are most needed, but to where they might benefit the donor by decreasing negative spillovers from underdevelopment while also, potentially, serving adaptation purposes. This suggests that adaptation aid will follow similar patterns to total aid flows rather than being diverted to the countries most in need of assistance. It also implies that donors will be more likely to respond to climate shocks with increased assistance if the shocks occur in proximate states, being less concerned about spillovers from more distant shocks. Tables 6.1 and 6.2 explore these hypotheses using the variables *Hot Shock* and *Dry Shock*.

Table 6.1 estimates models similar to those for foreign aid allocation in Chapter 4 for both adaptation aid (Models 1 and 2) and total aid (Models 3 and 4), with the variables *Hot Shock* included in Models 1 and 3 and *Dry Shock* included in Models 2 and 4. The results indicate that, on average, neither adaptation aid nor total aid increases when an already hot area experiences a temperature increase or an already dry area experiences a decrease in precipitation: the coefficients on both *Hot Shock* and *Dry Shock* show no evidence of a relationship between these variables and aid allocation. Of course, temperature and precipitation changes are only two of the potential impacts of climate

Table 6.1 **Determinants of Aid for Climate Adaptation 2010–2012**

	Model 1	Model 2	Model 3	Model 4
	Adaptation Aid	Adaptation Aid	Total Aid	Total Aid
Hot Shock	0.301		−0.366	
	(0.87)		(0.47)	
Dry Shock		−2.458		−0.104
		(0.29)		(0.91)
Distance	−0.858	−0.831	−1.478***	−1.482***
	(0.25)	(0.24)	(0.00)	(0.00)
Population	−0.519	−0.451	0.308**	0.314**
	(0.23)	(0.28)	(0.04)	(0.04)
US Military Assistance	0.110	0.129	0.054	0.055
	(0.34)	(0.26)	(0.13)	(0.14)
SIPRI Arms Transfers	0.029	0.025	−0.018	−0.018
	(0.64)	(0.68)	(0.21)	(0.22)
UN Vote Distance	2.528**	2.620***	0.224	0.267
	(0.01)	(0.00)	(0.51)	(0.45)
Security Council Member	1.127	1.018	0.040	0.043
	(0.36)	(0.40)	(0.94)	(0.93)
Colony	8.144***	8.041***	2.513***	2.480***
	(0.00)	(0.00)	(0.00)	(0.00)
Donor Exports	1.001***	0.993***	0.262***	0.252***
	(0.00)	(0.00)	(0.00)	(0.00)
Donor Imports	0.504***	0.477***	0.149***	0.163***
	(0.00)	(0.00)	(0.00)	(0.00)
Migration	0.616***	0.647***	0.346***	0.345***
	(0.00)	(0.00)	(0.00)	(0.00)
Income	−4.044***	−3.928***	−1.389***	−1.417***
	(0.00)	(0.00)	(0.00)	(0.00)
Disaster	0.457***	0.409***	0.139***	0.130***
	(0.00)	(0.00)	(0.00)	(0.01)
Civil War	−2.620**	−2.624**	−0.354	−0.353
	(0.04)	(0.04)	(0.43)	(0.44)

Continued

Table 6.1 **Continued**

	Model 1	Model 2	Model 3	Model 4
	Adaptation Aid	Adaptation Aid	Total Aid	Total Aid
Democracy	0.875***	0.749***	0.062	0.081
	(0.00)	(0.01)	(0.60)	(0.49)
Constant	−3.195	−4.209	20.649***	23.003***
	(0.71)	(0.62)	(0.00)	(0.00)
Sigma	10.261***	10.193***		
	(0.00)	(0.00)		
Fixed Effects	Donor	Donor	Donor	Donor
Observations	2,841	2,864	2,841	2,864
Censored	1,702	1,702		
Uncensored	1,116	1,116		
Industrialized Countries	23	23	23	23
Developing Countries	124	125	124	125

Dependent variable is the log of (one plus) aid commitments for adaptation or total aid commitments for the period 2010–2012. Tobit model specified when the dependent variable is adaptation aid; OLS model specified when the dependent variable is total aid. Cross-section analysis, p-values in parentheses; standard errors clustered on recipient. *Significant at the 10% level; **Significant at the 5% level; ***Significant at the 1% level.

change; it is possible that adaptation aid is responding to measures of increased vulnerability not captured here.

It does appear that adaptation aid is influenced by some of the same considerations that help determine bilateral aid allocation decisions more broadly. Many of the variables that are associated with higher overall bilateral aid allocation, as shown in Chapter 4, are also associated with increased climate adaptation aid: in Models 1 and 2 the coefficients on the variables *Colony, Donor Exports, Donor Imports,* and *Migration* are each positive and significant, consistent with the findings from Chapter 4.

The targeted development framework implies that donors will be most concerned with climate shocks in developing countries if they are likely to create negative spillovers for themselves. While on average there is no relationship between allocation aid and *Hot Shock* and *Dry Shock* in Table 6.1, the theory predicts that this relationship is likely to vary by distance, with donors more likely to respond to climate shocks in nearby countries. To examine this, the models in Table 6.2 include an interaction term between the shock variables and *Distance*. Models 5 and 6 show that the relationship between adaptation aid and both *Hot Shock* and *Dry Shock* varies with distance. The coefficients on the

Table 6.2 **Determinants of Aid for Climate Adaptation by Distance, 2010-2012**

	Model 5	Model 6	Model 7	Model 8
	Adaptation Aid	Adaptation Aid	Total Aid	Total Aid
Hot Shock	52.961***		1.700	
	(0.00)		(0.80)	
Hot Shock*Distance	−6.109***		−0.239	
	(0.00)		(0.74)	
Dry Shock		27.383*		11.729
		(0.06)		(0.24)
Dry Shock*Distance		−3.520**		−1.386
		(0.04)		(0.26)
Distance	−0.727	−0.701	−1.474***	−1.426***
	(0.33)	(0.33)	(0.00)	(0.00)
Population	−0.497	−0.453	0.309**	0.314**
	(0.25)	(0.28)	(0.04)	(0.04)
US Military Assistance	0.112	0.125	0.054	0.054
	(0.33)	(0.27)	(0.13)	(0.15)
SIPRI Arms Transfers	0.028	0.021	−0.019	−0.019
	(0.65)	(0.72)	(0.21)	(0.17)
UN Vote Distance	2.474**	2.545***	0.223	0.241
	(0.01)	(0.01)	(0.51)	(0.49)
Security Council Member	1.109	1.044	0.039	0.056
	(0.36)	(0.39)	(0.94)	(0.91)
Colony	8.141***	8.004***	2.513***	2.461***
	(0.00)	(0.00)	(0.00)	(0.00)
Donor Exports	0.995***	1.003***	0.262***	0.255***
	(0.00)	(0.00)	(0.00)	(0.00)
Donor Imports	0.499***	0.474***	0.149***	0.162***
	(0.00)	(0.00)	(0.00)	(0.00)
Migration	0.621***	0.649***	0.346***	0.348***
	(0.00)	(0.00)	(0.00)	(0.00)
Income	−4.025***	−3.936***	−1.388***	−1.421***
	(0.00)	(0.00)	(0.00)	(0.00)
Disaster	0.452***	0.405***	0.139***	0.128***
	(0.00)	(0.00)	(0.00)	(0.01)

Continued

Table 6.2 **Continued**

	Model 5	Model 6	Model 7	Model 8
	Adaptation Aid	Adaptation Aid	Total Aid	Total Aid
Civil War	−2.619**	−2.588**	−0.355	−0.348
	(0.04)	(0.04)	(0.43)	(0.44)
Democracy	0.864***	0.744**	0.062	0.081
	(0.00)	(0.01)	(0.60)	(0.50)
Constant	−4.376	−5.127	17.248***	16.961***
	(0.61)	(0.54)	(0.00)	(0.00)
Sigma	10.241***	10.187***		
	(0.00)	(0.00)		
Fixed Effects	Donor	Donor	Donor	Donor
Observations	2,841	2,864	2,841	2,864
Censored	1,702	1,702		
Uncensored	1,116	1,116		
Industrialized Countries	23	23	23	23
Developing Countries	124	125	124	125

Dependent variable is the log of (one plus) aid commitments for adaptation or total aid commitments for the period 2010-2012. Tobit model specified when the dependent variable is adaptation aid; OLS model specified when the dependent variable is total aid. Cross-section analysis with p-values in parentheses; standard errors clustered on recipient. *Significant at the 10% level; **Significant at the 5% level; ***Significant at the 1% level.

interaction terms are negative and significant, suggesting that countries near a donor that experience a climate shock are likely to receive more adaptation aid than is received by more distant countries. Coefficients on the same variables in Models 7 and 8, where the dependent variable is total aid allocation, show a similar pattern but are not significant. Given the limited timeframe and early stages of collecting data on adaptation aid, it is likely too early to determine whether the pattern of increased adaptation aid results in increases in total aid flows or simply a redirection or recoding of existing aid allocation to reflect adaptation relevance.

Attention to the need for adaptation aid is relatively new, as is the practice of marking aid data to reflect whether or not it is used for adaptation purposes. Given this, it would be inappropriate to draw strong conclusions from this analysis, and the results should be interpreted as suggestive rather than definitive. Within these limits, it is possible to say that allocation patterns of adaptation aid for the first years data were collected suggest that it may not go to the most vulnerable countries as measured by the temperature and precipitation shocks employed here. Additionally, adaptation aid does follow some of the same allocation patterns as overall aid flows, and the link between adaptation aid and shocks appears to vary with distance between donor and recipient.

Mitigation Results

Table 6.3 shows results for models of mitigation aid and total aid allocation, including several variables that might capture mitigation potential as well as other possible determinants of aid flows. The overall GHG emissions level does not appear to be related to either mitigation aid or total aid. However, greater growth in emissions from a country's level of emissions in 1990 is associated with modest increases in both mitigation and total aid, as is income growth. More rapid urban growth does not appear to be associated with higher aid flows. As with adaptation aid, Models 9 and 10 show that variables associated with higher total aid allocation in Chapter 4 are also associated with higher levels of mitigation aid. Less distant countries, trade partners, countries with larger migrant flows to the donor, former colonies, and those on the UN Security Council receive more climate change mitigation assistance.

Mitigation aid appears to be related both to mitigation potential, as measured by recent increases in GHG emissions and growth, and to other donor objectives. This fits the pattern predicted by the targeted development model, in which industrialized states seek to achieve reductions in GHG emissions (a public good) but the allocation pattern is skewed to also reflect donors' individual interests in development promotion. The result is likely to be a cross-country allocation of climate mitigation assistance that is inefficient from the standpoint of decreasing the level of future climate change.

Discussion

The allocation of resources by industrialized countries for climate change mitigation and adaptation in developing states is a relatively new development in international relations. As such, it is not possible to know how patterns will unfold as the area becomes more established, which is almost certain to occur given the importance of climate change as an issue linking industrialized and developing countries. The results presented in this chapter suggest that, at this early stage, financing is most likely not allocated based primarily on need for adaptation assistance or potential for climate change mitigation. Instead, the allocation of climate finance is consistent with an explanation based on industrialized states targeting their interactions with developing countries to maximize their own well-being. This results in inefficient allocation from the standpoint of achieving climate-related goals. While this type of skewing of

Table 6.3 **Determinants of Aid for Climate Mitigation, 2010–2012**

	Model 9 Mitigation Aid	Model 10 Mitigation Aid	Model 11 Total Aid	Model 12 Total Aid
GHG Emissions	−0.110 (0.83)		−0.151 (0.40)	
GHG Change from 1990		0.004** (0.05)		0.001*** (0.01)
Income Growth	0.394** (0.03)	0.388** (0.02)	0.107* (0.05)	0.104* (0.06)
Urban Growth	0.093 (0.80)	−0.045 (0.90)	−0.027 (0.83)	−0.085 (0.51)
Distance	−1.422** (0.05)	−1.446** (0.05)	−1.625*** (0.00)	−1.626*** (0.00)
Population	−0.136 (0.85)	−0.178 (0.71)	0.472* (0.06)	0.333** (0.02)
US Military Assistance	0.070 (0.55)	0.092 (0.44)	0.051 (0.14)	0.065* (0.07)
SIPRI Arms Transfers	−0.042 (0.46)	−0.045 (0.43)	−0.018 (0.21)	−0.021 (0.17)
UN Vote Distance	1.821* (0.07)	1.637 (0.10)	0.346 (0.29)	0.312 (0.34)
Security Council Member	1.970* (0.10)	2.106* (0.08)	0.158 (0.77)	0.244 (0.66)
Colony	6.928*** (0.00)	6.786*** (0.00)	2.601*** (0.00)	2.542*** (0.00)
Donor Exports	1.144*** (0.00)	1.168*** (0.00)	0.251*** (0.00)	0.252*** (0.00)
Donor Imports	0.582*** (0.00)	0.549*** (0.00)	0.161*** (0.00)	0.151*** (0.00)
Migration	0.597*** (0.00)	0.627*** (0.00)	0.314*** (0.00)	0.333*** (0.00)
Income	−3.726*** (0.00)	−3.915*** (0.00)	−1.402*** (0.00)	−1.545*** (0.00)
Disaster	0.305*** (0.00)	0.280*** (0.01)	0.125*** (0.00)	0.117*** (0.01)

Continued

Table 6.3 **Continued**

	Model 9	Model 10	Model 11	Model 12
	Mitigation Aid	Mitigation Aid	Total Aid	Total Aid
Civil War	−2.963**	−3.076**	−0.423	−0.447
	(0.03)	(0.02)	(0.36)	(0.33)
Democracy	1.279***	1.340***	0.080	0.131
	(0.00)	(0.00)	(0.50)	(0.27)
Constant	−9.395	−8.310	20.811***	22.244***
	(0.34)	(0.36)	(0.00)	(0.00)
Sigma	10.614***	10.579***		
	(0.00)	(0.00)		
Observations	2,921	2,921	2,921	2,921
Censored	1,772	1,772		
Uncensored	1,149	1,149		
Industrialized Countries	23	23	23	23
Developing Countries	128	128	128	128

Dependent variable is the log of (one plus) aid commitments for mitigation or total aid commitments for the period 2010–2012. Tobit model specified when the dependent variable is mitigation aid; OLS model specified when the dependent variable is total aid. Cross-section analysis, p-values in parentheses; standard errors clustered on recipient. *Significant at the 10% level; **Significant at the 5% level; ***Significant at the 1% level.

resources from efficient allocation for their stated purposes to pursue broader foreign policy goals is not new (think of "development" assistance during the Cold War), the fact that development goals are now behind the diversion of resources from other purposes marks a change from earlier periods. The evidence suggests that industrialized states wish to help with climate adaptation, but wish to do so in the countries where adaptation will lessen spillovers to themselves. These same states are willing to finance climate mitigation, but in choosing where to invest they are influenced by the same concerns that drive their development agendas more broadly.

The targeted development framework predicts that these patterns are not aberrations belonging to the early stages of a new issue area. Rather, diversion of promised resources from their efficient allocation from a climate perspective to simultaneously pursue other agendas vis-à-vis developing states—including promoting development where it suits their own interests—will likely remain the norm for industrialized country funders. For proponents of multilateral action on climate change, the findings in this chapter and predictions from the targeted development framework are not encouraging. From the point of view of an industrialized state seeking to maximize its own utility, it is not clear that delegation to an international body will yield better results than a bilateral policy. An industrialized state is likely to view a situation of bilateral decision-making in which it can simultaneously pursue multiple goals with climate finance as preferable to a situation in which a multilateral institution allocates financing in a way that increases climate efficiency at the expense of the industrialized state's private benefits.

This preference for bilateral provision will not necessarily result in worse results on adaptation and mitigation. The larger the role of private benefits in determining allocation, the less free-riding and more finance under bilateral provision compared to what would exist under an exclusively multilateral regime. Yet this funding is likely to be less efficient at producing desired climate-related outcomes, as it is skewed to provide benefits to donor states. The net impact on outcomes of this tradeoff between level of funding and efficiency is currently unknown.

It is worth noting that industrialized states may view sole reliance on bilateral provision as suboptimal. After states maximize their utility through bilateral allocation of resources, there are likely some situations where the marginal cost of funding additional adaptation or mitigation is less than the sum of the marginal benefits. These remain unfunded through bilateral provision if the marginal costs exceed the benefits to each industrialized state individually, even if collectively these are worth funding. There is a role for an institution to fill this gap, providing the remaining public good that bilateral action fails to finance. In this case, a mixed outcome of both bilateral and multilateral provision might provide the highest total benefit to industrialized states. The desirability of thinking of bilateral and multilateral responses as complements rather than substitutes is taken up in Chapter 7.

7

Conclusion: Rethinking Development

> The Cold War threat has been replaced by a diverse but interconnected set of threats and risks, which affect the United Kingdom directly and also have the potential to undermine wider international stability. They include international terrorism, weapons of mass destruction, conflicts and failed states, pandemics, and trans-national crime. These and other threats and risks are driven by a diverse and interconnected set of underlying factors, including climate change, competition for energy, poverty and poor governance, demographic changes and globalisation.
> —National Security Strategy of the United Kingdom, 2008[1]

Residents of industrialized countries do not live in an impenetrable bubble. They cannot insulate themselves from problems originating in other countries that have the potential to spill over borders. This was true of the 1918 flu pandemic, it was true of Nazi aggression in the 1930s, it was true of the nuclear arms race during the Cold War, and it is true for violent extremism today. It is also, increasingly, true for problems associated with underdevelopment. As Paul Collier rather colorfully notes, "a cesspool of misery next to a world of growing prosperity is both terrible for those in the cesspool and dangerous for those who live next to it."[2]

Development as Foreign Policy

Recognizing the growing ability of underdevelopment abroad to inflict costs on their own citizens, governments in industrialized countries have responded with a strategy of targeted development promotion. They seek to promote development when and where it will have a beneficial impact on themselves. One result is a higher priority for development on the foreign policy agenda in industrialized states. The opening quote of this chapter from the United Kingdom's National Security Strategy highlights the shift in both threats and responses as the world moved from the Cold War to an era of increased globalization. Concern for the role of underdevelopment in undermining security in the United Kingdom has not displaced concern over terrorism or weapons of mass destruction. Rather, it has risen to be a serious national security issue addressed alongside of, and seen as interconnected with, issues more traditionally found in the realm of security studies.

This change in thinking about development has been evident across industrialized states. In the United States the direction and scope of the shift came into focus soon after the attacks of September 11, 2001. This is seen in the National Security Strategy released by the Bush administration in 2002, in which the importance of overseas economic development is featured prominently. The 2010 National Security Strategy released by the Obama administration continued this emphasis; the phrase "diplomacy and development" appears seven times in the document, which also includes numerous other references to overseas development.[3] The Swiss Foreign Policy Strategy asserts that "in committing ourselves to preventing conflicts, alleviating poverty, and protecting the environment, Switzerland is fostering international stability, which in turn has a positive influence on the country's [Switzerland's] security, access to resources, and prosperity."[4] Japan's National Security Strategy discusses "development issues and global issues that could hinder peace and stability of the international community, such as poverty, energy issues, widening disparity, climate change, natural disasters, and food-related issues."[5] The importance of development is broadly recognized in these foreign policy and national security documents, not simply relegated to discussions in foreign aid charters. No longer are development concerns forced to the bottom of the foreign policy agenda, tangential at best to the well-being of industrialized states. In an increasingly connected world, development is a key component in foreign policy.

The purpose of this book has been to develop a theory of targeted, self-interested development and to demonstrate the theory at work in multiple issue areas. The linking of underdevelopment with the security and well-being of industrialized states has meant not only an increased focus on underdevelopment as an important foreign policy issue, but an emphasis on targeting development policy toward areas where it can have the most beneficial impact on policy making states. Conceptualizing development as self-interest breaks both from theories that relegate development to an area of "low politics" as well as from theories that suggest the increased emphasis on development is a manifestation of a "moral vision"[6] to help those in poorer countries. Instead, targeted development is a rational response on the part of the government in an industrialized country to promote development when and where it is likely to increase the utility of its own state. This does not mean that development is never superseded by other concerns, nor does it mean that development policy is never influenced by humanitarian concerns; there are certainly examples to support each of these possibilities. However, a systematic explanation of industrialized country interactions with developing states in the current international system requires a prominent place for the role played by the pursuit of targeted, self-interested development.

Issue Areas

The strategy of targeted development has influenced policy across multiple issue areas. In foreign aid, the area arguably linked most closely with development, the amount of aid flows has increased since 2001, its cross-national allocation has changed significantly from earlier periods, and a newfound appreciation for tailoring the composition of aid to the needs and capabilities of recipients has emerged. In some donors the increased importance of foreign aid has been remarkably stable across ideological dividing lines. Chapter 4 shows that across industrialized states this increased aid is targeted not necessarily toward the countries most in need of assistance, but toward the countries where development will provide the greatest increase in well-being for the aid-granting state.

The focus on increasing development has led to a proliferation of reciprocal trade agreements between industrialized and developing countries; such agreements between wealthy and developing states were almost nonexistent twenty-five years ago. As Chapter 5 demonstrates, these agreements are not only, or even disproportionately, with the most important developing country markets but also with small, poor states where underdevelopment has the ability to create spillovers for an industrialized country. Governments in industrialized states overcome significant domestic political economy constraints to obtain these agreements when they believe the development externalities are worth the domestic political cost.

The desire of industrialized states to enhance their own well-being through development abroad also appears to influence the allocation of resources in areas such as climate finance, where development is not the primary stated purpose of funds. An examination of the early years of climate finance in Chapter 6 suggests that mitigation and adaptation funds are being diverted to areas where they can provide development benefits to the donor states, rather than being spent where adaptation assistance is most needed or where mitigation resources can most efficiently combat climate change. The desire to promote targeted development results in the diversion of resources ostensibly allocated for other purposes, similar to the way development resources themselves were diverted to further other goals during the Cold War. More generally, the issues examined in this book should be viewed as representing a broader trend of increased importance for promoting development in a targeted manner, which can potentially influence any issue area in which industrialized countries are interacting with developing states.

Implementation and Effectiveness

The pivot toward focusing on development has created an opportunity for partnership between industrialized and developing states. When it comes to promoting development within a country the interests of the governments can coincide, with both desiring an increase in development that the industrialized state has the resources to finance. This convergence of interests has led to comparisons with the Marshall Plan, an early instance of targeted development abroad. In announcing the Millennium Challenge Corporation (MCC) in 2002, US President George W. Bush drew this parallel, noting that "In World War II, we fought to make the world safer, then worked to rebuild it. As we wage war today to keep the world safe from terror, we must also work to make the world a better place for all its citizens."[7] The approach of the MCC, in which the US government determines eligibility but requires potential recipient countries to draw up their own plans for assistance, also reflects the country-driven strategy of the Marshall Plan.

The more recently announced Alliance for Prosperity presents an even closer parallel to the US response to post–World War II Europe. The governments of El Salvador, Guatemala, and Honduras—the "Northern Triangle" countries in Central America—developed a joint, regional proposal to increase security and development in their countries and used this as the basis for a funding request to the United States. The Obama administration, concerned with the impact on the United States of increased violence, trafficking, and migration from the region, embraced the plan and requested a significant increase in foreign assistance for the 2016 fiscal year.[8] To increase support among Congress and the public, Vice President Joe Biden wrote an op-ed in *The New York Times* arguing that the United States has a "direct interest" in the area and that "the security and prosperity of Central America are inextricably linked with our own."[9] Funding approved by Congress in the amount of $750 million for 2016 includes a combination of increased security and development assistance for the region, with funds being tied to increasing development and decreasing migration, human trafficking, and corruption.[10]

While results, if any, of the increased funding will not be known for some time, the Obama administration's strategy of providing significant funding to a regionally developed plan that addresses both economic and security concerns—a move certain to evoke parallels with the Marshall Plan—provides important insights into the vision for a broader approach to combatting underdevelopment when it affects the United States. Interestingly, the early days of the Trump administration have not abandoned this plan, although it is too soon to predict the administration's overall strategy toward Central America. Soon after assuming office Secretary of State Rex Tillerson, while visiting Mexico, noted the importance of the Alliance for Prosperity for reducing violence and stimulating growth, which would in turn decrease undocumented migration.[11]

In spite of the increased importance placed on development and new strategies for promoting development abroad, there is no guarantee that these changes will result in effective development policies. The preceding chapters have documented a shift in intentions on the part of industrialized states. There is an increased understanding on the part of industrialized country governments that development promotion is in their own self-interest. This has led to new policy choices that reflect these changing priorities. Yet the book does not argue that these policy shifts will be effective in promoting development. This is an unanswered question that must be evaluated on an ongoing basis. After decades of engaging with developing countries, there is still no consensus within policy or academic circles on how, if, and/or under what circumstances outside actors can boost development. Perhaps industrialized states will simply prove ineffective at promoting development abroad, even when it is their goal to do so.

To stay with the example of Central America, in the last decade the United States has significantly increased foreign aid to Central America (even prior to the Alliance for Prosperity) and the Bush administration invested considerable political capital in gaining approval for CAFTA-DR in Congress, arguing that increased trade would lead to development in the region that would ultimately benefit the United States by decreasing migration and negative spillovers. Yet endemic violence has become a crippling problem in three of the targeted countries, and violence, drug trafficking, and the arrival of migrants—including large flows of undocumented minors and those claiming refugee status—continue to inflict costs on the United States. The Alliance for Prosperity may, or may not, be effective at combatting these problems.

An additional handicap in working toward development effectiveness comes from the age and size of institutions now tasked with development—both domestic agencies within industrialized states and international institutions that seek relevance in the development community. The US Agency for International Development was created in 1961 and for decades served as the primary "development" agency for the United States during the Cold War, funneling money to dictators in Africa, Asia, and Latin America in addition to performing more humanitarian-based tasks. It employs more than 7,000 people, including both direct hires and domestic and overseas contracts.[12] The World Bank is even older and larger; it came into being to address reconstruction in Europe in 1944 and, according to its website, employs more than 10,000 people worldwide.[13] Institutions of this size and longevity have developed organizational cultures that inform how they approach situations and problems; these are often path-dependent and slow to change.[14] Bureaucracies are prone to lag behind changing intentions of their principals.

The George W. Bush administration recognized this tendency when it created the MCC—a new organization with a new structure outside of the existing aid apparatus—to oversee the new type of foreign aid Bush was proposing. Catherine Weaver has written convincingly of the role of bureaucratic inertia in attempts to reform the World Bank in the 1990s, arguing that organizational culture "propelled change in a path-dependent direction that was not always congruent with the interests of external actors or even the intentions of internal reformers,"[15] making it difficult to adapt to a new international environment once it was "[deprived] of the Cold War rationale driving previous expenditures."[16] Effective development policy will require finding ways to work through or around existing organizational structures in support of development goals.

There is certainly the potential that the clear shift in intentions of industrialized states can lead to a change in development outcomes, at least in some cases. A key point is that we cannot seek to understand current and future outcomes of development promotion based on historical trends. There has been a change in the intentions of industrialized states, and development promotion now occupies a position of enhanced importance in foreign policy agendas. This may lead to more efficient development promotion; it also may not. However, given the fundamental shift in motivations guiding interactions between industrialized and developing states, examining the past, when interactions with developing states were dominated by non-development policy considerations, is highly problematic for understanding the expected impacts of current policies.

A New Periphery

A strategy of targeted development, if effective at increasing development in the targeted states, will lead to a new, smaller periphery. Targeted states will be brought further into the fold. Global prosperity will increase, the medium-term effect on industrialized states will be positive, but inequality between those left in the periphery and the rest will increase. This means that even if effective, industrialized states pursuing targeted development may be sowing seeds of future security problems in an attempt to deal with more immediate consequences of underdevelopment where it affects them most today.

An irony of the targeted development approach is that it will disproportionately leave behind developing countries most in need of outside assistance. Negative spillovers need a transmission mechanism, and this is more likely the greater the connections between states. Targeting is focused on developing states where connections with industrialized states are already relatively high. Yet the poorest countries—those most in need of outside assistance—are often less connected to other states and therefore less likely to become part of the targeted group. For instance, Chapter 4 finds that aid flows disproportionately to countries with larger migrant populations in the donor, in part to stem future migration by promoting development in these historical source countries for migrant flows. Yet even outside of aid, migration increases financial flows in the form of remittances. The World Bank estimate of officially recorded remittances to developing countries was $431.6 billion in 2015,[17] while foreign aid has averaged around $150 billion per year in recent years.[18] Clearly, remittances are related to the number of migrants living abroad. States with a connection to industrialized countries through migration thus see increased financial flows through remittances and foreign aid, while those developing countries without a strong migration connection to industrialized areas lag behind in both types of flows.

Chapter 5 examines the efforts by the Bush administration to pass CAFTA-DR in Congress. This trade agreement was enacted with countries that already received better than the standard treatment accorded to developing countries by the United States under the Generalized System of Preferences (GSP). All members of CAFTA-DR received preferential access to the US market through the Caribbean Basin Initiative (CBI) prior to signing CAFTA-DR, making this another instance of resources being expended in favor of states already connected to industrialized states rather than with those further in the periphery. Failure to be included in a trade agreement that encompasses other states can be particularly problematic for developing countries, as they will no longer operate on a level playing field for market access into the signatory states. The results in Chapter 6 show a clear trend of climate adaptation assistance being diverted from those most in need to those connected with industrialized states. These patterns are an anticipated result when industrialized states follow a strategy of targeted development promotion, but paint a bleak picture for developing countries not favored under these policies.

Aggregate statistics support the pattern of increased financial engagement with the developing world as a whole, while engagement with the poorest and neediest countries remains stagnant or falls. According to the OECD, foreign aid has risen to its highest levels in recent years, but the amount going to the poorest countries has decreased.[19] Foreign direct investment (FDI) flows to developing countries reached an all-time high of $681 billion in 2014, surpassing inflows of $499 billion into industrialized states, and five of the top ten recipients of FDI were developing countries.[20] Yet this growth is uneven across the developing regions of the world. FDI to Africa in particular remains low: for the 2012–2014 period flows to Africa were about $54 billion per year, about one-third of the amount flowing to Latin America and the Caribbean and one-ninth of the flows into "Developing Asia."[21] These trends are in keeping with the increasing connections and development of a core of developing countries, while others are left even further behind in a shrinking periphery. This new periphery might provide an opportunity for rising powers, such as China, to increase their influence abroad in areas neglected by wealthier states. This could represent another way in which neglect of the remaining periphery will have foreign policy ramifications for industrialized states in the future.

Rethinking the Role of International Institutions

The theory and analysis presented in the preceding chapters suggest that a new approach to understanding the role of international institutions in development may be warranted. While there can be various reasons for forming an international organization, one prevalent justification is the presence of suboptimal provision of an outcome due to market failure.[22] Externalities, in particular, are not usually considered by states acting out of their individual self-interest; when externalities are present, providing at a point where private benefit to the state equals private cost to the state, while individually rational, will lead to suboptimal provision from a collective perspective. In the case of global public goods it may never be individually optimal for a state to contribute to provision, leading to the well-known multiplayer prisoner's dilemma outcome in which no countries contribute to solving the problem (or they contribute only token amounts) even though all parties would be better off if they could agree to collectively fund a solution.[23]

The existence of divergent private benefits that partially coincide with the public benefit can lead to difficulties in bargaining over the exact form of the collective outcome.[24] In fact, there may be a tradeoff between the level of contribution for the "collective" good and the amount of control states cede over the makeup of the contributions and outcome.[25] When states have divergent preferences for the implementation of a collective strategy based on differences in private benefits, the greater control they maintain to increase their private benefit along with the collective benefit, the more they will be willing to contribute. However, the most efficient provision from a private benefit standpoint will be suboptimal from a collective standpoint (if they were identical there would be no increased benefit of maintaining control), meaning some collective gains are not realized when states maintain control of allocation decisions.

When examining an issue area characterized by some form of market failure, there is often a (perhaps implicit) comparison between the world with no institution covering the issue area and a world in which an institution is the prime coordinator of action across states in the issue area. For industrialized states pursuing targeted development abroad, this dichotomy may miss a third, optimal (from the industrialized countries' point of view) option: a hybrid approach in which bilateral targeting takes the lead and coordinated action through an institution provides collective benefits to the industrialized states that are left on the table after considering the outcomes of their bilateral actions. An example may be helpful here.

Consider a world with two industrialized states, Country i and Country j, and three developing states: Country a, Country b, and Country c. Suppose Country c is well governed and would be very efficient at turning resources into development outcomes but development in c does not provide many benefits to Country i or j. Instead, Country i receives significant benefits from development in Country a and Country j receives significant benefits from development in Country b, although they each receive at least some benefit from development in each of the three developing states.

Country i and Country j are deciding whether to coordinate through an international institution. One possibility would be to cede control over funds to the institution and allow the institution to allocate them where they have the greatest impact on development. Neither Country i nor Country j is in favor of this, as the institution would allocate more to Country c than is optimal from either of their perspectives. Alternatively, they could turn all their bilateral resources over to the institution and retain voting control over expenditures, but this would result in a bargaining problem over distribution and an end allocation that might not differ much from the bilateral pattern. In this case the industrialized countries may choose bilateral provision because it is actually superior to the purely multilateral outcome for maximizing their individual welfare. Note that this is only considering the point of view of the decision-making industrialized states, not global public welfare, as industrialized states seeking to maximize their utility will do so without regard to the collective utility of others. Now suppose a third option is open to the industrialized states: bilateral allocation combined with a supplemental role for an institution to collectively capture surplus that is left on the table after bilateral provision takes place. Returning to Country c, suppose that neither Country i or j provide it with any resources bilaterally; they would each benefit from development there, but the marginal private benefit (MB) is lower than the marginal private cost (MC) for both i and j. However, if preferences with regard to development in Country c are such that $MB_i + MB_j > MC$, then there is surplus left on the table after optimizing bilateral provision.

From the point of view of the industrialized states in this example, there is a much clearer case for an institution to fill a residual role than for an institution to play a leading role in the issue area. And it is not clear that this will, in practice, provide worse outcomes to developing countries than complete delegation to an international institution that is guided only by the idea of maximizing the well-being of developing states given its funding. Even if such an institution allocates its funds efficiently from the point of view of advancing global development, it might not have many funds to allocate.

Recognizing this tension between delegating control and funding is not new; Mancur Olson and Richard Zeckhauser were writing about it in the 1960s.[26] However, the lofty goals of even newly created institutions for addressing global issues linking industrialized and developing states, such as the Green Climate Fund, suggest that these insights are not guiding institutional expectations. The lack of buy-in from industrialized countries toward the Green Climate Fund (or the World Bank or the World Trade Organization on development matters) is consistent with these well-known difficulties of balancing bilateral priorities with multilateral provision. The increased importance of targeted development as a strategy pursued by industrialized states will exacerbate these tensions. It may be time to shift discussions regarding institutional design and best practices in areas linking industrialized and developing states. From the point of view of industrialized states contributing resources, the optimal role of institutions may be as a complement to, rather than as a substitute for, bilateral action. Failure to recognize this risks increasing irrelevance for institutions seeking to work in developing countries with resources provided by industrialized states.

Wrapping It Up

Governments have finite resources with which to address competing demands. As the relative importance of issues changes, the amount of political and financial resources channeled to these issues will reflect changing priorities. Yet absolute needs play a role as well. Globalization has increased the importance of underdevelopment as an area of concern to industrialized states both absolutely and relative to other issue areas. As a result, development is unlikely to become the primarily tangential concern it was during the Cold War.

Targeted development, as put forth in the preceding pages, is the account of a consistent strategy that explains a broad pattern of behavior by industrialized states toward developing countries in the post-2001 period. There will be deviations from this pattern, as no one theory can encompass all the individual actions of industrialized states. Yet as a concept it has considerable explanatory power across countries and issue areas. Furthermore, targeted development will likely remain a key component of the strategy pursued by industrialized states toward developing countries for the foreseeable future. Left unchecked, underdevelopment will continue to cause negative spillovers for other states. Governments in industrialized countries recognize this and will continue to pursue development abroad when and where it is in their interests to do so.

NOTES

Chapter 1

1. Inaugural address of US President Harry Truman, January 20, 1949.
2. Remarks at the first meeting of the United Nations High-Level Panel of Eminent Persons on Post-2015 Development Agenda, September 25, 2012, New York, NY. Cameron was co-chair of the panel.
3. The name derives from the fact that it was the fourth—and, by most, unexpected—point in Truman's speech.
4. Radelet (2003), pp. 107–108.
5. *White Christmas*, Paramount Pictures, 1954.
6. Keohane and Nye (2000, p. 112).
7. Blair (2006).
8. Fearon and Laitin (2004, p. 13).
9. Snyder (2011, p. 35).
10. See https://www.cgdev.org/initiative/commitment-development-index/inside.
11. See, for instance, Wolfensohn interview with Charlie Rose, available online at http://www.charlierose.com/view/interview/2912; also Mallaby (2004).
12. George W. Bush remarks at the UN Conference on Financing for Development, March 22, 2002.
13. Radelet (2003).
14. Doha WTO Ministerial 2001: Ministerial Declaration, paragraph 2.
15. Secretariat note on the Development Aspects of the Doha Round to the WTO's Committee on Trade and Development, November 28, 2005.
16. Kumar, Sanjay, "Green Climate Fund vows to up its game," *Nature* News, March 30, 2016, available online at http://www.nature.com/news/green-climate-fund-vows-to-up-its-game-1.19627.
17. Based on data from the OECD online database, DAC3a. Calculated using the "Multilateral, Total" percent of the sum of "Multilateral, Total" and "DAC, Total" categories. There are at times sizeable yearly fluctuations, but the average yearly percent multilateral using this measure is 30.04% for the period 1990–2000 and 30.61% for the period 2002–2014. The most recent years show a slight upward trend, but it is too soon to determine if this will be sustained.
18. See, for example, Martin (1992).
19. Koremenos, Lipson, and Snidal (2001, p. 767).
20. Keohane (1984).
21. Krasner (1991).
22. Olson and Zeckhauser (1966).
23. Olson and Zeckhauser (1966, p. 272).

24. This is not meant to imply that aid donors would not increase their own well-being by coordinating *within* recipient countries, to provide better outcomes that are valued by each donor present. It does suggest that coordination *across* countries is likely to be difficult and could result in lower overall aid flows, as donors whose most-preferred countries are not favored by coordination cut back on their giving.

Chapter 2

1. Statement to a Joint Meeting of the Senate Foreign Relations and House Foreign Affairs Committee, November 10, 1947.
2. Radio address April 28, 1947; quoted in Hitchcock (2010).
3. Leffler (2010).
4. Hitchcock (2010).
5. Ibid.
6. Hogan (1997).
7. Ibid.
8. See Hitchcock (2010) for a discussion of these variations across countries.
9. Leffler (2007).
10. Leffler (2010).
11. Ibid.
12. Foreign Assistance Act of 1948/Economic Cooperation Act of 1948; Title 1, Section 102 (a).
13. Hitchcock (2010).
14. Hogan (1997).
15. Quoted in Sanford (1982, p. 10).
16. Ibid.
17. Gaddis (2005, p. 30).
18. Waltz (1979, p. 171).
19. President Dwight Eisenhower news conference, April 7, 1954; in Public Papers of Dwight D. Eisenhower 1954, pp. 381–390; available online at http://quod.lib.umich.edu/p/ppotpus?cginame=text-idx;id=navbarbrowselink;page=browse.
20. Westad (2005).
21. Bradley (2010).
22. McGuire (1952, p. 345), emphasis in original.
23. Friedman (1958, p. 63); quoted in Kanbur (2006, p. 1565).
24. Latham (2010).
25. Quoted in Bradley (2010, p. 476). See also Engerman (2003).
26. Taffet (2007).
27. Latham (2010).
28. Westad (2005); see also Hochschild, Adam, "An Assassination's Long Shadow," *New York Times*, January 16, 2011.
29. Bradley (2010); see also Rochter, Larry, "Cheddi Jagan, Guyana's Founder, Dies at 78," *New York Times*, March 7, 1997.
30. Simpson (2008).
31. Based on data from the OECD DAC3a database; available online at stats.oecd.org.
32. Westad (2005).
33. Bradley (2010, p. 484).
34. President Lyndon Johnson, quoted in Leffler (2007, Kindle location 4032 of 13707).
35. Ibid., Kindle location 4243 of 13707.
36. US National Archives, available online at http://www.archives.gov/research/military/vietnam-war/casualty-statistics.html, accessed August 6, 2016.
37. Tirman, John, "Why Do We Ignore the Civilians Killed in American Wars?" *The Washington Post*, January 6, 2012.
38. Westad (2005).
39. Based on data reported to the OECD in database DAC3a.
40. Brands (1992).

41. On the role of the Safari Club, see Mitchell (2016).
42. Ibid.
43. Based on data reported to the OECD in database DAC3a.
44. Orr (1990); Miyashita (1999); Stein (1998).
45. Schraeder, Hook, and Taylor (1998); Berthélemy and Tichit (2004).
46. Based on data from the OECD, DAC3a database.
47. Westad (2005).
48. For an in-depth discussion of the Cold War in Latin America, including the 1970s–1980s in Central America, see Brands (2010).
49. Westad (2005).
50. Boys (2015).
51. Porteous (2008).
52. Copenhagen European Council, 21–22 June 1993, Bulletin of the European Communities, No. 6/1993.
53. US President William Jefferson Clinton, "Remarks to the 48th Session of the UN General Assembly in New York City, September 27, 1993." See also Brinkley (1997).
54. Reiff (1995).
55. Riehm (1997).
56. *New York Times*, "MISSION TO HAITI: DIPLOMACY; On the Brink of War, a Tense Battle of Wills," September 20, 1994.
57. Power (2001).
58. Lancaster (2007).
59. Radelet (2003, p. 107).
60. Stiglitz and Charlton (2005).
61. Bearce and Tirone (2010).
62. Remarks by the President on Foreign Policy, Grand Hyatt Hotel, San Francisco, CA, February 26, 1999; available online at https://www.mtholyoke.edu/acad/intrel/clintfps.htm.
63. Porteous (2008, pp. 13–14).
64. For the purpose of categorizing migrant stock in Figure 2.2, the sum of migrants from developing countries for which the major destination is listed as "developed areas" is included. Migrants from source countries that were high-income OECD countries by 1990 as well as the category "Other North" are excluded when summing the total migrants going to "developed areas."
65. PBS Frontline interview with John Lewis Gaddis; transcript available online at http://www.pbs.org/wgbh/pages/frontline/shows/iraq/interviews/gaddis.html; accessed August 13, 2016.
66. Girod, Krasner, and Stoner-Weiss (2009, p. 69).
67. See remarks by George W. Bush at the Inter-American Development Bank, March 14, 2002.
68. Radelet (2003).
69. Lancaster (2008, p. 4).
70. Swiss Foreign Policy Strategy 2012–2015, Federal Council report to Parliament on the strategic axes of foreign policy, March 2012, p. 5.
71. Japan's National Security Strategy, December 17, 2013, p. 6.
72. The National Security Strategy of the United Kingdom: Security in an Interdependent World, March 2008, p. 16.

Chapter 3

1. *Murders in the Rue Morgue*.
2. BBC online, "Migrant Crisis: Migration to Europe Explained in Seven Charts." March 4, 2016. Online at http://www.bbc.com/news/world-europe-34131911.
3. Renwick, Danielle, Council of Foreign Relations Backgrounder: "Central America's Violent Northern Triangle," January 19, 2016. Online at http://www.cfr.org/transnational-crime/central-americas-violent-northern-triangle/p37286. Preston, Julia, *New York Times*, "A Rush of Central Americans Complicates Obama's Immigration Task," January 8, 2016. Online at http://www.nytimes.com/2016/01/09/us/a-rush-of-central-americans-compounds-obamas-immigration-task.html.

4. Gberie, Lansana, 2016. "Crime, Violence, and Politics: Drug Trafficking and Counternarcotics Policies in Mali and Guinea." Online at https://www.brookings.edu/wp-content/uploads/2016/07/Gberie-Mali-and-Guinea-final.pdf.
5. Tavernise, Sabrina, and Donald G. McNeil Jr., "Zika Virus a Global Health Emergency, W.H.O. Says." *New York Times*, February 1, 2016. Online at https://www.nytimes.com/2016/02/02/health/zika-virus-world-health-organization.html.
6. Mullany, Gerry, and Chris Buckley, "China Warns of Arms Race After U.S. Deploys Missile Defense in South Korea." *New York Times*, March 7, 2017. Online at https://www.nytimes.com/2017/03/07/world/asia/thaad-missile-defense-us-south-korea-china.html.
7. Kadane (2009).
8. Edgar Allan Poe, *Murders in the Rue Morgue*, 1841.
9. It would also be possible for the αs to vary across countries, although for the sake of simplicity they are held constant here. This function can be thought of as analogous to country-wide production functions of the form $Y = AK^\alpha N^\beta$ where total factor productivity, A, varies across countries while α and β are held constant.
10. Carter and Stone (2015).
11. Kuziemko and Werker (2006).
12. Vreeland and Dreher (2014).
13. Vreeland (2011).
14. Lim and Vreeland (2013).
15. Rosen (2004).
16. Bender, Jeremy, *Business Insider*, "France's Military is All Over Africa," January 22, 2015. Online at http://www.businessinsider.com/frances-military-is-all-over-africa-2015-1.
17. Following similar logic, Carter and Stone (2015) find that the United States focuses vote buying in the United Nations on democratic countries.
18. It would be possible to separately specify the benefit that country i receives from developing country y in the utility function for scenario 2, so that $U_{i2} = \beta_x k_x [r_{ix2}]^\alpha + \beta_y k_y [r_{iy2}]^\alpha + v_i(R_i - r_{ix2} - r_{iy2} - f_{ix2})$. However, the donor will minimize cost with respect to r_{ix2} and f_{ix2} and then remaining expenditures from R_x will be distributed such that $\alpha \beta_y k_y [r_{iy2}]^{\alpha-1} = \frac{\delta v_i}{\delta g_{i2}}$ where $g_{i2} = r_{ix2} + r_{iy2} + f_{ix2}$, if the minimum-cost way of obtaining M_x yields $U_{i2} > U_{i1}$. Given this, nothing is gained by separating the impact on spending in country y from other opportunity costs of diverting resources to country x in exchange for providing M_x.
19. The first-order conditions for the constrained optimization show that the industrialized country i minimizes the cost of obtaining M_x by compensating country x with a mixture of r_{ix2} and f_{ix2} that satisfies the following (where $s_{ix2} = r_{ix2} + f_{ix2}$):

$$\frac{\alpha \gamma_x k_x (r_{ix2})^{\alpha-1}}{\frac{\delta v_x}{\delta f_{ix2}}} = \frac{\frac{\delta v_i}{\delta s_{ix2}} + \alpha \beta_x k_x (r_{ix2})^{\alpha-1}}{\frac{\delta v_i}{\delta s_{ix2}}}$$

The left-hand side is the ratio of the marginal benefit that country x receives from an additional unit of r_{ix2} relative to f_{ix2}, which represents the ratio of the amount of compensation that is "purchased" by country i for an additional unit of r_{ix2} relative to f_{ix2}. The right-hand side is the ratio of the cost to industrialized country i of providing r_{ix2} relative to f_{ix2}. The claim that the cost to country i of a unit of r_{ix2} is less than the cost of a unit of f_{ix2} follows from the fact that $\frac{\delta v_i}{\delta s_{ix2}} < 0$ and $\alpha \beta_x k_x (r_{ix2})^{\alpha-1} > 0$. The equation for r_{ix2}^{min} is obtained by rearranging this equation.
20. Berthélemy and Tichit (2004).
21. Amounts are constant dollars and exclude debt relief. Author calculations based on data from the OECD DAC3 (for commitments) database and CRS database (for debt relief).
22. Recall that in scenario 3 the utility that country i receives from development in country y is included in $v_i(R_i - s_{ix3})$ so that $\beta_y k_y [r_{iy4}^{min}]^\alpha - v_i(R_i - s_{ix3})$ captures, along with other opportunity costs in the $v_i(\cdot)$ function, the increase in utility provided by $r_{iy4} > r_{iy3}$. The same is true with regard to utility from development in country x: $v_i(R_i - s_{iy4}) - \beta_x k_x [r_{ix3}^{min}]^\alpha$ in inequality 3.16 includes the decrease in utility from forgone development in country x when moving from scenario 3 to scenario 4 and reducing r_{ix3} to r_{ix4}.

23. See Olson and Zeckhauser (1966) for a classic discussion of these issues with regard to both foreign aid and the NATO alliance.
24. Krasner (1991).
25. In the absence of bargaining costs and the costs of running an institution, it could still be optimal to use an institution to overcome remaining under provision due to free-riding. However, in reality both bargaining and maintenance are costly.

Chapter 4

* Portions of this chapter draw on the article "Aid Allocation and Targeted Development in an Increasingly Connected World," published in International Organization, 71(4), and reprinted with permission from Cambridge University Press.
1. https://www.theguardian.com/business/2009/dec/22/britain-still-in-recession.
2. Pimlott, Daniel, Chris Giles, and Robin Harding, "UK Unveils Dramatic Austerity Measures," *The Financial Times*, October 20, 2010. Online at http://www.ft.com/cms/s/0/53fe06e2-dc98-11df-84f5-00144feabdc0.html#axzz49JOPAtSC.
3. Data on aid as a percent of gross national income are from the OECD, available online at https://data.oecd.org/oda/net-oda.htm.
4. McKinlay and Little (1977, 1978); Maizels and Nissanke (1984); Schraeder, Hook, and Taylor (1998); Alesina and Dollar (2000); Bueno de Mesquita and Smith (2007, 2009, 2015).
5. Lumsdaine (1993); Noel and Therien (2002); Therien and Noel (2000); Tingley (2010).
6. PM speech at G8 Nutrition for Growth event, June 8, 2013. Online at https://www.gov.uk/government/speeches/pm-speech-at-g8-nutrition-for-growth-event.
7. "Clegg to push aid goal at UN Summit," September 21, 2010 http://www.standard.co.uk/newsheadlines/clegg-to-push-aid-goal-at-un-summit-6515846.html.
8. For example, McKinlay and Little (1977, 1978); Maizels and Nissanke (1984); Schraeder, Hook, and Taylor (1998); Alesina and Dollar (2000); Neumayer (2003); Berthélemy and Tichit (2004); Dollar and Levin (2006); Bueno de Mesquita and Smith (2009).
9. Fleck and Kilby (2010).
10. Dietrich, Mahmud, and Winters (2017).
11. Milner and Tingley (2010).
12. Lumsdaine (1993); Noel and Therien (2002); Therien and Noel (2000); Tingley (2010).
13. Although other donors may report voluntarily to the DAC, or have data available through other sources, these data are not consistently available over time. Therefore, to get a better comparison over time the analysis is restricted to DAC members, who are required to report their aid data to the OECD.
14. Data for Figures 4.1 and 4.2 and for the calculations in this section are taken from the OECD online database, available at stats.oecd.org.
15. McKinlay and Little (1977, 1978); Maizels and Nissanke (1984); Schraeder, Hook, and Taylor (1998); Alesina and Dollar (2000); Bueno de Mesquita and Smith (2007, 2009, 2015).
16. Maizels and Nissanke (1984, p. 880).
17. "Is Foreign Aid Working?" *Prospect Magazine*, Issue 128: November 2006. Online https://www.prospectmagazine.co.uk/magazine/isforeignaidworking.
18. Berthélemy and Tichit (2004); Boschini and Olofsgard (2007).
19. Lancaster (2007, p. 85).
20. Berthélemy and Tichit (2004, p. 266).
21. Brautigam and Knack (2004).
22. Woods (2005).
23. Bearce and Tirone (2010).
24. Dunning (2004); Wright (2009); Bermeo (2016).
25. Author calculations based on data from the OECD DAC3a database, available online at stats.oecd.org.
26. Quoted in Buzan (2006, p. 1106).
27. Bearce and Tirone (2010, p. 849).
28. Woods (2005, p. 393).

29. Quoted in Moss, Roodman, and Standley (2005, p. 3).
30. Fleck and Kilby (2010).
31. Press release, "Establishment of a National Security Council," May 12, 2010, UK Government Web Archive. Online at http://webarchive.nationalarchives.gov.uk/20130109092234/http://number10.gov.uk/news/establishment-of-a-national-security-council/; accessed August 13, 2016.
32. Kuziemko and Werker (2006); Vreeland and Dreher (2014).
33. See Carter and Stone (2015) for a review of this literature; the authors also point to the importance of analyzing "important votes," but such a measure is not available across donors.
34. Bueno de Mesquita and Smith (2009, 2010).
35. See Bermeo (2017).
36. Borjas (1993).
37. Bermeo and Leblang (2015).
38. Alesina and Dollar (2000); Fleck and Kilby (2010); Berthélemy and Tichit (2004); Dollar and Levin (2006); Neumayer (2003).
39. Maizels and Nissanke (1984) is an exception.
40. Moss, Roodman, and Standley (2005).
41. Fleck and Kilby (2010).
42. Clist (2011).
43. DAC members in the analysis (year of entry in parentheses): Australia (1961), Belgium (1961), Canada (1961), France (1961), Germany (1961), Italy (1961), Japan (1961), Netherlands (1961), Portugal (1961; withdrew in 1974 and rejoined in 1991), United Kingdom (1961), United States (1961), European Communities (1961; not included in country-level dyadic analysis), Norway (1962), Denmark (1963), Sweden (1965), Austria (1966), Switzerland (1968), New Zealand (1973), Finland (1975), Ireland (1985), Spain (1991), Luxembourg (1992), Greece (1999), Korea (2010); the following joined the DAC in 2013, after the time period covered in the analysis: Czech Republic, Iceland, Slovak Republic, Slovenia, Poland.
44. One is added to the value of aid before taking the natural log to preserve the zero values, which are then set as the lower-level censored value in Tobit regressions. The $1 amount is extremely small compared to aid values in the dataset: the lowest non-zero value is $10,000; when adding $1 to this the logged value remains unchanged through the third decimal place, so distortion from adding one before taking the log is unlikely.
45. Table DAC3a, constant US dollars, available online at stats.oecd.org; accessed July 15, 2014.
46. Accessed May 22, 2014.
47. EM-DAT: The OFDA/CRED International Disaster Database; www.em-dat.net, Université Catholique de Louvain, Brussels, Belgium; accessed June 3, 2014.
48. Gleditsch et al. (2002).
49. Online at https://freedomhouse.org/; accessed June 6, 2014.
50. Available at www.usaid.gov through the USAID "Greenbook"; accessed July 15, 2014.
51. Dreher, Sturm, and Vreeland (2009).
52. Online at http://www.cepii.fr/CEPII/en/bdd_modele/presentation.asp?id=6; accessed July 18, 2014.
53. Online at http://www.sipri.org/databases/armstransfers; accessed February 2, 2016.
54. Bailey, Strezhnev, and Voeten (2017). While a widely used variable, the direction of the relationship between similarity in voting in the UN General Assembly and foreign aid is theoretically ambiguous. A donor may give more aid to countries that have generally similar votes to itself, either as a reward for this practice or because UN votes are correlated with a general alignment of priorities that is associated with more aid (Alesina and Dollar, 2000). On the other hand, a donor may use aid to "buy" votes from countries that are generally more distant to itself, suggesting a negative relationship between aid and vote similarity.
55. Accessed July 17, 2014.
56. Coded from the CIA World Factbook.
57. Available at stats.oecd.org; accessed July 18, 2014.
58. Alesina and Dollar (2000); Alesina and Weder (2002); Berthélemy and Tichit (2004); Dollar and Levin (2006). In Bermeo (2017) I examine results using both the Tobit model and

another common approach, the two-part model, used by studies such as Neumayer (2003); Berthélemy (2006); Bueno de Mesquita and Smith (2009); Fleck and Kilby (2010); Clist (2011). Each specification has benefits and drawbacks, but the conclusions drawn regarding changes in aid allocation over time are similar with either specification.
59. Interaction terms can also be problematic in non-linear models such as Tobit (Greene, 2010), which provides an additional reason for also performing separate analyses by period.
60. Greene (2004) shows that the incidental parameter bias problem in Tobit models is unlikely to be an issue in panels of this length.
61. The results for *US Military Assistance* and *SIPRI Arms Transfers* are qualitatively similar if indicator values for receiving any military aid and any arms transfers are substituted for the current measures.
62. Post-estimation t-tests for equality of the difference between exports and imports across periods suggests that the difference has declined (p=0.00 comparing Models 1 and 3; p=0.11 when comparing Models 1 and 2).
63. I explore this in more depth in Bermeo (2017).
64. Donor fixed effects are included on their own and interacted with the two period effects, but not shown due to space constraints.
65. Germany does not have data on *UN Vote Distance* in the Cold War and so is excluded from the same dyads analysis in Table 4.2. To include Germany in the analysis by donor, *UN Vote Distance* is not included in the regressions for Germany.
66. For donors with sufficient data on migrant flows, analogous models were run separately including migration, and the coefficient for migration from the separate regression is reported at the bottom of the column for the post-2001 period. The main regressions exclude migration in both periods to allow a comparison over time (migration data are not available for the Cold War period). The Cold War period includes 1973–1988 or the years in that period for which a donor has data.
67. E.g., Burnside and Dollar, 2000. This premise is debated (e.g., Easterly, Levine, and Roodman, 2004), but still serves as a basis in the literature for using attention to governance to understand donors' commitment to development.
68. E.g., Claessens, Cassimon, and Campenhout (2009). Dollar and Levin (2006) find increased selectivity for multilateral but not bilateral donors. Berthélemy and Tichit (2004) claim to find increased selectivity, but use growth of GDP per capita as a measure of economic policies, which is uncommon in the literature.
69. Alesina and Dollar (2000); Svensson (2000); Alesina and Weder (2002); Collier and Dollar (2002); Neumayer (2003); Girod, Krasner, and Stoner-Weiss (2009).
70. Dollar and Levin (2006); Easterly (2007); Clist (2011).
71. de la Croix and Delavalladey (2014).
72. Easterly and Pfutze (2008); Easterly and Williamson (2011).
73. Kaufmann, Kraay, Mastruzzi (2010). The measure "voice and accountability" is not used, as it contains the Freedom House scores that are entered separately.
74. The creators' responses to some of the more important of these critiques appear on the WGI website (http://info.worldbank.org/governance/wgi/index.aspx#doc).
75. The MCC evaluates a country's scores relative to its peers, rather than the raw score.
76. There are no measures of governance with wide country coverage for the Cold War period. While some measures from the International Country Risk Guide (discussed further in the next section) begin in 1984, they have limited country coverage and only allow for including the last few years of the Cold War.
77. Log(*Distance*)=8.5 at approximately the 25th percentile for *Distance*.
78. Bermeo (2010); Akramov (2014); Nordtveit (2014); Winters and Martinez (2015).
79. Dietrich (2013).
80. I do not report results for sectors such as "multi-sector," where there is no clear prediction from the theory or "debt relief," the potential value of which varies based on the debt accumulated, which can be related to governance. Full descriptions available at http://www.oecd.org/dac/stats/purposecodessectorclassification.htm.
81. Percentages calculated from the OECD CRS dataset, accessed February 16, 2016.

82. Only aid classified by sector (including sectors not reported here) is used in the denominator (e.g. 100*(aid for social sectors/total aid classified by sector)).
83. Author calculation based on comparison of CRS and DAC datasets for DAC bilateral aid.
84. Easterly (2006, p. 4).

Chapter 5

1. Robert Zoellick, "CAFTA is a Win-Win," Op-Ed, *Washington Post*, May 24, 2005. Online at http://2001-2009.state.gov/r/pa/ei/speeches/2005/.
2. CNN, "House Narrowly Approves CAFTA," July 28, 2005. Online at http://www.cnn.com/2005/POLITICS/07/28/house.cafta/.
3. Andrews, Edmund L., "How CAFTA Passed House by 2 Votes," *New York Times*, http://www.nytimes.com/2005/07/29/politics/how-cafta-passed-house-by-2-votes.html. *The Economist*, "Finance and Economics: A Knotty Problem," June 4, 2005.
4. According to the Bureau of Economic Analysis, the GDP of Pittsburgh in 2003 was $94.7 billion; according to the World Development Indicators the combined GDP for CAFTA-DR countries in 2003 was $89.2 billion. Both figures in current dollars.
5. The dyads Australia–Micronesia and New Zealand–Micronesia only appear in Figure 5.1 after Micronesian independence in 1986, but the agreement was previously signed and so not "new" in that year. As a result the total number of dyads with a PTA increases in 1987 even though no new PTAs were signed.
6. E.g., Grossman and Helpman (1995); Milner (1997); Bagwell and Staiger (1999); Mansfield, Milner, and Rosendorff (2002); Maggi and Rodriguez-Clare (2007); Mansfield, Milner, and Pevehouse (2007); Mansfield and Milner (2012).
7. Gowa (1994); Gowa and Mansfield (1993).
8. Maggi (1999).
9. Özden and Reinhardt (2005).
10. Grossman and Helpman (1995, p. 687).
11. Mansfield and Milner (2012, Kindle Location 685).
12. See Hudec (1987); Özden and Reinhardt (2005); Hoekman and Ozden (2005); Shadlen (2008); Manger and Shadlen (2014).
13. Manger and Shadlen (2014).
14. Büthe and Milner (2008); Buthe and Milner (2014).
15. Özden and Reinhardt (2005).
16. See Manger and Shadlen (2014).
17. Manger (2009).
18. Manger (2009, p. 4).
19. The totals here are higher than those in Figure 5.1 because these include all countries that were developing at the time of signing while Figure 5.1 does not include countries for the years after they pass the high-income threshold, meaning some had dropped out by 2012.
20. Baccini and Dur (2012), applying Kahneman and Tversky (1979).
21. Hudec (1987).
22. Özden and Reinhardt (2005, p. 2).
23. Alt et al. (1996).
24. Gowa (1994).
25. Gowa and Mansfield (1993).
26. On time inconsistency and protection, see Hudec (1987); Özden and Reinhardt (2005); Maggi and Rodriguez-Clare (2007); Mansfield and Milner (2012).
27. Manger (2009, p. 22).
28. Mansfield and Reinhardt (2003).
29. *The Economist*, "A small victory for free trade as CAFTA," July 28, 2005.
30. Hornbeck (2012).
31. *The Economist*, "The Americas: Five Get Anxious; Central American Trade," May 29, 2004.
32. Pregelj (2005).

33. See, for example, Adduci II, V. James, "New U.S. Trade Act to Help Caribbean Nations Overcome NAFTA Disadvantage," *North American Free Trade and Investment Report*, May 31, 2000. Online at http://www.adduci.com/node/110.
34. Pregelj (2005).
35. *The Economist*, "The Americas: How to Trade Up," February 15, 2003, pp. 35–36. *The Economist*, "Nothing's Free in This World; Central America," August 6, 2005.
36. Sánchez-Ancochea (2008).
37. Schrank (2008).
38. Hicks, Milner, and Tingley (2014).
39. *The Economist*, "Trading Arguments; Central America," July 14, 2007.
40. Hicks, Milner, and Tingley (2014).
41. Hicks, Milner, and Tingley (2014).
42. See USTR website: https://ustr.gov/trade-agreements/free-trade-agreements/cafta-dr-dominican-republic-central-america-fta.
43. *The New York Times* reported leading up to the vote on CAFTA that US trade with other members accounted for 1.4% of total US trade ("Q&A: The CAFTA Debate," July 18, 2005). The USTR reported figures of $60 billion in trade in goods (exports+imports) between the United States and CAFTA-DR countries in 2013 and total US trade in goods of $3.88 trillion.
44. Andrews, Edmund L., "Small Trade Pact Becomes a Big Political Deal," *New York Times*, July 27, 2005.
45. *The Economist*, "The CAFTA conundrum; Trade," June 18, 2005.
46. Guisinger (2009).
47. *The Economist*, "The CAFTA Conundrum," June 16, 2005.
48. *The Economist*, "Stemming the Tide; Face Value," June 18, 2005.
49. *The Economist*, "The CAFTA conundrum; Trade," June 18, 2005.
50. Beehner, Lionel, Council on Foreign Relations Backgrounder, "What are the main issues in the debate over CAFTA?" July 18, 2005. Online at http://www.cfr.org/trade/main-issues-debate-over-cafta/p9050.
51. Pregelj (2005).
52. Bumiller, Elisabeth, and Edmund Andrews, "Bush Sells Trade Pact in Hostile Territory," *New York Times*, July 16, 2005.
53. Becker, Elizabeth, "A Push for a Central American Trade Pact," *New York Times*, May 13, 2005, Late Edition (East Coast).
54. Andrews, Edmund L., "Pleas and Promises by G.O.P. As Trade Pact Wins by 2 Votes," *New York Times*, July 29, 2005, Late Edition (East Coast).
55. *New York Times*, "A New Trade Deal: Harvesting Poverty," December 22, 2003, Late Edition (East Coast).
56. Andrews, Edmund L., "G.O.P. Hopes Bill on China Will Assist Trade Pact," *New York Times*, July 15, 2005, Late Edition (East Coast).
57. Andrews, Edmund, "Senate Approves Free Trade Pact: Central American Accord Faces Fight in House," *New York Times*, July 1, 2005.
58. Andrews, Edmund L., "White House Makes Deals For Support Of Trade Pact," *New York Times*, July 26, 2005 Late Edition (East Coast).
59. Andrews, Edmund L., "Small Trade Pact Becomes a Big Political Deal," *New York Times*, July 27, 2005.
60. *The Economist*, "The Americas: How to Trade Up," February 15, 2003, pp. 35–36.
61. "The Stakes in CAFTA," *Washington Post* Editorial, July 26, 2005. Becker, Elizabeth, "Central American Trade Pact Passes First Congressional Test," *New York Times*, June 15, 2005, Late Edition (East Coast).
62. "Statement by the President on the Central American and Dominican Republic preferential trade agreement," June 23, 2005. Online at http://2001-2009.state.gov/e/eeb/rls/rm/2005/48546.htm.
63. Zoellick, Robert, "CAFTA is a Win-Win," *Washington Post*, May 24, 2005, Online at http://2001-2009.state.gov/r/pa/ei/speeches/2005/.
64. Press release, US Department of Defense, May 11, 2005. Online at http://archive.defense.gov/Releases/Release.aspx?ReleaseID=8472.

65. CNN.com, "House Narrowly Approves CAFTA," July 28, 2005. Online at http://www.cnn.com/2005/POLITICS/07/28/house.cafta/.
66. The compacts with Honduras and Nicaragua were later terminated before the funds were fully disbursed; the decision to terminate the compact with Nicaragua (lowering the total amount disbursed to $113.5 million) followed the 2008 municipal elections in which widespread irregularities and fraud were alleged, and in Honduras the compact was terminated following the 2009 coup that ousted President Manuel Zelaya, although $205 million of the original $215 million was disbursed.
67. "CAFTA-DR Facts: Building Trade Capacity under CAFTA-DR," Office of the US Trade Representative, CAFTA Policy Brief, July 2007.
68. Figure 5.2 excludes data for 1999 in which the region was devastated by Hurricane Mitch and foreign aid was more than 10 times its average value in Honduras (the country hardest hit, with at least 5,600 killed and more than one-quarter of the population affected), more than 4 times its annual average in Nicaragua, and double its annual average in Guatemala. This surge was due to a humanitarian disaster and not a good indicator of long-term development commitment. On the impact of Hurricane Mitch in Central America, see Inter-American Development Bank, "Central America after Hurricane Mitch." Online at www.iadb.org.
69. I traveled to Managua, Nicaragua, in March 2006 and to Tegucigalpa, Honduras, in June 2006. In each country I was able to interview the head of the USAID office and MCC program, numerous USAID staff, and the heads of several non-US bilateral and multilateral aid agencies.
70. Author interviews with personnel from USAID and Michigan State University, Managua, Nicaragua, April 2006.
71. Accessed March 18, 2016.
72. Data for the Dominican Republic for the 1990s are not available, so no trend line is plotted for this country. The sharp drop for Guatemala in 2005 may be due to damage from Hurricane Stan, which caused extensive mudslides resulting in loss of life and damage to infrastructure in Guatemala in October 2005.
73. Hornbeck (2012).
74. Ibid.
75. Ibid.
76. Renwick (2016).
77. Zong and Batalova (2015).
78. Renwick (2016).
79. Kuek Ser, Kuang Keng, *PRI's The World,* "Map: Here are countries with the world's highest murder rates," June 27, 2016.
80. Renwick (2016).
81. Preston, Julia, "A Rush of Central Americans Complicates Obama's Immigration Task," *International New York Times,* January 8, 2016.
82. Zong and Batalova (2015).
83. Dyer, Zach, "Nicaraguan Migrants Don't Follow Other Central Americans to US, Choosing Costa Rica Instead," *Tico Times,* August 27, 2014.
84. Online at stats.oecd.org.
85. From the World Bank's *World Development Indicators.*
86. Manger and Shadlen (2014).
87. Mansfield, Milner, and Rosendorff (2002); Mansfield, Milner, and Pevehouse (2007); Mansfield and Milner (2012).
88. Online at https://freedomhouse.org/.
89. Beck et al. (2001).
90. Gowa (1994).
91. Gowa and Mansfield (1993).
92. Correlates of War Formal Interstate Alliance Dataset, Version 4; variable equals one if the variable for defense, neutrality, nonaggression, and/or entente is coded as one in the underlying data; zero otherwise.
93. The US GDP deflator is taken from the IMF's International Financial Statistics.
94. Data are from the GeoDist database. Online at http://www.cepii.fr; accessed July 18, 2014.

95. Coded by the author from the CIA World Factbook.
96. Carter and Signorino (2010). For an application in the context of trade agreements, see Manger and Shadlen (2014).
97. On separation, see Beck and Katz (2001). This is not simply a theoretical argument; in the current case separation would result if country fixed effects were included, which would be similar to selecting on the dependent variable as states not signing any agreements would be excluded from the analysis.
98. Including both GDP and trade results in an insignificant coefficient on GDP.
99. Classification cutoffs are based on 2005 criteria as income is measured in constant 2005 dollars in the analysis.
100. Manger and Shadlen (2014).
101. Mansfield and Milner (2012).
102. Mansfield and Milner (2012).
103. Gowa (1994).
104. Gowa and Mansfield (1993).
105. Mansfield and Milner (2012).
106. Manger and Shadlen (2014).

Chapter 6

1. The Copenhagen Accord can be found at http://unfccc.int/meetings/copenhagen_dec_2009/items/5262.php.
2. See, for example, Center for Global Development, "Climate Change and Development in Three Charts," August 18, 2015. Online at http://www.cgdev.org/blog/climate-change-and-development-three-charts.
3. See, for example, Intergovernmental Panel on Climate Change, Working Group II: Impacts, Adaptation and Vulnerability, 2014 report.
4. Ciplet, Roberts, and Khan (2013).
5. United Nations Environment Program, *The Adaptation Gap Report 2016*. Online at http://web.unep.org/adaptationgapreport/2016.
6. Terpstra, Pieter. "Is Adaptation Short-Changed? The Imbalance in Climate Finance Commitments," World Resources Institute, November 13, 2013. Online at http://www.wri.org/blog/2013/11/adaptation-short-changed-imbalance-climate-finance-commitments.
7. Center for Global Development, "Climate Change and Development in Three Charts," August 18, 2015. Online at http://www.cgdev.org/blog/climate-change-and-development-three-charts.
8. Mogelgaard, Kathleen, Heather McGray, and Niranjali Manel Amerasinghe, World Resources Institute, "What Does the Paris Agreement Mean for Climate Resilience and Adaptation?" December 23, 2015. Online at http://www.wri.org/blog/2015/12/what-does-paris-agreement-mean-climate-resilience-and-adaptation.
9. For a summary of findings regarding the link between climate/weather changes and economic variables, see Dell, Jones, and Olken (2014).
10. Moore and Diaz (2015).
11. McLeman (2014).
12. See, for example, Hsiang, Burke, and Miguel (2013).
13. Olson (1965).
14. Keohane (1984).
15. Busch, Jonah. "Snakes or Ladders at the Carbon Fund?", June 17, 2016. Online at http://www.cgdev.org/blog/snakes-or-ladders-carbon-fund.
16. Kumar, Sanjay, "Green Climate Fund vows to up its game," *Nature* News, March 30, 2016. Online at http://www.nature.com/news/green-climate-fund-vows-to-up-its-game-1.19627.
17. Available online at stats.oecd.org; accessed June 29, 2016.
18. Harris et al. (2014), data accessed March 31, 2017.
19. Accessed online July 2, 2016.
20. Accessed online May 22, 2014.

Chapter 7

1. The National Security Strategy of the United Kingdom: Security in an Interdependent World, March 2008, p. 3.
2. Collier (2007, p. 99).
3. US National Security Strategy, May 2010.
4. Swiss Foreign Policy Strategy 2012–2015, Federal Council report to Parliament on the strategic axes of foreign policy, March 2012, p. 5.
5. Japan's National Security Strategy, December 17, 2013, p. 31.
6. Lumsdaine (1993).
7. Remarks by George W. Bush at the Inter-American Development Bank, March 14, 2002.
8. Mayer, Peter J., and Clare Ribando Seelke, Congressional Research Services, "President Obama's $1 Billion Foreign Aid Request for Central America," July 21, 2015.
9. Biden, Joseph R., Jr., "Joe Biden: A Plan for Central America," *New York Times,* January 29, 2015.
10. Gonzalez, Elizabeth, Americas Societies/Council of the Americas, "Update: Central America and the Alliance for Prosperity," February 25, 2016. Online at http://www.as-coa.org/articles/update-central-america-and-alliance-prosperity.
11. Joint Statement by Secretary of State Rex Tillerson and Secretary of Homeland Security John Kelly on Bilateral Discussions in Mexico City, February 23, 2017.
12. Government Accountability Office report, GAO-10-496, "FOREIGN ASSISTANCE: USAID Needs to Improve Its Strategic Planning to Address Current and Future Workforce Needs," June 2010.
13. See http://www.worldbank.org/en/about/what-we-do.
14. Allison and Zelikow (1999).
15. Weaver (2008, p. 142).
16. Ibid., p. 140.
17. World Bank press release, "Remittances to Developing Countries Edge Up Slightly in 2015," April 13, 2016. Online at http://www.worldbank.org/en/news/press-release/2016/04/13/remittances-to-developing-countries-edge-up-slightly-in-2015.
18. Based on data from stats.oecd.org.
19. Anderson, Mark, "Foreign Aid Close to Record Peak after Donors Spend $135bn in 2014," *The Guardian,* April 8, 2015. Online at https://www.theguardian.com/global-development/2015/apr/08/foreign-aid-spending-2014-least-developed-countries.
20. United Nations Conference on Trade and Development, *World Investment Report 2015: Reforming International Investment Governance,* p. ix.
21. Ibid., p. 4, Figure 1.2.
22. Keohane (1984).
23. For a discussion of the multiparty prisoner's dilemma in this regard, see Mayer (2014).
24. Krasner (1991).
25. Olson and Zeckhauser (1966).
26. Olson and Zeckhauser (1966).

REFERENCES

Akramov, Kamiljon T. 2014. *Foreign Aid Allocation, Governance, and Economic Growth.* Philadelphia, PA: University of Pennsylvania Press.
Alesina, Alberto, and David Dollar. 2000. "Who Gives Foreign Aid to Whom and Why?" *Journal of Economic Growth* 5:33–63.
Alesina, Alberto, and Beatrice Weder. 2002. "Do Corrupt Governments Receive Less Foreign Aid?" *American Economic Review* 92(4):1126–1137.
Allison, Graham, and Philip Zelikow. 1999. *Essence of Decision: Explaining the Cuban Missile Crisis.* Second edition. New York: Longman.
Alt, James E., Jeffry Frieden, Michael J. Gilligan, Dani Rodrik, and Ronald Rogowski. 1996. "The Political Economy of International Trade." *Comparative Political Studies* 29(6):689–717.
Baccini, Leonardo, and Andreas Dur. 2012. "The New Regionalism and Policy Interdependence." *British Journal of Political Science* 42(1):57–79.
Bagwell, Kyle, and Robert W. Staiger. 1999. "An Economic Theory of GATT." *American Economic Review* 89(1):215–248.
Bailey, Michael, Anton Strezhnev, and Erik Voeten. 2017. "Estimating Dynamic State Preferences from UN Voting Data." *Journal of Conflict Resolution* 61(2):430–456.
Bearce, David H., and Daniel C. Tirone. 2010. "Foreign Aid Effectiveness and the Strategic Goals of Donor Governments." *Journal of Politics* 72(3):837–851.
Beck, Nathaniel, and Jonathan N. Katz. 2001. "Throwing Out the Baby with the Bath Water: A Comment on Green, Kim, and Yoon." *International Organization* 55(2):487–495.
Beck, Thorsten, George Clarke, Alberto Groff, Philip Keefer, and Patrick Walsh. 2001. "New Tools in Comparative Political Economy: The Database of Political Institutions." *World Bank Economic Review* 15(1):165–176.
Bermeo, Sarah Blodgett. 2010. "Development and Strategy: Aid Allocation in an Interdependent World." Manuscript, Duke University, available at http://fds.duke.edu/db/attachment/2430.
Bermeo, Sarah Blodgett. 2016. "Aid is Not Oil: Donor Utility, Heterogeneous Aid, and the Aid-Democratization Relationship." *International Organization* 70(1):1–32.
Bermeo, Sarah Blodgett. 2017. "Aid Allocation and Targeted Development in an Increasingly Connected World." *International Organization* 71(4).
Bermeo, Sarah Blodgett, and David Leblang. 2015. "Migration and Foreign Aid." *International Organization* 69(3):627–657.
Berthélemy, Jean-Claude. 2006. "Bilateral Donors' Interest vs. Recipients' Development Motives in Aid Allocation: Do All Donors Behave the Same?" *Review of Development Economics* 10(2):179–194.
Berthélemy, Jean-Claude, and Ariane Tichit. 2004. "Bilateral Donors Aid Allocation Decisions—A Three-Dimensional Panel Analysis." *Inernational Review of Economics and Finance* 13:253–274.

Blair, Tony. 2006. A Global Alliance for Global Values. Technical report. The Foreign London: Foreign Policy Center.

Borjas, George J. 1993. "Economic Theory and International Migration." *International Migration Review* 23(3):457–485.

Boschini, Anne, and Anders Olofsgard. 2007. "Foreign Aid: An Instrument for Fighting Communism?" *Journal of Development Studies* 43(4):622–648.

Boys, James D. 2015. *Clinton's Grand Strategy: US Foreign Policy in a Post-Cold War World*. New York, NY: Bloomsbury Academic.

Bradley, Mark Philip. 2010. "Decolonization, the Global South, and the Cold War, 1919–1962." In *Cambridge History of the Cold War: Volume 1, Origins*, ed. Melvyn P. Leffler and Odd Arne Westad. New York, NY: Cambridge University Press, pp. 464–485.

Brands, Hal. 2010. *Latin America's Cold War*. Cambridge, MA: Harvard University Press.

Brands, H.W. 1992. *Bound to Empire: The United States and the Philippines*. New York: Oxford University Press.

Brautigam, Deborah A., and Stephen Knack. 2004. "Foreign Aid, Institutions, and Governance in Sub-Saharan Africa." *Economic Development and Cultural Change* 52:255–285.

Brinkley, Douglas. 1997. "Democratic Enlargement: The Clinton Doctrine." *Foreign Policy* 106:110–127.

Bueno de Mesquita, Bruce, and Alastair Smith. 2007. "Foreign Aid and Policy Concessions." *Journal of Conflict Resolution* 51(2):251–284.

Bueno de Mesquita, Bruce, and Alastair Smith. 2009. "A Political Economy of Aid." *International Organization* 63(2):309–340.

Bueno de Mesquita, Bruce, and Alastair Smith. 2010. "Leader Survival, Revolutions, and the Nature of Government Finance." *American Journal of Political Science* 54(4):936–950.

Bueno de Mesquita, Bruce, and Alastair Smith. 2015. "Competition and Collaboration in Aid-for-Policy Deals." Manuscript, New York University.

Burnside, Craig, and David Dollar. 2000. "Aid, Policies, and Growth." *American Economic Review* 90(4):847–868.

Büthe, Tim, and Helen V. Milner. 2008. "The Politics of Foreign Direct Investment into Developing Countries: Increasing FDI Through International Trade Agreements." *American Journal of Political Science* 52:741–762.

Büthe, Tim, and Helen V. Milner. 2014. "Foreign Direct Investment and Institutional Diversity in Trade Agreements: Credibility, Commitment, and Economic Flows in the Developing World, 1971–2007." *World Politics* 66(1):88–122.

Buzan, Barry. 2006. "Will the 'Global War on Terrorism' Be the New Cold War?" *International Affairs* 82(6):1101–1118.

Carter, David B., and Curtis S. Signorino. 2010. "Back to the Future: Modeling Time Dependence in Binary Data." *Political Analysis* 18(3):271–292.

Carter, David B., and Randall W. Stone. 2015. "Democracy and Multilateralism: The Case of Vote Buying in the UN General Assembly." *International Organization* 69(1):1–33.

Ciplet, David, J. Timmons Roberts, and Mizan Khan. 2013. "The Politics of International Climate Adaptation Funding: Justice and Divisions in the Greenhouse." *Global Environmental Politics* 13(1):49–68.

Claessens, Stijn, Danny Cassimon, and Bjorn Van Campenhout. 2009. "Evidence on Changes in Aid Allocation Criteria." *The World Bank Economic Review* 23(2):185–208.

Clist, Paul. 2011. "25 Years of Aid Allocation Practice: Whither Selectivity?" *World Development* 39(10):1724–1734.

Collier, Paul. 2007. *The Bottom Billion: Why The Poorest Countries Are Failing And What Can Be Done About It*. New York, NY: Oxford University Press.

Collier, Paul, and David Dollar. 2002. "Aid Allocation and Poverty Reduction." *European Economic Review* 46:1475–1500.

de la Croix, David, and Clara Delavalladey. 2014. "Why Corrupt Governments May Receive More Foreign Aid." *Oxford Economic Papers*, pp. 51–66.

Dell, Melissa, Benjamin F. Jones, and Benjamin A. Olken. 2014. "What Do We Learn from the Weather? The New Climate-Economy Literature." *Journal of Economic Literature* 52(3):740–798.
Dietrich, Simone. 2013. "Bypass or Engage? Explaining Donor Delivery Tactics in Aid Allocation." *International Studies Quarterly* 57(4):698–712.
Dietrich, Simone, Minhaj Mahmud, and Matthew S. Winters. 2017 (forthcoming). "Foreign Aid, Foreign Policy, and Government Legitimacy: Experimental Evidence from Bangladesh." *Journal of Politics*.
Dollar, David, and Victoria Levin. 2006. "The Increasing Selectivity of Foreign Aid, 1984–2003." *World Development* 34(12):2034–2046.
Dreher, Axel, Jan-Egbert Sturm, and James Vreeland. 2009. "Development Aid and International Politics: Does Membership on the UN Security Council Influence World Bank Decisions?" *Journal of Development Economics* 88(1):1–18.
Dunning, Thad. 2004. "Conditioning the Effects of Aid: Cold War Politics, Donor Credibility, and Democracy in Africa." *International Organization* 58:409–423.
Easterly, William. 2006. *The White Man's Burden*. New York, NY: Penguin Books.
Easterly, William. 2007. "Are Aid Agencies Improving?" *Economic Policy* 22(52):633–678.
Easterly, William, Ross Levine, and David Roodman. 2004. "Aid, Policies, and Growth: Comment." *American Economic Review* 94(3):774–779.
Easterly, William, and Tobias Pfutze. 2008. "Where Does the Money Go? Best and Worst Practices in Foreign Aid." *Journal of Economic Perspectives* 22(2):29–52.
Easterly, William, and Claudia R. Williamson. 2011. "Rhetoric versus Reality: The Best and Worst of Aid Agency Practices." *World Development* 39(11):1930–1949.
Engerman, David C. 2003. "West Meets East: The Center for International Studies and Indian Economic Development." In *Staging Growth: Modernization, Development, and the Global Cold War*, ed. David C. Engerman, Nils Gilman, Mark H. Haefele, and Michael E. Latham. Amherst and Boston: University of Massachusetts Press.
Fearon, James D., and David D. Laitin. 2004. "Neotrusteeship and the Problem of Weak States." *International Security* 28(4):5–43.
Fleck, Robert K., and Christopher Kilby. 2010. "Changing Aid Regimes? U.S. Foreign Aid from the Cold War to the War on Terror." *Journal of Development Economics* 91:185–197.
Friedman, Milton. 1958. "Foreign Economic Aid: Means and Objectives." *The Yale Review* 47(4):500–516.
Gaddis, John Lewis. 2005. *Strategies of Containment: A Critical Appraisal of American National Security Policy During the Cold War*. Revised and expanded ed. New York, NY: Oxford University Press.
Girod, Desha M., Stephen D. Krasner, and Kathryn Stoner-Weiss. 2009. "Governance and Foreign Assistance: The Imperfect Translation of Ideas into Outcomes." In *Promoting Democracy and the Rule of Law: American and European Strategies*, ed. Amichai Magen, Thomas Risse, and Michael McFaul. New York, NY: Palgrave Macmillan.
Gleditsch, Nils Petter, Peter Wallensteen, Mikael Eriksson, Margareta Sollenberg, and Havard Strand. 2002. "Armed Conflict 1946–2001: A New Dataset." *Journal of Peace Research* 39(5):615–637.
Gowa, Joanne. 1994. *Allies, Adversaries, and International Trade*. Princeton, NJ: Princeton University Press.
Gowa, Joanne, and Edward Mansfield. 1993. "Power Politics and International Trade." *American Political Science Review* 87(2):408–420.
Greene, William. 2004. "Fixed Effects and Bias Due to the Incidental Parameters Problem in the Tobit Model." *Econometric Reviews* 23(2):125–147.
Greene, William. 2010. "Testing Hypotheses about Interaction Terms in Nonlinear Models." *Economics Letters* 107:291–296.
Grossman, Gene M., and Elhanan Helpman. 1995. "The Politics of Free Trade Agreements." *American Economic Review* 85(4):667–690.

Guisinger, Alexandra. 2009. "Determining Trade Policy: Do Voters Hold Politicians Accountable?" *International Organization* 63(3):533–557.

Harris, I., P.D. Jones, T.J. Osborn, and D.H. Lister. 2014. "Updated High-Resolution Grids of Monthly Climatic Observations - the CRU TS3.10 Dataset." *International Journal of Climatology* 34(3):623–642.

Hicks, Raymond, Helen V. Milner, and Dustin Tingley. 2014. "Trade Policy, Economic Interests, and Party Politics in a Developing Country: The Political Economy of CAFTA-DR." *International Studies Quarterly* 58:106–117.

Hitchcock, William I. 2010. "The Marshall Plan and the Creation of the West." In *The Cambridge History of the Cold War, Volume 1*, ed. Melvyn P. Leffler and Odd Arne Westad. Kindle ed. New York, NY: Cambridge University Press, pp. 154–174.

Hoekman, Bernard, and Caglar Ozden. 2005. "Trade Preferences and Differential Treatment of Developing Countries: A Selective Survey." World Bank Policy Research Working Paper 3566.

Hogan, Michael J. 1997. "Blueprint for Recovery." US Embassy Website in Germany; available at http://marshallfoundation.org/library/documents/blueprint-recovery/.

Hornbeck, J.F. 2012. "The Dominican Republic-Central America-United States Free Trade Agreement (CAFTA-DR): Developments in Trade and Investment." CRS Report for Congress.

Hsiang, Solomon M., Marshall Burke, and Edward Miguel. 2013. "Quantifying the Influence of Climate on Human Conflict." *Science* 341(6151):1235367.

Hudec, Robert E. 1987. *Developing Countries in the GATT Legal System*. Aldershot, Hampshire, UK: Gower Publishing Company.

Kadane, Joseph B. 2009. "Bayesian Thought in Early Modern Detective Stories: Monsieur Lecoq, C. Auguste Dupin and Sherlock Holmes." *Statistical Science* 24(2):238–243.

Kahneman, Daniel, and Amos Tversky. 1979. "Prospect Theory: An Analysis of Decision Under Risk." *Econometrica* 47(2):263–291.

Kanbur, Ravi. 2006. "The Economics of International Aid." In *Handbook of the Economics of Giving, Altruism and Reciprocity, Volume 2: Applications (Handbooks in Economics)*, ed. Serge-Christophe Kolm and Jean Mercier Ythier. Amsterdam: North Holland/Elsevier.

Kaufmann, Daniel, Aart Kraay, and Massimo Mastruzzi. 2010. "Governance Matters V: Governance Indicators for 1996–2005." World Bank Policy Research Working Paper 5430, available at https://elibrary.worldbank.org/doi/abs/10.1596/1813-9450-5430.

Keohane, Robert O. 1984. *After Hegemony: Cooperation and Discord in the World Political Economy*. Princeton, NJ: Princeton University Press.

Keohane, Robert O., and Joseph S. Nye. 2000. "Globalization: What's New? What's Not? (And So What?)." *Foreign Policy* 118:104–119.

Koremenos, Barbara, Charles Lipson, and Duncan Snidal. 2001. "The Rational Design of International Institutions." *International Organization* 55(4):761–799.

Krasner, Stephen D. 1991. "Global Communications and National Power: Life on the Pareto Frontier." *World Politics* 43(3):336–366.

Kuziemko, Ilyana, and Eric Werker. 2006. "How Much Is a Seat on the Security Council Worth? Foreign Aid and Bribery at the United Nations." *Journal of Political Economy* 114(5):905–930.

Lancaster, Carol. 2007. *Foreign Aid: Diplomacy, Development, Domestic Politics*. Chicago, IL: University of Chicago Press.

Lancaster, Carol. 2008. *George Bush's Foreign Aid: Transformation or Chaos?* Washington, DC: Center for Global Development.

Latham, Michael E. 2010. "The Cold War in the Third World, 1963-1975". In *Cambridge History of the Cold War: Volume 2, Crises and Detente*, ed. Melvyn P. Leffler and Odd Arne Westad. New York, NY: Cambridge University Press pp. 258–280.

Leffler, Melvyn P. 2007. *For the Soul of Mankind: the United States, the Soviet Union, and the Cold War*. New York, NY: Hill and Wang.

Leffler, Melvyn P. 2010. "The Emergence of an American Grand Strategy, 1945–1952." In *Cambrige History of the Cold War, Volume 1*, ed. Melvyn P. Leffler and Odd Arne Westad. Kindle ed. New York, NY: Cambridge University Press, pp. 67–89.

Lim, Daniel Yew Mao, and James Raymond Vreeland. 2013. "Regional Organizations and International Politics: Japanese Influence over the Asian Development Bank and the UN Security Council." *World Politics* 65(1):34–72.

Lumsdaine, David Halloran. 1993. *Moral Vision in International Politics: The Foreign Aid Regime, 1949–1989*. Princeton, NJ: Princeton University Press.

Maggi, Giovanni. 1999. "The Role of Multilateral Institutions in International Trade Cooperation." *American Economic Review* 89(1):190–214.

Maggi, Giovanni, and Andres Rodriguez-Clare. 2007. "A Political-Economy Theory of Trade Agreements." *American Economic Review* 97(4):1374–1406.

Maizels, Alfred, and Machiko K. Nissanke. 1984. "Motivations for Aid to Developing Countries." *World Development* 12(9):879–900.

Mallaby, Sebastian. 2004. *The World's Banker*. New York, NY: Penguin Press.

Manger, Mark S. 2009. *Investing in Protection: The Politics of Preferential Trade Agreements between North and South*. New York, NY: Cambridge University Press.

Manger, Mark S., and Kenneth C. Shadlen. 2014. "Political Trade Dependence and North-South Trade Agreements." *International Studies Quarterly* 58:79–91.

Mansfield, Edward D., and Helen V. Milner. 2012. *Votes, Vetoes, and the Political Economy of International Trade Agreements*. Princeton, NJ: Princeton University Press.

Mansfield, Edward D., Helen V. Milner, and Jon C. Pevehouse. 2007. "Vetoing Cooperation: The Impact of Veto Players on Preferential Trading Arrangements." *British Journal of Political Science* 37(3):403–432.

Mansfield, Edward D., Helen V. Milner, and B. P. Rosendorff. 2002. "Why Democracies Cooperate More: Electoral Control and International Trade Agreements." *International Organization* 56:477–513.

Mansfield, Edward D., and Eric Reinhardt. 2003. "Multilateral Determinants of Regionalism: The Effects of GATT/WTO on the Formation of Preferential Trading Arrangements." *International Organization* 57(4):829–862.

Martin, Lisa L. 1992. "Interests, Power, and Multilateralism." *International Organization* 46(4):765–792.

Mayer, Frederick W. 2014. *Narrative Politics: Stories and Collective Action*. New York, NY: Oxford University Press.

McGuire, Carl. 1952. "Point Four and the National Power of the United States." *American Journal of Economics and Sociology* 11(3):343–356.

McKinlay, R.D., and R. Little. 1977. "A Foreign Policy Model of U.S. Bilateral Aid Allocation." *World Politics* 30(1):58–86.

McKinlay, R.D., and R. Little. 1978. "A Foreign Policy Model of the Distribution of British Bilateral Aid, 1960-70." *British Journal of Political Science* 8(3):313–331.

McLeman, Robert A. 2014. *Climate and Human Migration: Past Experiences, Future Challenges*. New York, NY: Cambridge University Press.

Milner, Helen V. 1997. *Interests, Institutions, and Information: Domestic Politics and International Relations*. Princeton, NJ: Princeton University Press.

Milner, Helen, and Dustin Tingley. 2010. "The Domestic Politics of Foreign Aid: American Legislators and the Politics of Donor Countries." *Economics and Politics* 22(2):200–232.

Mitchell, Nancy. 2016. *Jimmy Carter in Africa: Race and the Cold War*. Stanford, CA: Stanford University Press.

Miyashita, Akitoshi. 1999. "Gaiatsu and Japan's Foreign Aid: Rethinking the Reactive-Proactive Debate." *International Studies Quarterly* 43(4):695–731.

Moore, Frances C., and Delavane B. Diaz. 2015. "Temperature Impacts on Economic Growth Warrant Stringent Mitigation Policy." *Nature Climate Change* 5:127–131.

Moss, Todd, David Roodman, and Scott Standley. 2005. "The Global War on Terror and U.S. Development Assistance: USAID Allocation by Country." Center for Global Development Working Paper 62.

Neumayer, Eric. 2003. *The Pattern of Aid Giving: The Impact of Good Governance on Development Assistance*. New York, NY: Routledge.

Noel, Alain, and Jean-Philippe Therien. 2002. "Public Opinion and Global Justice." *Comparative Political Studies* 35(6):631–656.

Nordtveit, Ingvild. 2014. "Partner Country Ownership: Does Better Governance and Commitment to Development Attract General Budget Support?" University of Bergen Working Papers in Economics.

Olson, Mancur. 1965. *The Logic of Collective Action*. Cambridge, MA: Harvard University Press.

Olson, Mancur, and Richard Zeckhauser. 1966. "An Economic Theory of Alliances." *Review of Economics and Statistics* 48(3):266–279.

Orr, Robert. 1990. *The Emergence of Japan's Foreign Aid Power*. New York, NY: Colombia University Press.

Özden, Çağlar, and Eric Reinhardt. 2005. "The Perversity of Preferences: GSP and Developing Country Trade Policies, 1976–2000." *Journal of Development Economics* 78:1–21.

Porteous, Tom. 2008. *Britain in Africa*. London: Zed Books.

Power, Samantha. 2001. "Bystanders to Genocide." *The Atlantic*, September.

Pregelj, Vladimir N. 2005. "Caribbean Basin Interim Trade Program: CBI/NAFTA Parity." CRS Issue Brief for Congress.

Radelet, Steven. 2003. "Bush and Foreign Aid." *Foreign Affairs* 82(5):104–117.

Reiff, David. 1995. *Slaughterhouse: Bosnia and the Failure of the West*. New York, NY: Touchstone.

Renwick, Danielle. 2016. "Central America's Violent Northern Triangle." Council on Foreign Relations Backgrounder, available at http://www.cfr.org/transnational-crime/central-americas-violent-northern-triangle/p37286.

Riehm, Peter J.A. 1997. "The USS Harlan County Affair." *Military Review* 77(4):31–36.

Rosen, Howard. 2004. "Free Trade Agreements as Foreign Policy Tools: The US-Israel and US-Jordan FTAs". In *Free Trade Agreements: US Strategies and Priorities*, ed. Jeffrey J. Schott. Washington, DC: Institute for International Economics, pp. 51–77.

Sánchez-Ancochea, Diego. 2008. "State and Society: The Political Economy of DR-CAFTA in Costa Rica, the Dominican Republic and El Salvador." In *The Political Economy of Hemispheric Integration in the Americas: Responding to Globalization*, ed. Diego Sánchez-Ancochea and Kenneth C. Shadlen. New York: Palgrave Macmillan.

Sanford, William F. 1982. "The Marshall Plan: Origins and Implementation." US Department of State Bulletin, Bureau of Public Affairs.

Schraeder, Peter J., Steven W. Hook, and Bruce Taylor. 1998. "Clarifying the Foreign Aid Puzzle: A Comparison of American, Japanese, French, and Swedish Aid Flows." *World Politics* 50:294–320.

Schrank, Andrew. 2008. "Export Processing Zones in the Dominican Republic: Schools or Stopgaps?" *World Development* 36(8):1381–1397.

Shadlen, Ken. 2008. "Globalisation, Power and Integration: The Political Economy of Regional and Bilateral Trade Agreements in the Americas." *Journal of Development Studies* 44(1):1–20.

Simpson, Bradley R. 2008. *Economists with Guns: Authoritarian Development and U.S.–Indonesian Relations, 1960–1968*. Stanford, CA: Stanford University Press.

Snyder, Jack. 2011. "Realism, Refugees, and Strategies of Humanitarianism." In *Refugees in International Relations*, ed. Alexander Betts and Gil Loescher. New York, NY: Oxford University Press.

Stein, Howard. 1998. "Japanese Aid to Africa: Patterns, Motivation, and the Role of Structural Adjustment." *Journal of Development Studies* 35(2):27–53.

Stiglitz, Joseph E., and Andrew Charlton. 2005. *Fair Trade For All: How Trade Can Promote Development*. New York, NY: Oxford University Press.

Svensson, Jakob. 2000. "Foreign Aid and Rent-Seeking." *Journal of International Economics* 51(2):437–61.
Taffet, Jeffrey F. 2007. *Foreign Aid as Foreign Policy: The Alliance for Progress in Latin America*. New York, NY: Routledge.
Therien, Jean-Philippe, and Alain Noel. 2000. "Political Parties and Foreign Aid." *American Political Science Review* 94(1):151–162.
Tingley, Dustin. 2010. "Donors and Domestic Politics: Political Influences on Foreign Aid Commitments." *Quarterly Review of Economics and Finance* 50(1):40–49.
Vreeland, James Raymond. 2011. "Foreign Aid and Global Governance: Buying Bretton Woods—the Swiss-Bloc Case." *Review of International Organizations* 6(3-4):369–391.
Vreeland, James Raymond, and Axel Dreher. 2014. *The Political Economy of the United Nations Security Council: Money and Influence*. New York, NY: Cambridge University Press.
Waltz, Kenneth N. 1979. *Theory of International Politics*. Reading, MA: Addison-Wesley.
Weaver, Catherine. 2008. *Hypocrisy Trap: The World Bank and the Poverty of Reform*. Princeton, NJ: Princeton University Press.
Westad, Odd Arne. 2005. *The Global Cold War*. New York, NY: Cambridge University Press.
Winters, Matthew S., and Gina Martinez. 2015. "The Role of Governance in Determining Foreign Aid Flow Composition." *World Development* 66:516–531.
Woods, Ngaire. 2005. "The Shifting Politics of Foreign Aid." *International Affairs* 81(2):393–409.
Wright, Joseph. 2009. "How Foreign Aid Can Foster Democratization in Authoritarian Regimes." *American Journal of Political Science* 53(3):552–571.
Zong, Jie, and Jeanne Batalova. 2015. "Central American Immigrants in the United States." Migration Policy Institute; online at http://www.migrationpolicy.org/article/central-american-immigrants-united-states.

INDEX

Figures, notes, and tables are indicated by f, n, and t following the page number.

Abbott, Tony, 63
Action Aid (NGO), 62
Afghanistan
    Cold War politics and, 23, 26
    foreign aid to, 60–61
    refugees from, 35
    Soviet invasion of, 25
Albania
    NATO membership of, 27
    trade agreements with, 123–125t
Alliance for Progress, 22
Alliance for Prosperity, 147, 148
American Farm Bureau Federation, 103
Angola, Cold War politics and, 2, 23–24, 25, 26
Arbenz, Jacobo, 22
Arias, Oscar, 101
Australia
    Cold War strategy and, 21, 26
    foreign aid from, 23, 24, 63, 76t, 88t
    trade agreements with, 121–124t
Australian Aid Agency (AusAID), 63
Austria, foreign aid from, 25, 62, 76t, 88t

Barre, Siad, 26
Bearce, David, 62
Belgium
    Cold War politics and, 23, 24, 26
    foreign aid from, 62, 88t
Benn, Hilary, 61
Berthélemy, Jean-Claude, 62
Biden, Joe, 147
Blair, Tony, 5, 27
Bosnia
    ethnic cleansing in, 28, 29
    trade agreements with, 124t
Bradley, Mark, 23

Brautigam, Deborah, 62
Brazil
    Cold War politics and, 23, 26
    foreign aid to, 25
    United States trade with, 102
Bulgaria
    EU and NATO membership of, 27
Busch, Jonah, 132
Bush, George H. W., 27
Bush, George W.
    CAFTA-DR and, 14, 89, 102–105, 120, 148, 150
    development policy, 33, 145, 147
    Millennium Challenge Corporation and, 9, 149
Büthe, Tim, 95

CAFTA-DR, 89, 100–111
    complementary engagement in region and, 105–107, 106f, 120
    developing countries, impact on, 100–102, 150
    development policy and, 14, 148
    results, 107–111, 108f, 110f
    United States, impact on, 102–105
Cambodia, trade agreements with, 97, 124–125t
Cameron, David, 1, 2, 57
Cameroon
    foreign aid to, 25
    trade agreements with, 97, 124t
Canada
    foreign aid from, 23, 63, 76t, 88t
    NAFTA and, 100, 101
    trade agreements with, 121–125t

Canadian International Development Agency (CIDA), 63
Carbon Fund, 131
Caribbean Basin Initiative (CBI), 101, 103, 115, 150
Carter, David, 42
Carter, Jimmy, 24, 25, 29
Castro, Fidel, 22, 104
CBI. *See* Caribbean Basin Initiative
Cédras, Raoul, 29
Center for Global Development, 8, 132
Central Intelligence Agency (CIA), 2, 21–24, 26
Chamber of Commerce, 103
Chávez, Hugo, 104
Cheney, Dick, 89
Chile
  Cold War politics and, 26
  trade agreements with, 96–97, 121–123*t*
China
  climate change and, 32, 126
  Cold War strategy and, 20, 21, 23
  rising power of, 151
  South China Sea conflict and, 36
  trade and, 103, 124*t*
Christian Aid (NGO), 62
CIA. *See* Central Intelligence Agency
CIDA. *See* Canadian International Development Agency
Clegg, Nicholas, 57
Climate change adaptation, 129, 132–140
  funding patterns, 136–139*t*
  targeted development and, 7, 127–131
Climate change mitigation
  funding patterns, 132–140, 141–142*t*
  targeted development and, 7, 127–131
Climate finance, 7–8, 10–11, 13, 15, 53, 55, 126–143, 146
  adaptation vs. mitigation, 129–131
  institutions for, 131–132
  targeted development and, 13, 15, 55, 127–132, 146
Clinton, Bill, 27–29, 33
Clist, Paul, 68
Cold War, 2–4, 17–26
  foreign aid allocation during, 69–79, 83–85
Colombia
  foreign aid to, 25
  trade agreements with, 123–125*t*
Commitment to Development Index, 8
Committee on Trade Capacity Building, 106
Conference of the Parties (COP), 126, 127
Conference on Financing for Development, 9
Congo, Democratic Republic of, 2, 23, 26, 46
Containment strategy, 2–3, 20–26
Copenhagen Accord (2009), 126, 128, 132
Costa Rica,
  CAFTA-DR and, 14, 100–111 106*f* 108*f*
  United States aid to, 105, 106*f*
Credit Reporting System (CRS) database, 82
Croatia, EU and NATO membership of, 27
Cuba
  Cold War politics and, 2, 24, 25
  revolution in, 22
Cyprus, EU membership of, 27
Czech Republic
  EU and NATO membership of, 27
  foreign aid from, 88*t*

DAC. *See* Development Assistance Committee
DeLay, Tom, 105
Denmark, foreign aid from, 25, 76–77*t*, 88*t*
Development Assistance Committee (DAC), 60, 68
Diaz, Delavane, 129
Doha Round, 10, 90, 102
Dollar, David, 161n68
Dominican Republic
  CAFTA-DR and, 14, 89, 100–110, 106*f*, 108*f*
  Cold War politics and, 23, 26
  trade agreements with, 122–124*t*
  United States aid to, 105, 106*f*
Dos Santos, Jose Eduardo, 25
Drug trafficking, 3, 32, 35, 107, 109, 148

Easterly, William, 86
EBA. *See* Everything But Arms
Economic Cooperation Act of 1948 (US), 17, 18
Economic Cooperation Administration (ECA), 19
The Economist, 100, 102
Egypt
  Camp David Accords and, 43
  foreign aid to, 25
  trade agreements with, 122–123*t*
Eisenhower, Dwight, 21, 22
El Salvador
  Alliance for Prosperity and, 147
  CAFTA-DR and, 14, 100–110, 106*f*, 108*f*
  Cold War politics and, 25
  MCC compact with, 105, 106–107
  refugees from, 35
  trade agreements with, 123–125*t*
  United States aid to, 105, 106*f*
Estonia, EU and NATO membership of, 27
Ethiopia, Cold War politics and, 23, 24
European Union, 27, 95
  preferential trade agreements with, 111–112, 114–115, 121–125*t*
European Coal and Steel Community, 20
European Recovery Program. *See* Marshall Plan
Everything But Arms (EBA) arrangements, 95

FDI. *See* foreign direct investment
Fearon, James, 5
Financial Times, 56
Finland, foreign aid from, 25, 62, 76–77t, 88t
Fleck, Robert, 58, 67
Foreign aid, 56–88. *See also specific donor and recipient countries*
  allocation patterns, 64–82, 65t, 71–72t, 74–75t, 76–79t, 81f
  CAFTA-DR and, 105–107, 106f
  climate finance and, 128, 131–133, 135–140, 136–137t, 138–139t
  commitments over time, 60f
  composition of, 82–84, 85t
  effectiveness of, 86
  official development assistance by OECD donor, 88t
  preferential trade agreements and, 92–93, 112–113, 115, 116t, 117–118, 117f, 120
  recipient governance and allocation patterns, 79–84, 81f, 85t
  targeted development and, 6–8, 13–14, 54, 57–59, 63–64, 146
Foreign direct investment (FDI), 31f, 32, 107–108, 108f, 150
France
  Cold War development policy, 18, 24, 26
  foreign aid from, 23, 62, 76–77t, 88t
  former colonies and, 42
  Marshall Plan and, 18–20
Free-rider problem, 11, 15, 50–52, 130, 131, 143
Free Trade Agreement of the Americas (FTAA), 104
Freedom House, 69, 114
Friedman, Milton, 22

Gaddis, John Lewis, 32
General Agreement on Tariffs and Trade (GATT), 94, 98
Generalized System of Preferences (GSP), 94, 95, 98, 101, 150
Germany
  Cold War politics and, 24, 26
  foreign aid from, 23, 24, 25, 77t, 88t
  Marshall Plan and, 18–20
Ghana, foreign aid to, 25
Girod, Desha, 33
Globalization, 3, 5, 29, 33, 34, 144, 153
Gowa, Joanne, 98, 114, 119
Green Climate Fund, 9, 10, 126, 131, 132, 153
Greenhouse gas (GHG) emissions, 7, 15, 30, 32, 38, 42, 47, 51, 127, 129–130, 135, 140, 141t
Grenada
  Cold War politics and, 25, 26
  trade agreements with, 124t

Grossman, Gene, 94
GSP. *See* Generalized System of Preferences
Guatemala
  Alliance for Prosperity and, 147
  CAFTA-DR and, 14, 100–110, 106f, 108f
  Cold War politics and, 2, 22, 25, 26
  refugees from, 35
  trade agreements with, 123–125t
  United States aid to, 105, 106f
Guisinger, Alexandra, 102
Guyana
  Cold War politics and, 23
  trade agreements with, 124t

Haiti, UN intervention in, 28–29
Helpman, Elhanan, 94
Hoffman, Paul, 21
Honduras
  Alliance for Prosperity and, 147
  CAFTA-DR and, 14, 100–110, 106f, 108f
  MCC compact with, 105, 106–107
  refugees from, 35
  trade agreements with, 123–125t
  United States aid to, 105, 106f
Human trafficking, 3, 32, 89, 107, 147
Humanitarian interventions, 5, 66–67, 83
Hungary
  EU and NATO membership of, 27
Hurricane Mitch, 164n68

IDB. *See* Inter-American Development Bank
IMF. *See* International Monetary Fund
Indonesia
  Cold War politics and, 23, 26
  foreign aid to, 25
  trade agreements with, 123–125t
Inter-American Development Bank (IDB), 33
International Country Risk Guide (ICRG), 81, 83, 84, 85t
International Monetary Fund (IMF), 69
Iran
  Cold War politics and, 2, 21, 23, 25, 26
  Middle East stability and, 35
Iran-Contra scandal, 25
Iraq, 35, 60, 61
Ireland, foreign aid from, 62, 88t
Islamic State, 35
Israel
  Camp David Accords and, 43
  foreign aid to, 2, 25
  trade agreements with, 42, 99, 121t
Italy
  Cold War politics and, 23, 24
  foreign aid from, 23, 25, 62, 77t, 88t
  Marshall Plan and, 18

Jagan, Cheddi, 23
Japan
    Asian Development Bank and, 42
    Cold War and, 18, 21, 23, 24, 26
    development policy in, 33, 56, 145
    foreign aid from, 23, 24, 25, 77t, 88t
    trade agreements with, 97, 122–125t
Johnson, Lyndon, 23–24
Jordan
    foreign aid to, 25
    trade agreements with, 42, 122–124t

Kaye, Danny, 3
Kennan, George, 21
Kennedy, John F., 22
Kenya, foreign aid to, 25
Keohane, Robert, 3
Kilby, Christopher, 58, 67
Knack, Stephen, 62
Korean War, 2, 20
Koremenos, Barbara, 10
Krasner, Stephen, 33

Laitin, David, 5
Lamy, Pascal, 10
Lancaster, Carol, 29, 33, 62
Latham, Michael, 22–23
Latvia, EU and NATO membership of, 27
Leffler, Melvyn, 23
Lerner, Daniel, 22
Lipson, Charles, 10
Lithuania, EU and NATO membership of, 27
Lumumba, Patrice, 23

Maastricht Treaty, 29
Maizels, Alfred, 61
Major, John, 27
Malawi, foreign aid to, 25
Malaysia, trade agreements with, 96–97, 123–125t
Mali
    foreign aid to, 25
    French military bases in, 42
Malta, EU membership of, 27
Manger, Mark, 95, 96–97, 99, 114, 119
Mansfield, Edward, 94, 98, 100, 114, 119
Mao Zedong, 20
Marcos, Ferdinand, 2, 24, 26
Marshall, George, 17, 18
Marshall Plan, 17, 18–20, 21, 147
MCA. *See* Millennium Challenge Account
MCC. *See* Millennium Challenge Corporation
McGuire, Carl, 22
McLeman, Robert, 129
Mexico
    Conference on Financing for Development in, 9
    NAFTA and, 100, 101
    Rex Tillerson visit to, 147
    trade agreements with, 96–97, 121–122t
    trade with, 102, 109
MFN. *See* Most favored nation status
Michigan State University, 107
Migration, 1, 3, 8, 30f, 32, 35, 36, 72, 111
    climate change and, 129, 136t, 137, 138t, 141t
    foreign aid and, 14, 57, 65–67, 65t, 69, 72, 72t, 76–79t, 86
    trade agreements and, 99, 104, 109, 111
Migration Policy Institute, 109
Military assistance, 64–65, 69, 72, 75
    climate finance and, 133, 136t, 138t, 141t
    foreign aid and, 25, 64, 65t, 69–75
Millennium Challenge Account (MCA), 9
Millennium Challenge Corporation (MCC), 33, 81, 105, 106, 147, 149
Millennium Development Goals, 29
Millikan, Max, 22
Milner, Helen, 94, 95, 114, 119
Mobutu Sese Seko, 2, 23, 24, 25, 26, 46, 47
Modernization theory, 3, 22
Monnet Plan, 19
Moore, Frances, 129
Morocco
    Cold War politics and, 24
    foreign aid to, 25
Moss, Todd, 67
Mossadeq, Muhammad, 21
Most favored nation (MFN) status, 94, 100
Mozambique, Cold War politics and, 23, 24

NAFTA. *See* North American Free Trade Agreement
National Association of Manufacturers, 103
NATO. *See* North Atlantic Treaty Organization
Netherlands, foreign aid from, 23, 25, 62, 78t, 88t
New York Times, 102, 103, 147
New Zealand
    Cold War strategy and, 21
    foreign aid from, 25, 62, 78t, 88t
    trade agreements with, 121–125t
Nicaragua
    CAFTA-DR and, 14, 100–110, 106f, 108f
    Cold War politics and, 2, 25
    MCC compact with, 105, 106–107
    trade agreements with, 97, 123–125t
    United States aid to, 105, 106f
Nissanke, Machiko, 61
North American Free Trade Agreement (NAFTA), 99, 100, 101

North Atlantic Treaty Organization (NATO), 19–20, 27, 29, 35
North Korea
  Cold War politics and, 20
  nuclear program in, 36
Norway
  foreign aid from, 25, 78t, 88t
  trade agreements with, 121–125t
Nye, Joseph, 3

Obama, Barack
  development policy and, 63, 111, 145, 147
Official development assistance (ODA). See Foreign aid
Olson, Mancur, 11, 153
Organization for Economic Cooperation and Development (OECD), 25, 28f, 30f, 32, 46, 60, 68, 82, 83, 84, 88t, 90, 112, 133, 150
Organization for European Economic Cooperation (OEEC), 19
Oxfam, 62
Özden, Çağlar, 98

Pakistan
  Cold War politics and, 25, 26
Paris Agreement (2015), 36, 127
PEPFAR. See President's Emergency Plan for AIDS Relief
Peru, trade agreements with, 97, 123–125t
Phare program, 27
Philippines
  Cold War politics and, 2, 23, 24, 26
  trade agreements with, 123–125t
Pinochet, Augusto, 26
Poe, Edgar Allan, 35, 36
Point Four, 2, 20, 22
Poland
  EU and NATO membership of, 27
  foreign aid from, 88t
Porteous, Tom, 27, 29–30
Portugal
  Cold War politics and, 24
  foreign aid from, 88t
Preferential trade agreements, 89–125. See also specific trade agreements
  dyadic analysis, 90f, 111–120, 116t, 117f, 118f, 121–125t
  targeted development and, 7–8, 14, 54–55, 91–93, 146
  theories of, 93–100
President's Emergency Plan for AIDS Relief (PEPFAR), 33

Quadrennial Diplomacy and Development Review (US), 63

Radelet, Steven, 2, 29
Reagan, Ronald, 24, 25
Reinhardt, Eric, 98, 100
Remittances, 150
Romania, EU and NATO membership of, 27
Roodman, David, 67
Rostow, Walt, 22
Rumsfeld, Donald, 105
Russia, 27, 35. See also Soviet Union
Rwanda, genocide in, 29

Safari Club, 24
Sánchez-Ancochea, Diego, 101
Saudi Arabia
  Cold War politics and, 24
  Middle East stability and, 35
Savimbi, Jonas, 25
Schrank, Andrew, 101
Security Council (UN), 28, 42, 65, 65t, 69, 70, 71t, 72, 74t, 76–79t, 133, 136t, 140, 141t
September 11, 2001 terrorist attacks, 8–9, 32–34, 58, 62, 145
Shadlen, Kenneth, 95, 114, 119
Slovakia, EU and NATO membership of, 27
Slovenia, EU and NATO membership of, 27
Snidal, Duncan, 10
Snyder, Jack, 5
Solis, Otton, 101
Somalia
  Cold War politics and, 24, 26
  US intervention in, 28
South Africa
  Cold War politics and, 24, 25
  trade agreements with, 122–123t
South China Sea, 36
South Korea
  Cold War politics and, 20
  missile defense system in, 36
Soviet Union, Cold War and, 19–26
Spain, foreign aid from, 62, 88t
Standley, Scott, 67
Stone, Randall, 42
Stoner-Weiss, Kathryn, 33
Sudan, foreign aid to, 25
Sugar industry, 103
Suharto, 23, 26
Sweden, foreign aid from, 62, 78t, 88t
Switzerland
  development policy in, 33, 145
  foreign aid from, 25, 42, 78t, 88t
  trade agreements with, 121–125t

Syria
  refugees from, 35
  trade agreements with, 121*t*

Tanzania, foreign aid to, 25
Targeted development
  climate finance and, 15, 55, 126–143, 146. *See also* Climate finance
  foreign aid, 13–14, 54, 56–88, 146. *See also* Foreign aid
  historical perspective, 12, 17–34
  international institutions and, 9–12, 151–153
  new periphery and, 149–151
  preferential trade agreements and, 14, 54–55, 89–125, 146. *See also* Preferential trade agreements
  strategy of, 4–8
  terrorism and, 8–9
  utility maximization, 12–13, 35–55. *See also* Utility maximization
Terrorism
  development policy and, 5, 8–9, 33, 42, 62, 144, 145
  September 11, 2001 attacks, 32–34
  targeted development and, 8–9
Thailand
  Cold War politics and, 23
  trade agreements with, 96–97, 122–123*t*
Tichit, Ariane, 62
Tillerson, Rex, 147–148
Tirone, Daniel, 62
Trade agreements. *See* Preferential trade agreements
Truman, Harry, 1–2, 17, 18, 20, 59–60
Trump, Donald, 36, 147
Tunisia
  foreign aid to, 25
  trade agreements with, 121–122*t*
Turkey
  foreign aid to, 25
  migrant crisis and, 43
  trade agreements with, 121*t*

United Kingdom
  Cold War development policy, 18, 26
  development policy in, 34, 144–145
  foreign aid from, 23, 25, 56–57, 62, 79*t*, 88*t*
  Marshall Plan and, 19–20
  post-Cold War development policy in, 27, 42, 62
United Nations 5, 70, 72, 71*t*, 74*t*, 76–79*t*, 109, 136–137*t*, 138–139*t*, 141–142*t*
United Nations Conference on Trade and Development (UNCTAD), 6, 31*f*, 108*f*

United Nations Environment Program (UNEP), 127
United Nations Framework Convention on Climate Change (UNFCCC), 126, 131
United States
  CAFTA-DR and, 14, 89, 100–111, 120, 148
  climate change and, 126
  Cold War development policy, 1–3, 18, 20–26
  foreign aid from, 23, 62, 67, 79*t*, 88*t*
  Marshall Plan and, 17–20
  migration to, 35, 109, 111
  military assistance from, 69, 71*t*, 72, 74*t*, 75, 76–79*t*
  post-9/11 development policy, 32–34, 145
  post-Cold War development policy, 26–32
  trade agreements with, 42, 97, 121–123*t*
Uruguay Round, 29
US Agency for International Development (USAID), 62–63, 107, 148
US Trade Representative (USTR), 102
Utility maximization, 12–13, 35–55

Vietnam
  Cold War politics and, 20, 21, 23
  trade agreements with, 124–125*t*
Vietnam War, 2, 23–24, 26

Waltz, Kenneth, 21
Washington Consensus, 16
Weaver, Catherine, 149
Wolfensohn, James, 8
Woods, Ngaire, 62
World Bank 9, 131, 132, 148, 149, 153
World Development Indicators, 68, 110*f*, 114, 135
World Trade Organization (WTO), 9, 10, 29, 99–100
  Doha Round, 10, 90, 102
Worldwide Governance Indicators (WGI), 80–84, 81*f*, 85*t*

Zaire
  Cold War politics and, 2, 24, 25, 26
  foreign aid to, 25, 46
Zambia, foreign aid to, 25
Zeckhauser, Richard, 11, 153
Zelaya, Manuel, 164n66
Zimbabwe
  foreign aid to, 25
  trade agreements with, 125
Zoellick, Robert, 89, 104

www.ingramcontent.com/pod-product-compliance
Ingram Content Group UK Ltd.
Pitfield, Milton Keynes, MK11 3LW, UK
UKHW021903240426
12048UKWH00037B/1192